Enforcer Notices:

practical guidance for local authority enforcement officers

by **Julie Barratt**

edited by **Chris Lewis**

Julie Barratt Legal Training

First edition 2014
First reprint 2020

British Library Cataloguing in Publication Data.
A catalogue record for this book is available from the British Library.

ISBN 978-1-910676-05-9

Printed and bound by The Print Co. (West)Ltd.

Contents

Preface

In 2014 after several years of prevarication I finally decided that I would get my finger out and, in response to at least two, possibly three people who had requested me to do it, write a book based around the legal columns I had been writing, on a more or less monthly basis, for Environmental Health News. I must admit I thought it would be a straightforward proposition; line the columns up in some sort of sensible order, write couple of paragraphs stitching them together and the job would be done. I recruited an unsuspecting friend and professional colleague, Chris Lewis, to act as editor to make the book more credible and we set off down the road to literary fame and glory. About eight months down the line we produced 'Investigation and prosecution: practical guidance for local authority enforcement officers' and launched it onto an unsuspecting world. In the course of doing so we had some lively debates about the minutiae and not so minutiae of legal process, the relative weight and prominence to be given to certain topics and issues and the authority for certain propositions but we managed not to fall out and to produce the required manuscript on time.

'I & P' as it will ever been known to us was well received by enforcement officers and was favourably reviewed. We were basking in its glory and hanging up our respective keyboards when we were assailed by enforcement officers who told us that it was a good job, but a job only half done. While investigation and prosecution are part of the job of an enforcement officer, so is the service of enforcement notices which we had conspicuously failed to address. Since denial of either point was pointless we considered our position. We had set off with more enthusiasm than was proper to write 'I & P', having only a vague idea of how much work would be involved. We swiftly realised that my glib assertions about just writing a few paragraphs and doing a bit of cut 'n' paste were a pipe dream and put in a lot of hard hours writing, honing and fine tuning and occasionally wholesale rejecting to come up with what we produced and hoped would be more than a vanity project. Other than to our respective partners Mike and Gillian, who had relished the peace and quiet while we were working, the prospect was not hugely appealing so soon on the heels of our first effort, but we did concede that was there another book out there if we were minded to go for it.

As is now clear, after more gin and tonic than is good for a person, we took a collective deep breath and agreed that we should produce what we see as a companion volume to Investigation and Prosecution, a book similar in style that looks at enforcement notices from cradle to grave; from their rationale, the types of notices through drafting, service, appeals against and enforcement of, high lighting pitfalls and mantraps, busting myths and attempting to provide pragmatic advice. Once more we have not set out to produce a textbook, a book of authority or a good practise guide. We have produced a book of practical guidance based on our collective experience as enforcement officers and lawyers in the hope that we can save some from making the mistakes of others and improve the knowledge and awareness of the rest.

As will be evident from the text there are a huge variety of enforcement notices; some straightforward and as subtle in their effect as an air raid, others creatures of much more sophistication with the potential to be as damaging to the enforcement officer serving them as to the recipient receiving them. We agreed it was impossible to try to address all of them as discrete notices ranging from the Housing Acts through Environmental Protection to Food Hygiene and Safety, Town and County Planning, Building Control and on and on; rather we have grouped notices together by what they do and how they do it. Some inevitably will slip though the net, their variance from the norm being such that they do not fit comfortably within our somewhat blunt classification, but the principles of drafting, service and enforcing compliance will hold true and lessons learned are transferable from one type of notice to another irrespective of the area of practise from which they arise.

As with its companion volume this book is one that we hope readers will dip into taking from it nuggets of good advice. It is not to be followed slavishly, neither is it a complete guide to everything an enforcement officer will ever need to know about enforcement notices. It is a book of practical guidance and good sense and we hope that it will be useful. Given that is the case any discussion of the law is not exhaustive, and recourse should be had to statute or case law for a complete understanding of the topics covered.

Once more I am indebted to Chris Lewis for his editorship of this book. His measured consideration and balanced approach are invaluable in shaping my somewhat frantic draft into a sensible manuscript that says what we want it to in a clear and concise way, all in good humour and with a commendable lightness of touch. This book is as much his as mine and I am very much in his debt for his assistance, encouragement and friendship.

Chapter 1

What are enforcement notices?

For the purposes of this book an enforcement notice is one of any number of notices, having statutory origin, that are served by local authority enforcement officers on individuals or organisations to require them to do or to stop doing something. They have a variety of names depending on the statute under which they arise; Improvement or Prohibition notices if they arise under the Health and Safety at Work etc. Act 1974, Planning Enforcement and Stop Notices if they arise under the Town and Country Planning Act 1990, Abatement Notices if they have their origin in the Environmental Protection Act 1990 to name but a few. Invariably they have more familiar handles – a Sec. 79 notice means something to an environmental health practitioner while a Sec. 179 notice is bread and butter stuff to a planner. Irrespective of their name the common link between enforcement notices across the piste is that they all have their origins in statute. Every enforcement notice is specifically created by a section of a statute and often the creating section will be very specific about what has been created, specifying what the enforcement notice shall be called, what it shall be used for and by whom, its limitations and restrictions and will generally make other specific provisions or requirements relating to its use or service. As creatures of statute there is nothing fluffy or flexible about enforcement notices. The rules of statutory interpretation require that the power to serve a notice should be read narrowly, therefore an enforcement notice may not exceed in its ambition, the reason for which it was created, and may not be used to achieve something that the legalisation does not allow. Enforcement notices are directed and specific. Should there be any doubt about the reach or the scope of a notice, or the circumstances in which it can be used, the doubt can be readily resolved by reference back to the section of the legislation that created it, and additionally in some cases the interpreting case law that surrounds it.

Enforcement notices are one of the basic tools of an enforcement officer's trade and are used day in day out to tackle whatever issue the local authority is focusing its attention on.

What is the purpose of an enforcement notice?

Moving on, what is the purpose of an enforcement notice? In its simplest sense the answer is quite straightforward; it's to get something done. More than that it is to get it done in the way that the Enforcement Officer wants it done and in the time he wants it done; it really is as simple as that. From the point of view of an Enforcement Officer it is a useful tool for making the reluctant do something, stop doing something, or face the consequences. Up to a point it is an extremely powerful though fairly blunt instrument.

From the point of view of the recipient an enforcement notice can have very significant consequences. It may cause him to undertake an action he didn't want to undertake, spend money that he did not intend or cannot afford to spend or stop doing something profitable for reasons with which he doesn't agree. Or it may not. He may choose to ignore it and take the consequences of doing so. Irrespective of whether the recipient of the notice decides to comply with the requirements of the notice, challenge them or ignore them he is going to have to do something, even if that something is to actively choose to do nothing and to see what transpires.

As an aside, but reflecting reality, it is also true that the fact that an enforcement notice has been served often becomes a withering disappointment to the complainant. Looking at matters from his point of view he may have complained about the matter in hand for some time. In some cases he may have been party to evidence gathering, for example in the form of collating a diary of noise events or antisocial behaviour incidents, but contrary to his hopes the service of an enforcement notice is not a whizz bang solution to his problems. In fact, unless the enforcement notice is of the type that has immediate effect he probably won't notice anything has happened. To add insult to injury he will have to be told that in the short term it is quite possible that nothing will happen as the enforcement notice will have an appeal period that will have to pass before it becomes live, and thereafter a compliance period by the end of which compliance has to be achieved. The matter may be resolved but resolution may not be speedy, and it probably won't be dramatic.

Myth Busting

So that we all start off in the same place before moving on to the more technical and legally challenging issues around serving of enforcement notices it helps to do a bit of myth busting, and it would be fair to say that there are a few myths attached to enforcement notices.

The first, much beloved by both members of the public who may have complained vociferously to the local authority about the issue that the enforcement notice will address and a not inconsiderable number of elected members, is that the notice itself is a cure-all, and that once it has been served all will be well and the matter about which complaint has been made will be resolved immediately and for ever. They believe that serving an enforcement notice is akin to firing a magic bullet and that once it hits its target the solution sought will naturally follow as night follows day.

The second myth is that enforcement notices are a quick, cheap and easy way to tackle an issue. All the enforcement officer has to do is identify the problem, formulate a solution, write it all down on the notice and send it to the recipient and the job is done. What could be easier, cheaper and more convenient?

The third myth, less a myth perhaps than a fervent hope, is that the matter of serving an enforcement notice is one between the council and the recipient of the notice and that no-one else is or needs to be involved.

Myth 1. There cannot be many enforcement officers who have not had some experience of serving an enforcement notice and finding that far from moving things along and delivering the solution desired, the enforcement notice itself has taken on a life of its own. The enforcement officer and the recipient are led on a merry dance that may or may not include Magistrates Court appeal hearings, repeated site visits, public meetings on through to further Magistrates Court appearances alleging non-compliance and all still with no tangible result in sight. Throw in for good measure threats of or actual engagement with the Local Government Ombudsman, which may achieve little in furthering the matter so far as achieving compliance is concerned but certainly adds some spice to it, and it may not be until the works in default stage some long way down the line that the remedy sought is actually achieved. This is all well and good when works in default of compliance are an option, but where they are not an option, or in times of financial difficulty not a wholly practical proposition, it may be the case that at the end of a long and tortuous process the enforcing authority is no nearer to a practical solution than it was when it started.

It also has to be said that persons engaged in nefarious but very profitable activities may view receipt of a Prohibition Notice, Stop Notice or notice of similar intent as something of an occupational hazard and take no notice at all of its requirement to cease forthwith the activity complained of, believing that there is more money to be made through carrying on the activity than they are likely to be fined for non-compliance. In some happy cases enforcement notices do work and deliver the solution required but in other cases where they take on a life of their own they deliver nothing but frustration and knockbacks and generate more work in pursuing compliance that will ever be justified when the end is finally achieved.

Whatever else enforcement notices can do they cannot guarantee success. They cannot deliver the solution. They can certainly keep the matter complained of in the front of the mind of the recipient, they can drag him through the court process and can cause him to be fined a considerable amount of money, but they cannot compel him to do what the local authority wants him to do. On some sorry occasions at the end of a long and tortuous process, in all probability punctuated by repeated complaints from members of the public and elected members alike, it will fall to the local authority to step into the shoes of the recipient and deliver the remedy required. It is success of a sort, but hardly a triumph of the process. The complainant who goes away with a warm glow because the council has served an enforcement notice may be about to become sadly disillusioned with the process.

Having despatched the first myth what about myth 2 – that enforcement notices are a quick, cheap and easy remedy? That they can be quick and cheap is certainly true. Identifying a problem, coming up with a solution, filling in a standard computer-generated template and sticking it in the post is about as quick, cheap and easy as it gets. Unfortunately, it is also the road to disaster. It will almost certainly spawn appeals based on numerous potential procedural irregularities. These can range from the powers available to the council or the competence of the officer serving the notice to technical defects in the way in which the notice is drawn up. The identity of the person on whom the notice is served, the way that service was achieved or not and the reasonableness of the notice's requirements are fruitful areas for exploration. Enforcement notices, blunt instruments though they may be, require a certain level of technical consideration, legal and procedural knowledge and sophistication in the way in which they are drafted and served. There are very few that can be 'knocked out' at the drop of a hat and still withstand the rigours of the legal nit picking and challenges to which they will be subject. Sometimes the enforcement officer will be certain of what he says, will do everything in a procedurally correct way, the notice will be without error in its drafting or service and complete compliance with its requirements will be achieved within the compliance period. When this happens enforcement notices are a quick, cheap and easy way of dealing with an issue. The occasions where this does happen however are very much the exception rather than the rule.

The third myth is that the issue is one for the enforcement officer and the recipient of the notice alone. That whilst the complainant has a walk on role at the beginning of the matter once the enforcement officer gets hold of it the presence of the complainant is no longer required and it is a simple issue for the enforcement officer and the recipient of the notice to thrash out between themselves. What a lovely closed circle that would be, but it isn't and in reality it shouldn't be. In addition to the complainant, and quite possibly his elected member, both of whom will be keen to know what is going on, there is the significant background presence of the Local Government Ombudsman. He may also take an interest in what is happening. It is not for him to say that decisions made were right or wrong; the merits of the issue are a matter for the council, just as the technical solution devised is one for the enforcement officer, but the Ombudsman can take a view on the way in which the matter was handled. Did the council respond to the initial complaint quickly enough? Did matters progress with sufficient speed and intent? If things went wrong, why did they go wrong? Was it due to failure to do all of the necessary checks? Was it carelessness? If compliance has not been achieved what is the council going to do about the problem? The lurking presence of the Ombudsman means that once a problem has been identified there is no do-nothing option, no do something slowly option and no throw your hands up in the air, give up and walk away option. Every action, inaction and reaction will potentially be subject to scrutiny and comment and any comment will be made public. Right from the point when issues are identified as being worthy of addressing by an enforcement notice they are the Ombudsman's business and enforcement officers do well to remember that.

As I said at the start of the chapter enforcement notices are a mechanism for getting someone, the recipient, to do something that the enforcement officer wants him to do, for reasons that can be justified within the terms of the legislation under which the enforcement notice arises. They can compel, direct or prohibit. They may have immediate effect. Their requirements may have very significant effects for individuals or businesses and may have considerable financial implications in the immediate or longer term. In some cases they may cause operations to cease or businesses to close. They may be a blunt instrument, but they are a big, blunt instrument and can have far reaching consequences. As you might expect therefore they are a not a gun to be fired wildly and at will. Serving an enforcement notice is a many staged process, and all of the steps of the process have to be taken in the right order and by the right person. Just about every stage of the process can be challenged and, in some cases, a successful challenge can have a catastrophic financial impact on the local authority that got it wrong.

What can possibly go wrong?

Just what can go wrong? Lots, actually. There may be no power to serve an enforcement notice or the wrong enforcement notice may be served. The officer who served it may not be authorised to serve a notice, or at least to serve the notice that was served. The notice may be flawed because it fails to comply with statutory requirements. It may have been served on the wrong party, in the wrong way or at the wrong place. Good service may not have been effected at all. The works required may be considered to be excessive or the proposed compliance period too short, giving rise to an appeal and the delay involved in hearing it. Unmeritorious appeals may be launched for no reason other than to delay the need for compliance. It may become clear once the enforcement notice does take effect that the compliance period is too long and that the complainant will continue to suffer in consequence. Compliance may not be achieved at all or be achieved in part only.

These are hazards enough, but then there are the nightmare scenarios. Everything goes exactly to plan but compliance with the requirements of the notice does not achieve the solution to the complaint. Or by way of slight variation, compliance with the requirements of the enforcement notice is achieved, the recipient changes his behaviour, but this gives rise to further issues that then need to be addressed. Or after an initial period of compliance the recipient reverts to his old ways and 6 months down the line everything is as it was, and it is necessary to start all over again. And finally when the recipient of the notice is prosecuted for failing to comply with its requirements, in part or at all, the sentence handed down by the court is derisory in the circumstances and makes non-compliance appear to have been a good judgement call on the part of the offender.

So why bother to serve enforcement notices?

While the mantraps into which the unwary can plunge are many, successfully serving enforcement notices is not a black art to be practised by the few. As I noted, enforcement notices are basic tools of the enforcement officer's trade and can be extremely effective in bringing issues to a swift resolution. They do however require the enforcement officer to be clear about the what, why, how and when of the matter in hand before going down the route of serving an enforcement notice and, just as importantly, being able to justify every part of his thinking should the need arise. The officer must be cognisant of both the legal and practical restrictions on what he may do using an enforcement notice. In practical terms he needs to determine what needs to be done, how it can and should be done, when it should be completed and who is the correct person to do it. And he should get it right first time.

The following chapters will look at each of the stages in detail examining the requirements and how they are satisfied.

Some initial thoughts

1. Enforcement notices are creature of statute. They only exist if created by statute and exist only in the form and for the purpose they were created.
2. An enforcement notice is not a particular sophisticated tool. It will not change hearts and minds. It can however be extremely effective if used correctly.
3. When a situation that merits service of an enforcement notice arises there is rarely a do-nothing option.
4. Service of an enforcement notice is the start of a procedure that has to be played out to the end. It cannot be abandoned part way through.
5. Serving an enforcement notice in not a guarantee that the matter it addresses will be resolved. It may not and the process of establishing that may be long and torrid.
6. Officers proposing to serve an enforcement notice need to be clear about what they want to achieve and how it should be achieved.

Chapter 2

Types of Notice

There are a number of reasons for serving a notice; because you want to know something, stop someone doing something or require them to do something and in consequence there are a number of different types of notice that can be used. They can be served proactively, before something has happened or reactively, after the event to prevent a recurrence or to control the way the activity continues. Generally, for the purposes of this book notices can be grouped into four groups, those being Inquisitorial, Assertive, Permissive or Prohibitive and each bears consideration as they are distinctly different in mode of action and result.

Inquisitorial Notices

The purpose of an Inquisitorial notice is to find out something. Examples are the Sec 16 Local Government (Miscellaneous Provisions) Act 1976 Requisition for Information or the Sec 171C Town and Country Planning Act 1990 Notice to require information about Activities on Land. These are served on the recipient, by the local authority, with the purpose of finding out information which is essential to the authority's inquiries. Typically the information will be the nature of the recipient's interest in a property or piece of land or the identity of others who may have an involvement in the land or business or something similar. The local authority will have some specific reason for requiring this information e.g. to progress its inquiries or more specifically to ensure that when it serves another notice, in order to control or stop an activity, it serves it on the correct parties in the correct place.

It might appear at first blush that Inquisitorial notices are fairly innocuous as all that they do is require the recipient to provide the information requested or give an indication that he has no interest in the property or land or advise that he does not have the information required. This is of course not the case. The serving of an Inquisitorial notice is usually the firing of the starting gun for enforcement action which will be thwarted if the notice that commences it is served on the wrong party or parties or is wrong in some other material particular. Most recipients of an Inquisitorial notice have a pretty shrewd idea that they are looking at the first stage in a potentially long and expensive procedure and therefore may be less than inclined to provide the information required. Failure on the part of the recipient of an Inquisitorial notice to return the information has consequences for the enforcement officer who served it. The fact that he served it indicates that he did not have all the information that he needed to confidently proceed to the next stage of enforcement, and so he may remain hamstrung. To proceed without being sure of all the necessary facts would be folly, since there is a possibility that any action taken would be challenged and potentially overturned, occasioning delay and cost. Equally to do nothing on the grounds that he doesn't know enough to proceed with confidence is not an option.

Although Inquisitorial notices may appear passive, in that they only require an individual to provide information or confirm that he does not possess it, they nonetheless have a sting in their tail. Effectively for the recipient there is no 'do nothing' option. He is obliged to respond, and more than that he has to confirm that his response is true. He is told on the face of the notice that he can be prosecuted for failing to provide the required information or for providing false information or information that he does not believe to be true. This ups the ante somewhat and puts many recipients between a rock and a hard place. If they fail to return the information required they can be prosecuted for failing to do so. If they make up information that will send the local authority off on wild goose chase they will be prosecuted for doing so. If they just misrepresent the truth a little bit they can also be prosecuted. However, if they provide the information required, in all probability they will find themselves the subject of rather more rigorous action. What they chose to do so a matter for them, but as I said there is no 'do nothing' option. Whatever the recipient may think it is right that the penalties for failing to respond or for providing a response more rooted in fiction than fact should be significant. However annoying it may be to the recipient to provide information which is unknown to the local authority but that will allow it to progress some action, which is most likely to the recipient's detriment, it should be remembered that the local authority is not asking for this information out of casual or passing interest; it will have a legitimate reason for wanting to know. It will be investigating a complaint or seeking to take action to prevent a nuisance or some similar activity for the benefit of adversely affected individuals or the wider community and will be thwarted if it does not have the information it requires and has requested. It will be legitimately aggrieved if the necessary information is known to the recipient and is withheld or provided in a less that wholly accurate way.

The Inquisitorial notice is not however a magic bullet. It has one important safeguard for the recipient who may think that he is staring down the barrel of a gun and is obliged to pull the trigger. That safeguard is the privilege against self-incrimination. No one can be compelled to provide information that directly incriminates himself and have that information used to convict him. The information provided can be used for the purpose for which it was required , such as to serve another type of enforcement notice on parties with an interest in land or the owners of a business but the provider of the information cannot be prosecuted solely on the basis of the information he is compelled to provide.

The most obvious non-local authority example of this is one that may be familiar to some; the request by the police that the owner of a vehicle to advise them of the identity of the driver of their vehicle, index number ABC 123, at a specific time and date in a specific named place when it was clocked exceeding warp factor 4. If you were not the driver at the time you are required to advise as to who was, but even if you are unfortunate enough to have to admit that it was indeed you who was driving at the time the police will still have to prove all of the other elements of the offence of driving at excess speed to the court, should you require them to do so, before you can be convicted. Of course, such is the procedure that we all know that we are probably dead in the water when the letter falls through the letter box and our rolling over and admitting our identity merely closes a circle, but if we don't make the necessary admission it remains for the prosecution to prove the identity of the driver; hence the penalty for failing to accurately provide the information required.

Inquisitorial notices are administrative in nature but are an important step for enforcement officers in making sure that any action that is founded on the information they secure is soundly based. More than that the use of such notices allows the enforcement officer to show that he has acted properly in ensuring that the information on which he relies has been obtained from the best source and that he is therefore justified in placing reliance on it.

Assertive Notices

Assertive notices do pretty much what their name says that they do – they assert what must be done by the individual or organisation on which they are served; they require them to behave in a certain way. They can do this in a number of ways, but the thread that runs through all of the notices in this group is that they allow something to happen or to continue subject to conditions. This is perhaps best described by way of examples.

Assertive notices can require that a process or activity be carried out in accordance with conditions that attach to it, such as planning conditions attached to a grant of planning permission. If the individual having the benefit of the planning permission fails to adhere to the conditions that are attached he can be required, through service of the appropriate notice (sec 187A of the Town and County Planning Act 1990), to comply with the requirements within a specified time period: if he does not, he can be prosecuted for failing to do so. Similarly, where a permit to do or carry out a certain activity is granted it may be made subject to constraints such as not to exceed specified levels of emissions or not to operate outside specified times, and should the operator fail to comply with the conditions a notice can be served on him requiring him to fall in line.

In most cases when the recipient of an Assertive notice fails to comply with its requirements he can be prosecuted, not for the failure to comply with the original condition but for failing to comply with the requirement in the notice; usually the penalty on conviction will be a financial penalty. The reason that failing to comply with a requirement of an Assertive notice is a criminal offence is quite straightforward. Any activity for which permission is granted subject to conditions, is one which has been the subject of consideration. The very reason that permission has to be sought in advance is because it is recognised that the activity may have an adverse impact on others e.g. through the release of emissions. That is not to say that the process or activity itself is undesirable, just that its impact has to be mitigated as far as possible. There has therefore been a trade off, and permission for the activity, process or development has been granted subject to conditions that have been tailored to ensure that any impact that does flow is minimised such as to make it acceptable. The *quid pro quo* is the requirement that the operator must operate subject to the conditions.

In most cases there will have been negotiation around the conditions and their specific requirements. The operator will wish to ensure that the conditions are not so restrictive as to fetter the way in which he operates, making it uneconomic or impractical and the local authority will wish to protect the population or the environment while encouraging development or enterprise that may bring jobs or other benefits to the area. Where the parties cannot agree on the conditions there is usually the facility to appeal to a third party, such as a Licensing Committee, Tribunal or the Planning Inspectorate which will hear both sides and then determine what conditions should be attached to the notice. It should be a win- win situation with both sides getting what they want, albeit subject to conditions.

The *quid pro quo* argument however does not always commend itself to the party that has obtained the permission or consent and who wishes to operate in merry disregard of the conditions. In such cases the Assertive notice will demand that he reverts to compliance within a specified period or else face the consequences in court, usually a fine. The court can only deal with the issue of breach. It has no discretion to alter or amend the condition. In some cases the court can impose fines that are tailored to take account of any financial gain that may have flowed from the breach, but it has no discretion to examine the reasonableness or practicality of the condition. That has already been done, and it cannot be revisited merely because it has been breached.

From the foregoing it is obvious that conditions attached to consents or permissions must be carefully considered. They must be reasonable and unambiguous and tailored to ensure that the business, operation or development can proceed without being unduly or unnecessarily constrained. If the operator conducts a cost benefit analysis and finds that if he breaches the condition/s attached to his consent the consequences of his being caught and prosecuted are less significant than the benefit to him of operating in breach he will be unlikely to comply and the local authority will be put to considerable inconvenience and frustration attempting to ensure that he does. It may be a fine balancing act to get conditions right, and as circumstances change the condition may become more or less onerous, but the acid test must be that a condition must be do as little as is necessary to achieve the aims of both parties.

In summary Assertive notices are fairly unsubtle instruments; they require compliance with pre-set conditions without debate as to reasonableness, practicality or collateral benefit, and in the event of non-compliance result in the prosecution of the recipient. They are not particularly sophisticated as a tool, but neither do they need to be to achieve their objective.

Permissive Notices

Permissive notices take us a step further up the ladder of sophistication. Unlike Assertive notices that are clear about what the recipient of the notice is required to do there is a degree of fluidity about the requirements of Permissive notices. The fluidity is not in the demands of the notice, which as before will be to do or to stop doing something, but in the manner in which compliance is to be achieved; that is left to the recipient to determine. An example is Statutory Nuisance Abatement notices (sec. 79 of the Environmental Protection Act 1990) which require the recipient to abate a nuisance within a specified time period, but which leave it to him to determine how to do it. Such notices are characterised by having an appeal period and /or mechanism which is integral to the process. The purpose of this period is to allow the recipient time to decide whether to appeal against the notice by notifying the court or a specified tribunal of his intention to appeal. During this period the provisions of the notice are held in abeyance and in the event that there is an appeal the notice will remain inactive until the appeal is either determined or withdrawn.

Whilst these notices contain a provision to appeal it is not an unfettered right. The grounds of appeal are limited to those that the legislation specifies, and the appeal must be properly made and expeditiously pursued by the appellant, in whose interest it should be to obtain a speedy resolution of the matter. That is not to say all appellants do pursue their appeals with diligence: most enforcement officers will have endured the frustration of the appellant who is playing the delay game and launches an appeal purely and simply to put off the inevitable day when he will have to comply, but such tactics and the response to them will be considered later.

The strength of the appeal process lies in the fact that it should ensure that by the end of the appeal both parties, the local authority and the recipient, will have had their views about the requirements of the notice, (actions, restrictions, limitations or time period for compliance) heard by an independent third party who will come to a determination. The decision may not please either particularly but will at least be informed by the views of both. That being the case both should be able to live with it, the local authority from an enforcement standpoint and the appellant from a compliance standpoint. It may not represent a meeting of minds, but it should be a meeting of understanding.

The other singular feature of Permissive notices is that they may have very long, if not open ended, compliance periods. Compliance with the notice requirements may take many months due to the complex nature of the work necessary to achieve compliance. On other occasions full compliance may never be achieved as the nature of the activity will always need to be controlled by the restriction in the notice, as uncontrolled it would present an unacceptable risk. Such notices can control successors in title to land or property and can sterilise activity. For that reason, they must be public documents so that those who can claim their protection are aware of their existence and those whose activity will be controlled by them are similarly informed. It is also the case that even though they have been served long ago in the annals of time they must be subject to regular review to ensure that they do not persist after the need for the protection they bestow has ceased to be necessary. They remain a living document even though they appear to all intents and purposes to be dormant.

Whilst it may be something of an exaggeration to say that the requirements of a Permissive notice, either accepted initially or resolved on appeal, have been reached by agreement, it is fair to say that both parties, enforcers and recipient, are cognisant of the requirements of the notice and, so far as it is possible, recognise that it represents the best that both could have hoped for. It follows therefore that the legislature presumes that the recipient of the notice will be moved to comply with its requirements, willingly or otherwise. The legislation that contains such notices therefore creates offences of failing to comply with requirements to take specific steps during the time period for compliance or alternatively for carrying out activities when prohibited from doing so. The size of fine imposed can be very significant depending on the nature of the breach or non- compliance, reflecting the attitude of Parliament to those who agree with (or at least fail to successfully dispute) what they are required to do or not do, but then fail to comply with the restrictions or requirements.

Prohibitive Notices

These are the most unsubtle of all of enforcement notices. Their purpose is to stop something happening and their impact is immediate. They take effect from the moment they are served and breach of their requirement to cease whatever activity is the subject of the notice has very serious consequences. Examples of such notices are the Sec 183 Town and Country Planning Act 1990 Stop notice, or Sec 20 Health & Safety at Work etc Act 1974 Prohibition notices. There is no room for horse trading or debate as to merits; the Prohibitive notice is served and takes effect immediately and ongoing compliance is required until such time as the local authority lifts the notice.

Unsubtle such notices may be but effective they certainly should be as the activity to which the local authority objects should grind to a shuddering halt. It probably goes without saying however that the service of a Prohibitive notice which may cause an industrial process to stop, a business to close or a development to cease, all with immediate effect, can have potentially catastrophic financial or business continuity consequences. As you might expect given the seriousness of the circumstances that attract service of Prohibitive notices, a breach of their requirements is taken extremely seriously. In some cases the legislation specifically empowers the courts to impose fines that not only reflect the gravity of the breach of the notice but also take account of any financial benefit that has flowed from the breach of the notice. In other cases a custodial sentence can be imposed on those who breach the requirements. They are serious notices with very serious consequences.

The seriousness of the consequences flows two ways. Given the potentially catastrophic consequences of a Prohibitive notice being served in error, the consequences for the local authority officer who pulls the trigger without getting his aim right are also considerable. Recipients of Prohibitive notices who can show the court that they should not have been served with the notice, or that the terms of the notice were excessive or unjustified, will be entitled to recover from the local authority all of the losses they have sustained in consequence of complying with the terms of the notice. That thought alone should be enough to make even the most enthusiastic advocate of Prohibition notices pause to reflect on his proposed course of action, however briefly.

It cannot be in anyone's interest for anything other than the most undesirable of activities to be brought to a grinding halt while the recipient of the notice and the local authority circle each other endlessly; it has to be assumed that both sides want compliance and a resolution of the matter as quickly as possible. That having been said it is also true that by the time the local authority finds itself in the position of being compelled to serve a Prohibitive notice the time for casual chit chatting about the subject of the notice are long gone and the parties are down to bare knuckle fighting. To promote a swift resolution of the issue between the recipient of the notice and the local authority the legislation usually contains provisions allowing for an urgent hearing of an appeal against either the notice or its conditions such that is either upheld or dismissed or potentially suspended as soon as possible.

Generally

Not all of the enforcement notices served by local authorities fall neatly into the above classification, some are best described as being 'unique to their own circumstances', but the most commonly used notices will fall within one of the identified groups. That having been said, to most enforcement officers the nature of the notice they are serving, whilst of interest for what it will achieve is no more than academic. What is more important is getting the legalities and technicalities of serving the notice right. A notice that is incorrect in some material particular is just a piece of paper with words on it that has no power to compel any one to do anything. In the next chapters I will consider what those legalities and technicalities are and how to avoid offending against them.

Notes about Notices

1. Most notices fall into one of four categories depending on what they do and how they achieve it.
2. The greater the impact that a notice has the more sophisticated or immediate is the appeal mechanism against it.
3. The greater the impact that a notice has on its recipient the greater the punitive sanction on the local authority that served it, if it is found to have done so wrongly.

Chapter 3

Getting the technicalities right

Before I launch into an exploration of both the drafting of notices and the does and don'ts of getting them right, I think it is helpful to consider some of the things that have the capacity to inflict a fatal blow to their validity, notwithstanding the fact that the content and all the details on the face of the notice are correct. The first consideration has to be whether the technicalities that precede the issuing of the notice have been correctly observed. Despite its importance this always seems to be a considerably less sexy topic than most others from most officers' point of view.

The strict requirements of administrative law probably don't appear on most officers' checklist of things to consider when serving an enforcement notice, or else they are subliminal things, done automatically without any real consideration and certainly without being accurately recorded. In most cases they are the things that cause officers to look mildly affronted or even deeply wounded when I ask them if they have not only considered but satisfied them, and they have the ability to taint our ongoing working relationship. They are, in the order I will consider them, the officer's authority to serve the proposed notice and the issues around the use of template notices. I know that officers think they are boring, but then so is a landmine right up until the minute you step on it.

Authority and Authorisation

Starting with the officer's authority to serve the proposed enforcement notice the first question is a simple one; 'Is the officer authorised to serve the notice?' It isn't just simple, it is fundamental. If the officer has not been authorised by the correct person in the local authority to serve the enforcement notice it doesn't matter how technically correct the drafting is, how reasonable the requirement and how beyond reproach the proposed compliance period the notice will be null and void. Local authorities are creatures of statute, created by statute and having only those powers, duties and responsibilities given to them by statute. Put simply, if there is not something in the legalisation that says that this shall be discharged by a local authority or council, or whatever description is used, the local authority may not lawfully do whatever action is prescribed. I have picked my words carefully there, because a local authority can do anything, but unless it has the power to do something, as laid out in a statute it cannot do that thing lawfully, and an unlawful action is null and void and lays the authority open to claims for damages or actions for trespass or some other tort with all the publicity and mortification that goes with such claims.

In most pieces of legislation the power to do something is given to 'the council', being the body corporate, in effect all of the elected members as a group. They are the council: the officers, from the Head of Paid Services right down to the humblest member of staff, are the vehicle by which the council discharges its obligations. The staff have no power to do anything unless directly given that power by the council through the process of delegation. No one, least of all Parliament, expects the council's functions to be discharged by the elected members and everyone knows, and fully expects, that the council's functions will be discharged by the council's officers, but just knowing and believing that is not enough. The council must actively consider how it is going to discharge a particular function and then delegate the necessary power to discharge that function to the appropriate officer. So, for the sake of argument, should a new piece of food safety legislation come into force requiring all food premises be painted blue and making local authorities the responsible authority for ensuing that this particular requirement is satisfied, the elected members, whether in full council or in cabinet or howsoever the particular council is structured, will firstly have to decide which department of the council should be responsible for enforcing the requirement. Then they have to delegate the power to discharge the function to the most appropriate person in that department. As with Parliament when they delegate the power, the councillors have no expectation that e.g. the Director of Environmental Health, to whom they have delegated the power or duty, will be out there with a big stick making people paint their food premises or agreeing that a particular colour of paint is blue as required; they know it will be the officers within the department who will actually discharge the function, and so they will also need to delegate to the Director of Environmental Health the power to appoint and authorise officers to perform the task. There is also an expectation that the Director will only authorise those members of his staff whom he believes to be capable, competent and able to enforce the requirements so that the legislation is enforced lawfully and properly. In simple terms that is how the game is played, except that it is not a game. It is a strict legal requirement and it must be done properly.

It is also important to recognise that authorisations come in different guises and merely being 'authorised' is not enough. Authorised to do what? An officer can be given a wide authority under the act which enables him to exercise all of the powers given to the local authority; on the other hand he may have been given only a very limited and circumscribed authority which enables him to exercise only a few, limited powers. So when I ask an officer whether they are authorised to serve a notice it is not an academic inquiry or an intended slight. It is to make sure that the Notice, whatever its requirements, whether significant or trivial, at least started out on a lawful basis; that the person who served it was lawfully entitled to do so; that the officer was authorised to do exactly what he has done. Does he have either general authority, to do anything and everything under the act, or does he only have limited authorisation, and if so has he acted within those limits?

The potential impact of enforcement notices varies considerably as I noted in Chapter 2, from those which merely make inquiries to those which can bring a process or development to an immediate and shuddering halt. As I also pointed out there can be fairly seismic consequences for the local authority if one of the prohibitory notices is wrongly served, whether through an administrative error or through error of circumstance. That this is the case is hardly a secret. It is well recognised by local authorities that serving a prohibitory notice can be something of a double edged sword, hence many take the view that it is not appropriate to authorise Mr Justoutofcollege to do all of those things that they might expect Mr Rathermoreexperienced to be competent to do. Authorisation therefore may be progressive; as an officer moves up the career ladder, so the level of his authorisations will increase, with more responsibility attaching to more senior posts. This is fairly common practise amongst local authorities, but each has its own ideas, and the authorisations attaching to officers at a particular level in one local authority will not be the same as in the neighbouring local authority. In the ideal world each officer should be cognisant of those things that they are authorised to do and stay firmly within the boundaries of their authorised activities, including serving only those notices that they are authorised to serve. Unfortunately, on occasions, whether through misplaced enthusiasm or ignorance, some will stray outside their authorisation, and if they do whatever action they have undertaken, including the serving of notices is *ultra vires* and so void. Where this does happen and where the individual served with the void notice has acted in reliance on it there may be consequences both for the local authority and for the individual officer concerned, hence the need to make sure that officers know the extent of their authorisation and remain within it.

The reason I want to underline the importance of officers being properly authorised and acting within the limits of their authorisation in purely pragmatic. In my experience as a practising Environmental Health Officer and as a lawyer there was rarely an occasion when the council's lawyers were involved in the practical process of serving an enforcement notice. Service of a notice was the exclusive remit of the enforcement officer, with assistance where required from within the department. The issues of concern tended to be the legalities of the notice rather that the technicalities of authorisations. Even when the matter did proceed to litigation the question of whether the enforcement officer who had generated the notice was both authorised and acted within his authorisation was not asked; it tended to be taken as read that it was the case, and at that point of course it was too late if an error had been made.

You may think that the foregoing is all lawyerly pedantic nit picking. A quick 'finger in the air poll' in the office may establish that no-one has ever been asked by an appellant or a defence lawyer whether they are authorised and if so the limits of their authorisation. Well maybe not. But I would just say a word to the wise. Some of the sharper lawyers who understand the way in which local authorities work will ask the question particularly where the structure of the local authority is such that there are generic officers whose titles are not as recognisable as the traditional environmental health/ planning /trading standards officers, and whose jobs, and the powers that attach to them, are not so obvious. Equally those with absolutely nowhere else to go may also make the same inquiry as they flail about desperately looking for a straw to grasp. Either way it is best to make sure that the inquiry is fruitless by ensuring that the officer who served the notice was properly authorised to do so and stayed within the limits of his authorisation. As I said it's not sexy, but it is important to get it right.

Template notices and their risks

And so to the second of my unsexy administrative issues, that of template notices. I want to be clear that I think templates are a good thing. I am quite happy to endorse the idea that constantly reinventing the wheel is an unnecessary exercise and that a job done well once is done well enough. What I do have concerns about is the practise of a template notice, once generated, becoming set in stone, to be used by countless generations of officers without ever being reviewed, refreshed or redrafted. When I qualified in the pre-personal computer era it was common practise for local authorities to purchase pre-printed notices from commercial companies, and for the exercise of serving a notice to be one of filling in the gaps on the notice with the relevant information, giving little or no thought at all to the pre-printed text which was just assumed to be correct. This practise, as well as giving rise to the only joke I know about template notices (*A- "Have you got the Shaws"? B- "What Shaws"? - A "Thanks, I'll have a gin and tonic" It helps to know that Shaws was the company producing the template notice*) meant that most officers never gave the printed content of the notice a second thought, it was just there because someone at the printers had put it there and that was good enough for them. The advent of computers has meant that pre-printed notices have been consigned to the same drawer as lawyers' quill pens and local authorities now generate their own template notices.

My experience of local authority template notices is this. At some point, not long after the department took delivery of the first gas fired computer someone, usually the most junior typist, was told to copy a pre-printed notice, add a few flourishes such as the name and logo of the local authority and fill in the certainties such as the address and telephone number of the Town Hall or Civic Offices. As time went on and necessity prevailed, more and more templates were generated until such time as the department was satisfied that it had as near as possible a complete suite of template notices at its disposal. There are obvious advantages to this system; once a notice has been 'templatised' the department will never run out of them; officers can make a hash of drafting them and just delete and start again at no cost to the department, and once drafted an infinite number of copies of a notice can be printed off at the press of a button. Most local authority departments now have comprehensive suites of template notices as well as informations, advice leaflets and standard letters all stored on a shared departmental drive that can be accessed by all staff. I make no criticism of this at all, and I can't imagine anyone mourns the demise of multi-layers of carbon paper and random blobs of typist's correction fluid.

What does concern me however is the tendency for templates, once generated, to be regarded as the finished product. We all know that familiarity breeds contempt and that is all too often the case with template notices. Everyone uses them but no-one actually considers them. The view tends to be that they are used, have always been used, and in all probability will continue to be used. New officers are told that these are the notices we use, and they should use them too. Consistency is assured, efficiency is promoted and original thought is not required. Then the world changes but the template does not.

We all know that things don't remain the same. Our common experience is that the law changes. The mother act under which a notice was generated may remain but in the years that follow there are many changes to it, some minor and some major, but all of which should be reflected in any notice generated under its provisions.   Realistically everyone will know about the major changes to the legislation; some may have contributed to the changes through working groups and consultation responses that have informed the changes and others will have been offered training courses once the changes have come into force. The changes are usually introduced on a much heralded date with everyone knowing what will change and how. Minor changes and little tweaks may be less obvious, and some changes may sneak in under everyone's radar.   Nonetheless whilst the minor changes may be less obvious enforcement officers will be able to get themselves up to speed and to change their practises accordingly. The changes that should concern us more are the very minor tweaks, that may not affect the practise of enforcement or the procedures for carrying it out, but rather the administrative changes that will have an impact, such as changes to mechanisms of appeal or similar which are not in any way related to the law that is being enforced but to the surrounding issues.

Why should such changes concern an enforcement officer using a template enforcement notice that has stood the test of time? Surely the issue is that the requirements of the notice should be clear and readily understandable, reasonable and proportionate and all of those things that their notices will be tested against? Well yes, but not in isolation. The rest of the notice, including all the notes attached to it must be accurate. To understand the importance of the accuracy of every element of the notice we need to go back to first principles. An enforcement notice is required to tell the person on whom it is served everything that person needs to know about all of the issues that arise from it. It should be clear who serves the notice, the intended recipient, why the notice is served, what is alleged, what is required, the time scale for achieving it and the consequences of failing to comply. It should make clear if there is an appeal process and if so within what time, on what grounds and how the notice can be appealed. In many cases the legislation that gives rise to the enforcement notice will go into considerable length describing the contents of the notice, from the name by which it is to be known to the notes that must accompany it. The theory is that the recipient of an enforcement notice should be able to get all of the information he needs about what is required, and when, and what to do if he disputes the notice from the notice itself. There should be no need for him to drop 'What do I do about a Planning Enforcement Notice' into Google or trot off to a solicitor to ask him what a Statutory Nuisance Abatement Notice is all about and what to do if he doesn't like the answer. Everything the recipient needs to know should be in his hand when he holds the notice, and he should be able to rely on the notice and its accompanying notes being right in law. I don't suppose too many people would dissent from that as a proposition, but there is a sting in the tail. The notice and its accompanying notes necessarily have to be accurate and correct in law. They have to be bang up to date and represent the law and the legislative procedure as it stands on the date that the notice was served.

The consequences of an Enforcement Notice or its accompanying notes being incorrect and stating the law and the procedure inaccurately can be calamitous. Looked at in isolation we have the first party to a dispute, the enforcing agency, serving a notice on the other party to the dispute, the recipient, and not only advising them of the current state of the law but at the same time encouraging them to rely on the accuracy of what they've been told when deciding what to do. Clearly the party being informed of the law in this way should be entitled to believe not only that he is being properly informed but that he can form a judgement about what is in his best interest based on what he has been told. Indeed he can. Article 6 of the European Convention on Human Rights, as incorporated into UK legislation by the Human Rights Act 1998, gives every individual the right to a fair hearing. A 'fair hearing' is not restricted to the rules of court procedure such that everyone has a go at speaking at some prescribed point before the verdict is returned. It is more than that. It is the right to be fairly treated at all stages of any procedure where the rights of an individual are being interfered with, restricted or restrained. It includes being properly informed of your rights, the consequences of a particular action, time scales and anything else that may affect a decision made by an individual. I don't suppose anyone would disagree with that. Otherwise we would have a system where an authority can take action against someone without providing any information about what they can do in response or worse, provide information that they know to be misleading or about whose accuracy they are unconcerned. The recipient would be left either not knowing what to do or taking action founded on the erroneous information, action which would almost certainly be to their detriment. Such a system is hardly going to commend itself to anyone. Hence the requirement that every part of a notice and its accompanying advice notes must be accurate, from the legislation at the top of the notice to the final note. If the recipient is to rely on information, it must be correct.

So back to where all this started, template notices that may not have changed since they were first painstakingly generated back in the dim and distant past. While there may have been enthusiasm for them at the time they were created as the modern and up to date way forward, that enthusiasm may not have carried itself forward to the necessary regular review of the templates to ensure that they remain accurate and the information in them remains correct. Even something as apparently petty as details of appeal stating that the appeal can be filed at a local magistrates' court when that court has been closed means that the notice is flawed. A notice that suggests the maximum fine for failing to comply with its requirements is £100 when changes to the legislation have increased that maximum fine to £500 is flawed because the recipient who decides £100 for breaching the notice is a price worth paying might have taken a different view had he been correctly advised that the maximum penalty was five times that amount. The potential appellant who strolls up to the door of the magistrates' court at ten minutes to closing time on the last day of the appeal period to find that the specified court is now a trendy wine bar and the nearest appropriate court is thirty miles away is prejudiced in the same way.

Having considered the impact of an out of date or inaccurate notice on the recipient it is worth considering how he might deal with it. He may take the view that the notice is so fundamentally flawed as not to be a notice at all, and that he may therefore ignore it with impunity. If that is his view he is not going to advise the local authority that served the notice to that effect, he will just go about his business merrily letting the local authority go through the next stages of the 'fail to comply with notice procedure' right up to issuing summonses to that effect and then pleading in his defence that the notice was not a notice, therefore there could not be in law be any offence of failing to comply with it. This will be followed by local authority red faces and mortification all round. Or he could comply with the requirements and then claim he was misled by the council and acted to his detriment on the basis of that incorrect information and commence proceedings claiming breach of Article 6, the right to a fair hearing, with the requisite claim for compensation that would accompany it. Or he could ask for a meeting with officer where he points out the error, in the hope that the officers will feel compelled to look favourably on whatever misdemeanour is represented on the face of the notice and take some less rigorous action or none at all. Either way it is not a particularly edifying prospect for the officer who served the notice. I should just note it may also be a bit of a car crash for other officers too if word gets out. Other less eagle eyed or legally savvy recipients of the same notice, who have fallen into line with its requirements at great cost or inconvenience, may feel a little aggrieved and suffer from an attack of late onset compensation fever as well.

The moral of this story is that officers should always check their template enforcement notices, and any other form of templatised document that they use for that matter. The importance of making sure that the information in template enforcement notices, and any accompanying notes, is correct really cannot be overstated. I am not saying for one minute that updating templates is fun. I remember when I was a student the mind numbing tedium of inserting update pages into the various loose leaf encyclopaedias of practice areas that we relied on, but I can't deny that they were useful resources and much relied on: that they were accurate and up to date was of paramount importance. If template notices are generated by a local authority someone must be charged with ensuring they are slap bang up to date and they should carry, as a footer or a file note, the date of their last update and a version number so that everyone who uses them can check that they are using the most recent, and therefore, the correct version. If the local authority buys in notices from an online supplier, or they form part of an enforcement package, the authority must be satisfied that the supplier has a rigorous checking and updating procedure in place. If the notice is flawed it will be the local authority that will be at fault not the legal draftsman who created it.

I said at the beginning of this chapter that the technicalities of enforcement notices are none too sexy. I don't suppose anything I have said has persuaded the reader to the contrary, but the fact is that if the technicalities are not correct the legalities don't matter. The lovingly collected and collated evidence, the carefully drafted witness statements and the hours and hours of painstaking surveillance will count for nothing because we will never need to consider them. Neither, more importantly, will a solution be delivered for the complainant or the party affected by whatever it is that the enforcement notice was served to prevent or stop. As far as they are concerned everything will be as it was, and they probably will be less than happy about it. Getting the technicalities right is not difficult but dealing with the fallout if the technicalities are wrong can be very messy indeed.

Tedious technicalities that will repay consideration

1.   Officers should be sure that they are properly authorised to serve enforcement notices before doing so, and
2.   Should only act within the limit of their authorisation.

3. It is extremely important that the information contained in enforcement notices and any accompanying notices is up to date and accurate. Notices that fail this test may not be notices at all and have no effect in law.

4. Beware of template notices; they may not have been updated. The fact that everyone uses them does not make them right!

Chapter 4

Preliminary considerations

For most enforcement officers serving an enforcement notice is second nature. They see a situation that merits the service of a notice and they just get on with it. Serving the notice is the next and obvious step, so that is what happens; the more experienced an officer gets the less they need to think about the what and why of serving a notice. Obviously this is not done without thought; the decision to serve the notice is clearly underpinned by a thought process but for most enforcement officers the process is automatic; asked what they were thinking many would struggle to answer. A simple analogy is that of driving.

When you start having driving lessons the whole process seems more complicated than a moon launch. You have to know what your hands and your feet are doing as well as looking ahead and behind, all at the same time. Within a very short space of time getting into the car is like putting a coat on, you just do it as part of a 'getting there' process; it is no longer the previously mind boggling complicated process of mirror, signal, manoeuvre and, in my case, stall. If at the end of a journey, even a relatively short one, someone was to ask you how you had driven there you would think in terms of the route taken not the gear changes and the mirror checking, which are just part of the process and not really worthy of thought. So it is with serving notices. Officers get to a point where they recognise that they should serve a notice and they just do it because that is what they do when they get to that point. But importantly there is a thought process that underpins what they are doing, albeit it is automatic and unrecognised, and I think it merits some exploration. Just occasionally the 'Why did you think what you thought at that stage' question gets asked, and the correct answer is rarely if ever 'I didn't think anything, I just did it'.

In respect of each of the four types of notice that I discussed in Chapter 2 I want to consider the thought processes that should underpin an officer's considerations when deciding whether to serve an enforcement notice. The thought process in each case is important, not least because in every case the officer is faced with a decision; being whether to serve an enforcement notice or not. In deciding whether or not to serve a notice and when considering what the notice should contain the officer has a considerable degree of discretion. In some cases there may be obvious driving factors. A flagrant health and safety risk must be addressed as a matter of urgency and the discretion in such circumstances is limited, but in most cases there are alternative courses of action that could have been taken, and it is important that the enforcement officer can justify why he acted as he did rather than choosing one of the other alternatives available to him. It may be some way down the line before the officer's conduct of a particular case is challenged. He may find himself accused of being overly passive or excessively aggressive and be asked why he did or did not serve a notice and what he anticipated achieving by the course of action he took. At that point the officer's decisions will come under scrutiny and he will need to justify the enforcement notice he served explaining what it was intended to achieve, and why it was reasonable for him to believe that it was the correct course of action. Whilst those enforcement officers with more experience may have to think back upon why they did what they did, and what they had intended to achieve, it is only because they know and understand the process so well that they no longer see the 'thinking' as a stage to be gone through; rather like driving, they just do it. The newly qualified may be more cautious and more obviously think through the process, but whether subliminally or not the underpinning thought process has to be done.

Inquisitorial Notices

As I have noted in Chapter 2 Inquisitorial notices are a means to an end. Of themselves they achieve nothing other than to provide information that will allow the enforcement officer to take further action should that be appropriate. The thought process behind service of an Inquisitorial notice such as a Local Government (Miscellaneous Provisions) Act 1976 sec. 16 Requisition for Information (about interest in land) or a Town and Country Planning Act 1990 sec. 171C Notice Requiring Information about Activities on Land is fairly straightforward. In either case something will be happening in or on land that the enforcement officer considers to be worthy of further investigation or of further action. As we all know however there is a marked difference between boldly going and safely arriving. All too often a notice served on the party presumed to be the owner of land, or the person having control, falls at the first hurdle because the person identified as the one on whom the notice should be served turns out to be the wrong person and the enforcement action grinds to a shuddering halt, leaving the enforcement officer no further on and still in the position of having to discover the true identity of the person on whom the notice should be served. In order to avoid this unfortunate outcome the Inquisitorial notice is used to obtain accurate information about who is doing what to land or who has an interest in land and the nature of that interest. There is a two pronged reason for the enforcement officer seeking this information through use of an inquisitorial notice; the first being to ensure that any further action is taken against the correct person in the appropriate capacity, the second so that the enforcement officer can protect himself against allegations of not carrying out all proper inquiries before taking action. This latter criticism can often arise if the matter becomes protracted or falls apart at some later stage. The belt and braces approach may seem pedantically overdressed but generally my less than original advice is that it's better to be safe than sorry.

I think it would be helpful to look at the thought processes involved in serving an Inquisitorial notice one stage at a time. Using the Local Government (Miscellaneous Provisions) Act 1976 sec. 16 Requisition for Information by way of example, it goes like this. Before the local authority can consider serving an Inquisitorial notice (which it will do through its duly authorised enforcement officer), it must be satisfied that it is carrying out one of its functions: so says the Act and that should go without saying. However before the enforcement officer can serve the notice he must have come to the conclusion that he needs more information about the identity of persons having an interest in the land, and the nature of their interest than he currently has at his disposal. As part of their 'getting it right first time' policy most departments will endorse that conclusion, and where there is any suggestion that the information already held by the department about the identity of parties or the nature of their interest may be out of date further investigation is clearly the proper way forward. Even where the enforcement officer may be in no doubt at all that he has the necessary information there is still much to be said for ensuring that the information is correct; it is a helpful way of shutting the door on any appeal against a subsequent enforcement which is based on various grounds such as the alleged misidentification of the person or persons on whom the notice was served, the failure to accurately identify the nature of the interest in property or the failure to serve the notice on all of the interested parties.

Having decided that a Requisition for Information should be served the enforcement officer will have to make a judgement about on whom it should be served. Serving the notice on everyone with an active pulse within the surrounding square mile in the hope of hitting on the right person is not a valid option; the Act is quite specific about who can be served with the notice, being:

(a) *the occupier of land , and*
(b) *any person who has an interest in the land either as a freeholder, mortgagee or lessee or who directly or indirectly receives rent for the land; and*
(c) *any person who, in pursuance of an agreement between himself and a person interested in the land, is authorised to manage the land or to arrange for the letting of it.*

That is it. The list is conclusive and if the enforcement officer wants to serve a Requisition for Information on a person who cannot be shoe horned into one of the classes of people specified in (a) – (c) inclusive he has a problem since that person cannot validly be served with the notice. The statutory rules of interpretation are clear and require the powers contained in legislation to be read narrowly so the classes of parties specified cannot be stretched by expansive interpretation. They are what the subsections say they are and that is it. In the case of this section (sec 16) it should be noted that subsections (a) and (b) both end with the word 'and', therefore they are inclusive and all or any of the persons specified can be served with the notice. Building on the first stage of this thought process i.e. the enforcement officer's decision that he needs more information, the question that arises is upon whom should the Inquisitorial notice be served? Not only must the officer be able to justify his decision to serve an Inquisitorial notice in logic but he must also be able to justify the selection of the person or persons on whom the notice was served by virtue of their inclusion within one of the groups in subsections (a) – (c).

The next question concerns what information can be sought in the notice. Quite obviously the information is going to be about the nature of the notice recipient's interest in the land in question, but some things are outside the scope of the notice. Once more we have to look to the strict wording of the section which tells us that the notice must provide the recipient with certain information; it must tell the person on whom it is served the identity of the land about which inquiries are made, the function that the local authority is discharging and the legislation that confers the power on the local authority to discharge that function. Basically the recipient is being told that the local authority has the right to do what it is doing by asking for information, and furthermore where he should go to check if he doesn't believe them. Having told the recipient of the notice by what right he asks for the information the enforcement officer then asks the recipient to tell him

- *within a period specified in the notice (which may not be less than 14 days beginning with the day the notice is served) the nature of his interest in the land and the name and address of each person he believes is the occupier of the land and of each person he believes is, as respects the lands, such a person as is mention in the provisions of subsections (b)-(c).*

Again, that is it. Regardless of how interested the enforcement officer may be about other matters such as how much the recipient of the notice may have paid for the land, his future intentions with respect to development and so on he may not lawfully ask for that information. All he can ask for is the nature of the recipient's interest and the names and addresses of anyone else that the recipient believes has an interest in the land. No independent thought is required, the Act tells the enforcement officer what he can ask and that must be the limit of his inquiries.

It doesn't matter which of the Inquisitorial notices is under consideration, the parameters will be the same. The Act under which the notice arises will tell the enforcement officer on whom a notice can be served and for what reason and the limits of the information that may be sought. The notice is, after all, an enforcement tool and as such it is more akin to a precise scalpel than a blunt sledgehammer.

As I said in chapter 3 one of the requirements of a notice is that it should tell the recipient absolutely everything he needs to know. In each and every case the Inquisitorial notice must advise the recipient of the consequences of either failing to provide the enforcement officer with the information required or of sending back information that he knows to be false or he does not know to be true. The recipient is therefore forewarned that ignoring the notice or sending back information designed to mislead or confuse will have consequences, and more than that, he is clear as to what the consequences will be. He can't be made to respond or to respond truthfully, that is his choice, but he knows the potential consequences of his choice.

Let us suppose that the recipient of the notice does follow the path of righteousness and returns the information requested to the enforcement officer within the prescribed time. So far as the enforcement process is concerned to the casual observer nothing obvious will have happened. Whatever matter it was that was engaging the enforcement officer will still be ongoing and, so far as the complainant is concerned, everything will be the same. There may even be dark mutterings about nothing happening even though the matter has been in the hands of the officer for several weeks. To the casual observer it probably does seem that little or no progress has been made, but assuming that the information returned is correct something will have happened, in that the enforcement officer will have put himself in a position to take the next step in the enforcement process, which is to take action against the appropriate party or parties. At this point however the officer can be safe in the knowledge that those parties against whom he is taking action are the ones he should be engaging with and that, subject to all the legalities of the next step he takes being taken correctly, a substantive remedy should be achievable. The information obtained through the Inquisitorial notice is a means to an end, or perhaps more accurately, it is a means to the next stage of the process.

Before I leave Inquisitorial notices I want to make a couple of points which arise out of practical experience. The first is that enforcement officers should remember that things change and included in things that change is ownership of property. A property held in title absolute today may well be subject to mortgage tomorrow, and a property occupied by an owner occupier last week may be stuffed full of tenants this week. Even if the enforcement officer *thinks* he knows the detail of property ownership it is important to remember that he may have to *prove* that, and that he knew it at the time he served the notice. It will not be enough to show that he knew with exquisite accuracy all of the details relating to ownership six months before the date of serving the notice, he will need to be able to show he knew the up to date details immediately before serving the notice so that he was sure that the information on which he relied was current. The few days delay incurred in securing accurate and contemporaneous information before sending out and awaiting the response to an Inquisitorial notice requiring details about interest in land may repay the prudent officer several times over if it means that any action taken based on the information is secure from challenge.

The second point I want to make relates to recipients of Inquisitorial notices who fail to return the information required, return inaccurate information, return information that is intentionally false or false because they don't care one way or the other about its veracity. Obviously the former is easier to spot than the latter as on the day prescribed for the return of the information to the enforcement officer it will not have been provided and so, subject to the officer being able to prove the notice was properly served, of which more later in this book, it will be pretty much an open and shut case. False information whether deliberately or carelessly provided will be less easy to spot. To all intents and purposes the recipient of the notice will have responded according to the instructions on the notice and the officer will have proceeded to take the appropriate action based on the information provided. It will not be until there is an appeal filed or a prosecution brought that it will become obvious that the party against whom the action has been taken was the wrong one and that wool has been figuratively pulled over the enforcement officer's eyes. Finally, getting to the point I want to make, in such cases I would encourage local authorities in the very strongest terms to do something about it.

Where information has not been provided as required or where false information has been provided there should be an active presumption in favour of prosecution. The recipient was warned on the face of the notice that prosecution was a potential consequence of either failing to respond or of providing false information and so he can hardly claim to have been hijacked if he is prosecuted. He will however have scored a very real victory over the local authority if he isn't. Prosecute him and make sure that the court is told either of the consequences of his failing to respond in terms of its effect on the local authority's ability to progress their intended action or of the implications of his providing false information, for both the authority and the complainant and any other persons affected. Lay it on with a trowel so that the court understands that this is not some trivial administrative 'fail-to-send-back- some- bit-of-paper' type offence but an offence that has far reaching consequences and one that impacts on real people in a significant way. Such action sends a message to others who may be considering acting in the same way and it may also be some small crumb of comfort to the complainant to know that what they see as delay or cock up is not the fault of the local authority. Who knows, it may also be helpful one day if the Local Government Ombudsman comes calling and wants to know how a case was investigated. Unless there is a very compelling reason not to do so, prosecute! As a Chief Planning Officer I used to work with liked to say 'Only rugs and mugs are walked on'. Enough said.

Words to the wise – Inquisitorial notices

- An Inquisitorial notice is not just a means to an end, it is an essential step in making sure any action that flows from it is targeted at the right parties,
- An Inquisitorial notice can only be served in circumstances prescribed in the Act that gives rise to it,
- The Act from which the Inquisitorial notice arises will tell the enforcement officer on which parties the notice can be served, and
- The Act from which the Inquisitorial notice arises will tell the enforcement officer what information he can require the parties to provide,
- The consequences of failing to provide the information required in time or at all must be made clear on the face of the notice, to ensure the recipient is forewarned of the potential consequences should he fail to comply.

- In the event of the recipient of a notice not complying with its requirements the local authority that served it should prosecute, alleging non-compliance with its requirements.

Assertive Notices

To my way of thinking the service of an Assertive notice will almost invariably follow the service of an Inquisitorial notice. If an enforcement officer is proposing to serve a notice on someone requiring them to do something they must be certain that they are going to serve it on the right person. To do that they will have to conduct some inquiry to establish that the right person has been identified. The type of Inquisitorial notice that is used will depend on the Assertive notice proposed; in most cases the Act that gives rise to the Assertive notice will contain a provision that allows inquires to be made. If we consider the Town and Country Planning Act 1990 for example, we see that there is a provision in the Act (sec 171C) which gives the local authority power to require information about activities on land. The information gathered from the response to that notice will inform any Town and Country Planning Act notices subsequently served, but it can only be used in respect of such notices. The Act is clear; the Inquisitorial notice can only be used where the local authority considers that there has been a breach of planning control. It would be wholly inappropriate and an abuse of process to attempt to use the Inquisitorial notice authorised by sec. 171C Town and Country Planning Act to try to obtain information about ownership of a food business for the purposes of serving a notice arising under food legislation.

Using my classification of enforcement notices, an Assertive notice is the bluntest of notice 'instruments' in the enforcement notice toolbox. Put crudely it identifies something that the local authority is not happy with and requires the recipient of the notice to do something about it within a specified time or suffer the consequences. There is no avenue for the recipient to argue about the merits of the requirement; he either complies or not as he sees fit. Typical examples are Town and Country Planning Act 1990, sec 187A Enforcement of Planning Conditions; Sec 215 Notices requiring the maintenance of land, and Detention Notices served under Reg.10 of the Food Safety & Hygiene Regulations 2013.

Quite clearly if the local authority is going to use a 'Do as we require or we will prosecute you' type mechanism there are some pre-requisites and they need to be satisfied before the notice is served. Assuming that the necessary information about the ownership of land or of a business is to hand the critical requirement is that there must be something tangible that the local authority can lawfully require from the proposed recipient of the notice; there must be something for them to do. For the enforcement officer to compel the proposed recipient to do something, for example detain food for the purpose of sampling, or comply with a planning condition or clear up land where the condition of the land is considered to be detrimental to the amenity of neighbouring land, there must be a specific section in the relevant Act that says that he can serve a notice making that demand. That might seem quite obvious, but what is important is what the section of the legislation that creates the notice actually says. It will tell the enforcement officer what the pre-requisites are before a notice can be served.

To explore this we can take as an example Regulation 10 of the Food Safety and Hygiene (England) Regulations 2013, reproduced below.

> **10.**—*(1) An authorised officer of an enforcement authority may, at an establishment that Article 4(2) of Regulation 853/2004 requires to be approved, by a notice in writing (in this regulation referred to as a "detention notice") served on the relevant food business operator or duly authorised representative require the detention of any animal or food for the purpose of examination (including the taking of samples).*

Reading the Regulation is instructive because it tells the enforcement officer everything he needs to know. The Regulation firstly tells him that only an authorised officer can lawfully use its provisions; that is a duly authorised officer, one who can show that he is authorised to enforce food safety legislation, including these specific Regulations. It then tells him that for him to have the power to serve a notice, the premises must be one that requires approval under Article 4(2) of Regulation 853/2004. He will have to be able to prove that this is the case. It should be noted that the strict wording of the Regulation is that the establishment *requires* to be approved, not that it *is* so approved, so a notice can be served on a premises that is or should be approved; the fact that approval has not been sought or has not yet been granted is not a fetter to serving a notice under this Regulation.

The Regulation also prescribes both the form and name of the notice; it shall be in writing and it shall be called a 'Detention Notice'. There is no room for creative thinking; the Regulation is definitive about name and form. It also tells the enforcement officer what the notice can do; it can require the detention of any animal or food for the purpose of examination and that examination can include the taking of samples. That is the limit of what the enforcement officer can do with the animal or food, he cannot sell it or destroy it; he may only examine it. If he wants to take matters further as the result of the examination process he may be able to do so, but he cannot do so under this Regulation. And finally, the Regulation tells us on whom this Detention Notice is to be served; it is to be served on the food business operator or any duly authorised representative, and no-one else. Careful reading of the just over 60 words contained in the Regulation tells the enforcement officer everything he needs to know and needs to be able to prove in order to lawfully serve this notice.

Every Assertive notice will start from a particular circumstance that the notice is intended to address; it may be for example that the enforcement officer believes that there has been a breach of a planning condition. For him to prove that such is the case there must be both a valid planning condition in force and the proposed recipient of the notice must be in breach of the planning condition. By way of further example, it may be a notice served under sec 4 of the Prevention of Damage by Pests Act 1949, in which case land with which the enforcement officer is concerned must be infested by rats or mice. And importantly, the enforcement officer must be able to prove the presence of rats or mice. There may be no appeal against the requirements of an Assertive notice where the reasonableness of the officers beliefs can be tested but in the event of there being a prosecution for non-compliance with it the officer will be required to prove to the court that his notice was properly served, and as part of that he will need to be able to show that the pre-requisites that preceded the serving of the notice, including all of the conditions that were required to be met to justify it were satisfied.

The Assertive notice will tell the recipient what he has to do to comply with its requirements. With notices of this sort the action to be taken is usually pretty straightforward. It will be a simple matter of 'Comply with the planning condition by doing XYZ 'or, 'Take such action as is necessary to remove rats or mice from the land'. The breach of the legislation will be relatively straightforward and therefore the steps to be taken to achieve compliance will also be. The notice will also tell the recipient how long he has to comply. This will be bald figure, 14 days or 28 days or 3 months or whatever the enforcement officer considered to be appropriate. This time period is important to a number of people. It is important to the recipient of the notice. It tells him how long he has to get the necessary work done; not started, not half finished, not even 99% finished, but completed. It is important to the enforcement officer (and anyone who takes over the case in his absence) because it tells them at what point compliance should be achieved so he knows when he may either consider the case closed or consider what further action he needs to take. It is also important to the complainant or any others affected by the problem that the notice addresses because it is only at the end of the period that they can anticipate that the problem from which they are suffering will stop. It may just be a figure, but a number of people will be interested in it.

As with Inquisitorial notices, the Assertive notice has to tell the recipient the consequences of failing to comply with its requirements. In most cases the non-compliant recipient will be liable to prosecution in the magistrate's court and on conviction to a fine, the level of which will have to be indicated on the notice. As with Inquisitorial notices it is a matter for the recipient whether or not he complies with the Assertive notice, but he is left under no illusions about what may happen if he doesn't, and he can factor that into his decision as to how to respond.

As I did with Inquisitorial notices, I want to make a couple of points about Assertive notices. I think it is fair to say that if a local authority has gone to the trouble of responding to a complaint, or has proactively established that something has happened and on the basis of its findings has made the effort to serve a notice, we are entitled to assume that the matter is important to them. As night follows day so the issue of compliance must also be important to them. So it should be reasonable to assume that at the end of the compliance period the officer who served the notice will go hot foot to the site in question to check that compliance has been achieved, and if it hasn't, will immediately spring into action and do something about it. Wandering along some months after the end of the compliance period and happening to notice that compliance is some way from being achieved doesn't really help if the matter then proceeds to court and the prosecutor is trying to explain to the magistrates the importance the local authority places on compliance. The local authority must not just want compliance it must be seen to want it.

The second point is a repetition of the one I made regarding Inquisitorial notices – if the recipient of the notice fails to comply with it, do something about it. Serving an Assertive notice has to be more than a gesture; it is a statement of intent, and the intention must be to resolve the issue addressed by the notice. If at the end of the compliance period compliance has not been achieved, do what your notice says on its face and prosecute the non-compliant recipient. It will not get the matter resolved, and I concede quite freely that such action won't win over everyone's' hearts or minds, but at least you will be seen to mean what you say. It is also the case that despite having been successfully prosecuted for non-compliance in the magistrates' court the recipient, now a convicted defendant, will not necessarily learn from his experience and may still refuse to comply. If he doesn't, go back to the start and serve another notice, and if he doesn't comply with that one, prosecute him again. And repeat as necessary. The matter is not concluded until compliance is achieved and serving a notice of itself is not enough. Complete compliance with its requirements and all of them is the conclusion of the matter; enforcement officers need to be in there for the long haul.

Words to the wise – Assertive notices

- Remember that serving an Assertive notice may be stage 2 of the enforcement process and you may need to serve an Inquisitorial notice first to be sure that you have accurate and up to date information available,
- Make sure you have the evidence to show that the remedy you demand through the Assertive notice is justified,

- Make sure your notice contains all those elements that the legislation requires and if the legislation is definitive on a point, such as the title of the notice, follow its instructions,
- Visit the site promptly at the end of the compliance period to check whether compliance has been achieved,
- If compliance has not been achieved at the end of the compliance period do something about it!

Permissive Notices

Up to now I have considered notices that are one sided in their construction. By that I mean that the local authority decides to serve them, decides what is required for compliance, serves the notice and prosecutes any non-compliance. The recipient is very much the minor partner; he must do what he is told before the end of the compliance period or else. Permissive notices are different beasts; what the local authority says on the face of the notice may not define the eventual outcome because the recipient of the notice is entitled to have his say about the requirements for compliance, the time period and in some cases whether service of the notice is appropriate at all. Permissive notices are distinguished from the other types of enforcement notice because attached to the Permissive notice is a right of appeal. Inquisitorial Notices have no right of appeal against them, but they are short term notices and require the recipient to do only one thing; to provide information to the enforcement officer. There is no need for an appeal provision; if the recipient of the notice has no interest in the land to which the notice relates all he has to do is say as much in his response and the matter is closed. Assertive notices do not have a right of appeal against them because, as noted above, there is no issue between the parties about the requirements of the notice. The enforcement officer must be able to show through e.g. the pre-existence of a planning condition or clear evidence of an infestation of rats or mice that the service of the notice is objectively justified; if there was no such breach or evidence he would not be involved in the matter at all.

Permissive notices however are quite different in the way that they operate. Taking some specific examples; Health and Safety at Work etc Act 1974 sec. 21 Improvement Notices can require owners of businesses to make significant changes to their operations that may require the spending of huge sums of money; Environmental Protection Act 1990 sec. 80 Abatement Notices can control the way individuals behave; Town and Country Planning Act 1990 sec. 172 Breach of Planning Control Notices allow the local authority to control the way in which landowners use or develop their own land and Food Safety and Hygiene Regulations 2013 reg. 6 Hygiene Improvement Notices can specify works that a business owner will be compelled to take in order to continue trading. All these Permissive notices contain very big sticks indeed and in many cases the owner of the land or business on whom they are served will feel more than a little aggrieved to be the recipient of one of them.

To add further grist to the mill, the justification for serving Permissive notices is nothing like as cut and dried as that for Assertive notices. The justification for Assertive notices as we have seen is readily identifiable; it is e.g. a pre-existing planning condition which is known to both parties or clear and compelling evidence of an infestation of mice or rats as proven by evidence such as damage caused, droppings, dead animals and possibly even live sightings. The enforcement officer is not required to form an opinion as to the necessity for an Assertive notice to be served based on speculative consequences should he fail to do so, he merely points to the evidence justifying it and goes right ahead and starts drafting. A Permissive notice however is much more sophisticated in its genesis since it requires the enforcement officer to form a view about the circumstances with which he is presented and to decide what, if anything, should be done about them. Sec.21 of the Health and Safety at Work etc. Act 1974 starts with the words *'If an inspector is of the opinion that…';* sec 80 of the Environmental Protection Act 1990 commences with the words *'(..) where a local authority is satisfied that a statutory nuisance exists…';* and reg. 6 of the Food Safety and Hygiene Regulations 2013 begins *'If an authorised officer of an enforcement authority has reasonable grounds for believing…'.* Permissive notices are not served in circumstances where something has to be blue and it isn't. They are served when the enforcement officer thinks either that something should be done, or should be done in a different way to the way that it is being done, and he is sufficiently convinced of the merits of his opinion as to require the business operator or land owner to fall in with his view and change the way they are operating.

That one person should have the power to make another act according to his opinion is an anathema to most people. Imagine the uproar if one individual could say to another 'In my opinion your hair style does nothing for you, therefore you must change it to a style of my choosing' or 'I am satisfied that as you live in the city you have no need of a sports car, therefore you must get rid of your car and replace it with a bicycle'. We live in a society where you can do what you like with your hair, from shaving it all off to colouring it orange and making it stick up in spikes; where, subject to you being able to afford it, you can drive anything you like, whether it suits your apparent needs or not. Eyebrows are raised when huge 4x4 off road vehicles are used for the school run in town but whatever the opinion of the school gate parents there is nothing they can do to force the determined 4x4 owner to downsize their vehicle. An orange Mohican hair may not be to everyone's taste, but even when the opinion of 99% of the population is that the style is hideous no-one can force someone whose taste in hairstyles verges on the more exotic to adopt a more traditional style and colour. As a culture we support the right of individuals to be individual and to 'do it their way'. Permissive notices fly in the face of this support for the individual and authorise an enforcement officer to require another, usually a business owner or landowner, to do it his way.

Dwelling as we do in the real world, we know that the power of an enforcement officer to serve a Permissive notice is not an unfettered one. The man or woman from the council cannot strut into a business and throw his or her weight about with impunity, expecting or demanding instant compliance. It is precisely because Permissive notices are such a powerful tool that they are subject to a number of restraints. In every case the legislation under which they arise imposes limits on the circumstances in which they can be served. Consider by way of example the power which authorises an enforcement officer to serve a sec. 80 Environmental Protection Act 1990 Abatement Notice in circumstances where the enforcement officer, exercising the power duly delegated to him by the council, is satisfied that a statutory nuisance exists. It is not for the enforcement officer to decide what constitutes a statutory nuisance. He has no discretion to run about determining what should and what should not be a statutory nuisance. The clue to what is a statutory nuisance is in the name. Something is a statutory nuisance because the statute says that it is. Sec.79 of the

Environmental Protection Act 1990 specifies in considerable detail what constitutes a statutory nuisance. It describes a particular set of circumstances, such as a premises in such a state or an animal kept in such a manner and then further requires that state or manner to be prejudicial to health or a nuisance before the officer can be satisfied that a statutory nuisance exists and consequently that the service of an Abatement Notice is justified. However offended an enforcement officer may be by a particular circumstance, to use my earlier example, … *'any hair style so extreme as to be wholly unflattering to the wearer…',* it is not a statutory nuisance unless somewhere in the mother act, the Environmental Protection Act 1990, or somewhere in other enactments, it is defined as being a statutory nuisance. Similarly, an enforcement officer cannot just serve a sec 21 Health and Safety at Work Act 1974 Improvement Notice because he has some innovative idea about how safety at a premises should be improved. He may only serve the notice if someone

(a) is contravening one or more of the relevant statutory provisions; or

(b) has contravened one or more of those provisions in circumstances that make it likely that the contravention will continue or be repeated.

For the enforcement officer to serve the notice he must be satisfied that there is at least one statutory provision that is either being contravened at the time of his visit, or has already been contravened and is likely to be contravened again.

There are therefore two constraints on the right of the enforcement officer to serve a Permissive notice. Firstly, that the legislation prescribes that a particular set of circumstances must exist and secondly that the officer must be of the view that the circumstances required do indeed exist. In the event of both requirements being satisfied the enforcement officer may serve the notice. It is at this point that Permissive notices diverge further from Assertive and Inquisitorial notices. In the case of both Inquisitorial and Assertive notices the requirement for compliance is straightforward. For Inquisitorial notices it is to provide the information required; for Assertive notices it is to comply with the condition or requirement that is in place and currently being ignored or contravened. It is a black and white situation and there is no room for negotiating or horse trading about how compliance is to be achieved.

The requirements for compliance with Permissive notices are much less prescriptive. In many cases the enforcement officer can pretty much require the recipient of the notice to 'take such measures as may be necessary to ensure compliance' or 'abate the nuisance' 'or 'remedy the contravention'. The enforcement officer is not required to prescribe how compliance is to be achieved by saying 'Do X, Y and Z and then paint everything a fetching shade of purple': rather he says 'Achieve X' and leaves it to the recipient of the notice to determine the best, most appropriate, most pragmatic or even cheapest way to achieve that. Going back to my comments about the right of an individual to run their life as they see fit, we can see where this sort of flexibility has its roots. If I am a business owner I can pretty much run my business as I wish. My product can be as cheap as old chips or high end, exclusive and out of the reach of most consumers. It can be an everyday essential or a pointless luxury. As a landowner I can use my land as I wish. I can develop it or I can leave it undeveloped; the choice to farm crops or animals or leave it as wilderness is a matter for me. That having been said a total *laisse faire* non-interventionist policy by government allows for chaos of every variety to proliferate. Hence health and safety legislation developed to protect employees from the risk of injury or illness arising from their working conditions. Environmental protection legislation developed to protect the health of the public from the products of industrialisation initially and latterly, from the consequences of modern living, such as noise and artificial light pollution. Food safety and hygiene legislation recognises the danger to consumers that is presented by unfit, contaminated or unhygienically produced food, and planning legislation recognises that the land bank is a finite asset that must be protected for the benefit of future generations irrespective of current ownership. The legislation that gives rise to Permissive notices recognises that, subject to an individual not endangering his workforce or others; affecting the health of the public; poisoning them; making them ill or causing permanent or lasting damage to land, he should be allowed to do what he wants in the way that he wants. It accords with this underpinning theory that when required to do something by an enforcement officer, and subject to him actually doing it, the recipient of a Permissive notice should be able to achieve the required outcome in the way that he thinks best. It is not for the enforcement officer to direct him as to how compliance is to be achieved, just to require him to achieve it. Hence I can be served with an Abatement notice requiring me to stop my cockerel crowing at 4.30am every morning if it is causing the neighbours sleep disturbance and stress, but I cannot be told how to curb its vocal enthusiasm. It is a matter for me whether I lock it in a dark hen house, send it away to live in the countryside or encase it in pastry. Provided my chosen method is effective the choice of method is mine.

From a practical point of view I think it is important to note that where the enforcement officer has formed a view that something is occurring that should be addressed by the service of a Permissive notice he should be certain that he can justify, at least to himself, the reasons for his serving the notice. I cannot overstress the importance of recording the reasons for serving the notice in a file note prior to the drafting of the notice and making sure that the note is retained. It may be that the reasons for serving the notice are clear, but the particulars may not be. The reasons for drafting it in the particular way it is drafted, for selecting the time period for compliance and so on, may be less obvious to the casual observer and, since the notice has the potential to be appealed, the reasoning behind its terms and requirements should be recorded for future reference and to rebut any allegation of post event justification that may be made at a later date.

It is said that for every action there is an equal and opposite reaction. It is also true to say that for every opinion there is an equal and opposite opinion. As I have said Permissive notices are served because in the opinion of the enforcement officer there is a beach of the legislation that should be addressed. It is fair to say that in many cases the recipient of the notice will not share that opinion. He may disagree with some or all that the enforcement officer opinion and because of his disagreement take the view that it is unfair or unreasonable that he should be required to comply with it. It is hard to think of any situation in a democratic country when the individual is required to say to an official 'I reject your view entirely but I am powerless to do anything about it other than roll over and accept it'. Such is certainly not the case with Permissive notices. If the recipient of a Permissive notice disagrees with the opinion of the enforcement officer serving it, he is entitled to appeal against it. His appeal will be heard by a third party, whether a magistrate sitting alone, a bench of magistrates , a tribunal or a Planning

Inspector and it is that third party who will make a ruling that is binding on both parties to the notice.

Such is the importance of the right to appeal that the Permissive notice must have the details of the right to appeal on its face; how the appeal is to be made, the time for making an appeal and the mechanics of making it. It is not in the interests of justice that the recipient of a notice who is aggrieved by its contents should have to hunt high and low to find out how he can object to it; he is to be given that information in a clear and comprehensible way so that nothing prevents him from exercising his right to appeal. As I discussed in chapter 3 the information must be correct in all respects, so that the potential appellant who relies on it is not prejudiced by doing so.

Having said that there is a right of appeal, it should be emphasised that this right of appeal is by no means unfettered. The appeal may only be founded on one of the grounds of appeal that are contained within the legislation. The appellant is not free to dream up his own ground of appeal based on his particular gripe with the requirements of the notice. However vehemently he may object to the requirements of a notice, unless his objection is on all fours with one of the statutory grounds of appeal, he cannot lawfully make it. Specifying the grounds on which an appeal can be founded is a pragmatic stance by the legislators. It recognises that there may be disagreement between the enforcer and the enforced against, but is not minded to allow them to slug out all and every difference the enforced against may have with the requirements in an appeal scenario, with consequent delays in compliance with the notice. Rather the legislator specifies those grounds under which an appeal may be brought, and they are exclusive.

The guardian of the appeal process is the tribunal before which it is to be heard. Before the tribunal decides the merits of the appeal it must decide whether or not the appeal is validly brought under the terms of the legislation. If it decides that the appeal is not validly brought under the terms of the legislation it must reject the appeal without considering its merits. If the appeal is rejected the Permissive notice will stand and the recipient will be required to comply with its requirements. If the appeal is accepted, in most cases, the notice will be held in abeyance pending the determination of the appeal. The holding of the notice in abeyance is clearly in the interests of the recipient, now the appellant, since it means he is not required to expend resources complying with requirements that may be quashed or amended. Unfortunately, as we shall discuss later, it can also become the source of frustration and delay. Appeals are discussed in more detail later in this book, for the present it suffices to say that they are a feature of Permissive notices and that their outcome has the ability to fundamentally affect the notice by quashing it, altering or amending its requirements or the time scales for compliance.

If a Permissive notice is quashed on appeal we need consider it no further. If however it is upheld or survives in an amended form the appellant is required to comply with it within the time scale prescribed. At the risk of repeating myself, I think it is important to say that just as it was important to ensure that compliance has been achieved in the case of Assertive notices it is important to ensure that compliance with Permissive notices is achieved. In some cases this will be a simple matter of looking over the fence and seeing that the necessary action has been taken or visiting the business and seeing that the required steps have been taken. In other cases the compliance requirement will be ongoing, the business owner will be required to keep on keeping on, and in such cases compliance monitoring will also have to be an ongoing process and may continue for years to come.

Words to the wise – Permissive notices

- Offences addressed by Permissive notices are subjective; the enforcement officer must be of the opinion that an offence has been committed, therefore justification is critical,
- In a Permissive notice the enforcement officer will prescribe what compliance will look like, but not how it should be achieved
- There is a right of appeal to a third party from a Permissive notice
- Permissive notices do not take effect immediately. They only take effect after the appeal period has elapsed, and then only if there has been no valid appeal

- The final terms of a Permissive notice may not be settled until after it has been subject to appeal
- Compliance with a Permissive notice may not be a one-off act. It may be ongoing, and in such cases monitoring of compliance must be the same.

Prohibitive Notices

The fourth class of notice is the one that is most extreme in its impact; the Prohibitive notice. Prohibitive notices do exactly what they say on the tin, they prohibit an activity and they do it with immediate effect. They are, in a manner of speaking, the biggest gun in the enforcement officer's armoury and as their effect is so dramatic they are not to be sprayed about with impunity.

The first point that needs to be made is that officers planning to serve Prohibitive notices should make certain that they are authorised to do so. A local authority cannot be criticised for being risk averse if it declines to authorise the newly qualified to serve Prohibitive notices. Quite the reverse; a degree of experience is required to my mind before an enforcement officer is competent to serve Prohibitive notices. Nothing is lost if an officer who is not authorised to serve such a notice has to return to the office or call up one of his more experienced colleagues to ask him to step into the fray and serve a Prohibitive notice. If anything, it shows that the officer is aware of the limitations of his authorisation and respects them. Certainly when I was in practice if I was briefed to advise someone who had been served with a Prohibitive notice my first line of inquiry would be whether the serving officer was authorised to serve a Prohibitive notice or not. It did occasionally happen that an enforcement officer, in the white heat of the moment, forgot he was not authorised or maybe did not even consider the question. It has occasionally happened that an enforcement officer has been doing the job for so long that everyone, including the officer himself has assumed that he must be fully authorised but, unfortunately, although his experience might have merited full authorisation, for whatever reason, his authorisation had not been reviewed and extended. Whatever the reason for the failure, such cases made it a very easy day in the office for me and a rather more torrid one for the local authority officers concerned.

The rationale for Prohibitive notices is that they should be used when an enforcement officer comes across a situation where the danger presented is so potent, the risk to health so severe or the potential damage to the environment so great that it must be addressed immediately. Allowing the matter to continue unabated until an appeal is heard would be unacceptable due to the continuing danger, risk or damage that would present during that time; hence the Prohibitive notice stops it in its tracks. Examples of Prohibitive notices are the Stop Notice served under sec 183 of the Town and Country Planning Act 1990; the Prohibition Notice served under sec 22 of the Health and Safety at Work Act 1974; and Hygiene Emergency Prohibition Notices and Orders under reg. 8 of the Food Safety and Hygiene Regulations 2013.

As with Permissive notices, Prohibitive notices are served where in the view of the enforcement officer there is some activity taking place that requires an urgent response. However, unlike Assertive notices the view of the enforcement officer is not tested at appeal before the notice takes effect. On appeal the Assertive notice is held in abeyance until such time as the appeal takes place, and, should the appeal be upheld and the view of the enforcement officer not win the day, no harm is done. In the case of a Prohibitive notice the activity giving rise to the notice being served in most cases stops immediately after service, despite the fact that the recipient may lodge an immediate appeal. If the recipient of a Prohibitive notice is aggrieved by its requirement, and given that he is likely to be, at least in his view suffering some loss or damage, he will want to appeal and to do so as quickly as possible. I hardly need to note again that the appeal provisions must be included on the face of the Prohibitive notice and, given the impact of a Prohibitive notice, the recipient of one is likely to be fervently interested in them.

As important as making sure that the appeal provisions are on the face of the notice and are clear and unequivocal is the need for the enforcement officer to record his justification for serving the Prohibitive notice. What was it about the conditions or circumstances that he found that made serving a Prohibitive notice imperative? Why would an Assertive notice not do? What damage was being done and why could it not continue in the short term? The reasons will probably be clear and will most likely have been discussed with colleagues and senior officers. All of the alternatives, palatable or unpalatable will have been weighed until the combined view of the team was that a Prohibitive notice was the only realistic option for the local authority. Given the potential consequences if the decision proves to be wrong, or if the terms of the notice are successfully challenged, the Prohibitive notice and its wording will almost certainly have been chewed over by lawyers and signed off by someone very high up the departmental pecking order. Despite this, and however the decision was arrived at, and however thinly shared the responsibility, the decision to serve the Prohibitive notice and the terms of its requirements are the responsibility of the officer who serves it and he will be the one required to defend it at any appeal. It is therefore critical that he records his reasons and justification for doing so. This recorded thinking will never be more important than at an appeal where the tribunal of fact does not take the same view as the enforcement officer and overturns or amends the Prohibitive notice or, perhaps worse where, for whatever reason, the local authority withdraws the Prohibitive notice. In such cases the very real threat of having to pay compensation to the appellant rears its ugly head. By way of example, under the Town and Country Planning Act 1990 compensation is payable under sec. 171H, for 171E Temporary Stop Notices and under sec. 186, for sec 183 Stop Notices. I don't want to raise undue alarm; it certainly is not the case that anyone who serves a Prohibitive notice is at a risk of seeing a massive compensation claim riding over the hill in their direction. It is however a very foolish enforcement officer indeed who does not consider, even if only briefly, the risk that he may get it wrong and be looking a claim for compensation squarely in the face. That is why there are usually strict protocols wrapped around the serving of Prohibitive notices.

Compensation is usually only payable in cases where the Prohibitive notice is quashed or varied because the justifications for the notice or its contents were outside those that constitute a valid reason for service; in such a case the local authority will have exceeded its power and in doing so will have caused loss or damage to the appellant. Equally if the local authority suddenly loses the courage of its convictions or further evidence comes to light that suggests it may have acted in error, and it consequently withdraws its Prohibitive notice, it is right that it should pay compensation to the party that has been adversely affected by its error.

The thought process for the serving of Prohibitive notices is exactly the same as for Assertive notices. Once the enforcement officer has decided that there is justification for an Assertive notice he should ask himself about the urgency of the matter. Will an Assertive notice do, or is there a compelling reason for the matter that gives rise to complaint being stopped and resolved more quickly? If there is, what is that reason? Notwithstanding the potential for compensation being awarded to someone who has an unjustified Prohibitive notice served on them, where circumstances dictate that a Prohibitive notice should be served, it is extremely important that it is served. I have been told by officers from more than one local authority that their authority does not use certain Prohibitive notices on the grounds that they are 'too dangerous'. The purpose of such notices being included in the legislation is that they should be used; for local authorities to banish them from their armoury through fear of repercussions is worse than foolish; it fetters their ability to do the job they are required to do to best effect. As long as all of the necessary issues have been considered and recorded and the local authority protocol for authorising such notices has been followed they should be used.

In respect of the other 3 classes of notice I have stressed the importance of following up the service of the notice to ensure compliance is achieved or to take further action if it is not. I hardly need underline how important it is to follow up the service of a Prohibitive notice. Unlike the other classes of enforcement notice the response to a Prohibitive notice should be immediate and should continue until such time as the notice is withdrawn or there is a successful appeal. The local authority that serves a Prohibitive notice must police it and ensure that compliance is immediately achieved. If it is not, further action must be taken. It is an offence for the recipient of a Prohibitive notice not to comply with its requirements and in some cases the sentencing magistrates can take account of any financial benefit that has accrued to a recipient who continued with his activity in disregard of the notice; they may impose a financial penalty that not only penalises the offender for the breach of the notice but also has regard to any financial benefit which has accrued or appears likely to accrue to him in consequence of the failure to comply. Of course, the court can only use the full extent of its sentencing power if it has evidence before it to justify doing so, which underlines the importance of continuous monitoring of the land or property concerned.

The final comment regarding Prohibitive notices relates to their ongoing nature and the fact that they must be withdrawn by the local authority as soon as the steps necessary to achieve compliance have been taken. It is a fair bet that the recipient of a Prohibitive notice who has carried out all of the works necessary to secure compliance will be very quick to inform the local authority to that effect and to request that the notice be withdrawn, but equally the local authority should be on the ball and ensure that as soon as conditions are such that the notice can be withdrawn, they withdraw it.

Words to the wise – Prohibitive notices

- Enforcement officers proposing to serve Prohibitive notices should check that they are authorised to do so
- Prohibitive notices should only be used where there is an urgent need to remediate the situation and officers should record their justification for serving them
- When a Prohibitive notice has been served it is essential that compliance with its requirements is monitored, and that failure to comply is addressed
- Prohibitive notices should be withdrawn as soon as the necessary steps to achieve compliance have been taken.

We are now four chapters into this book and so far have only considered the theory that underpins enforcement notices. I now intend to move on to the practical aspects of serving notices, including the whys, wherefores and what should be done and discussing what can go wrong and why.

Chapter 5

The contents of an enforcement notice

Up to this point I have talked about the theory underpinning enforcement notices and the technicalities that precede their service. I've said that most people never consider the underpinning theory and that whilst most enforcement officers will be aware of the need to satisfy the technical requirements, they also occasionally slip down their 'to do' list. Important the requirements may be, riveting they most certainly are not. What most enforcement officers will want to know is what do we have to do to make sure that we serve them properly and make certain that the recipient does what we want him to do? Skim readers rejoice, from this point on that is what I am going to consider.

What must an enforcement notice contain?

The constituent elements of an enforcement notice are not a secret. They are laid out in the legislation that creates them. That is not to say that in each and every statutory instrument that creates an enforcement notice there will be a Section X – 'Enforcement notice – contents thereof', there won't be, but by picking through the sections that talk about the enforcement notice and its contents the officer will be able to identify what the elements are and make sure that they are all present and correct. Whilst there is no such thing as a generic form of notice there are some requirements that are standard to all enforcement notices, and it is worth considering what they are, the reasons for them and what happens if any one of them is missed off the notice.

An enforcement notice must contain

1. The identity of the local authority serving it
2. The name and address of the party on whom it is served
3. Clear identification of the issue that the notice is served to address and the statute under which this requirement arises
4. The steps that are required to achieve compliance with the notice
5. The time period for compliance to be achieved
6. Details of the consequences of failing to comply with the requirements of the notice

7.   Information about any right of appeal that may exist, including how to appeal, to whom to appeal and the time period for the appeal to be lodged.

Each of the requirements is important and failing to include any one of them will either give rise to grounds of appeal or will render the notice null and void. Given their importance there is merit in considering why each is required and the effect of their absence.

1.   The identity of the local authority serving the notice

In most cases this is a given. In-house generated templates will usually feature the name of the local authority as well as other less relevant information, such as the corporate logo or heraldic crest or the council's strap line about X-shire being a great place to work, rest and play or whatever it happens to be. Whether the notice is a template notice, a standard form of words printed on corporate headed paper or is a purchased-in standard document, the name and address of the local authority that serves it must appear on it. This is not just to prevent a corporate identity crisis; it serves a purpose in law. The purpose is to ensure that the local authority's action is *intra vires*. A local authority, except in some rare cases, only has power to act within its own administrative boundaries. Outside that boundary, e.g. inside a neighbouring authority they have no such authority and any action they take there is unlawful; they are restricted to their home soil. The presence of the name, and in most cases the address, of the local authority helps tells the recipient of the notice whether the local authority that serves the notice has any lawful authority to do so; he will be able to check whether the land, property or business concerned does indeed lie within the administrative area of that authority. Being realistic, in most cases it will; most local authority officers are all too aware of where their local authority boundaries lie and have enough to do without wandering off into next door to get involved in their problems. But in large rural authorities, where the boundaries wander around over hill and dale and where the big black line is not on the ground for all to see, it is usually worth checking that the property concerned and all of it does indeed lie within the local authority's administrative area before serving an enforcement notice, or taking any other form of action for that matter.

Getting it wrong

There is no ground of appeal against an enforcement notice served by a local authority in respect of anything outside its own boundaries. There doesn't need to be because the enforcement notice is void *ab initio* (from inception) i.e. it was never an enforcement notice, and it has no force in law. All it amounts to is a piece of paper with words on it and the recipient is free to ignore it. He cannot appeal against something that does not in law exist. This presents certain difficulties for the local authority that does not work out that it has trespassed into the area of another council, but the recipient does. As far as the local authority can see they have served a notice on someone who is choosing to ignore both it and them and, in consequence, at the end of the compliance period they may lurch off down the path of prosecution before their error comes to light. Of course, any summons served on the recipient of an unlawful notice will also be void as the offence alleged will not exist. It is to be hoped that the local authority will realise that their notice is fatally flawed or, if they do not, that the Clerk to the Justices, who considers the Information alleging non-compliance will pick it up and refuse to issue a Summons. Unfortunately, on occasions, the checks are not as rigorous as they might be, and things slip through the net. I know of at least one local authority that has paid for grant aided works in a property in its neighbouring authority and of two that have served notices requiring works to private water supplies that were not theirs to deal with.

The implications of getting wrong something as simple as not knowing where the local authority boundary is are both embarrassing and potentially expensive. The embarrassment goes without saying; the potential expense arises from two sources. The first is because any money spent by the local authority that has taken the unlawful action is not money lawfully expended and so it cannot be recovered from the local authority in whose area it acted or indeed from anyone who has directly benefitted, such as the recipient of grant monies. That is bad enough, but secondly we should not lose sight of the fact that an enforcement notice is often served because someone has complained about something that is affecting them and, by the time it is serving enforcement notice of whatever type, the local authority generally shares that view. The fact that it has acted outside its jurisdiction may not come to light until much time has elapsed but nothing substantive by way of remedy has been delivered, during which time the complainant will still be suffering from whatever it was that has caused his complaint. His obvious next step is to complain, first to the local authority and thereafter to the Local Government Ombudsman. Most of us would rather avoid such references which can be embarrassing and expensive.

One final point under this heading. The fact local authority A may have made something of a hash of things doesn't means that the recipient of the first, flawed notice can disappear into the sunset without a care in the world. He can't. Chances are that the neighbouring local authority, B, will share the same view as local authority A and, once acquainted with the position, will in all probability serve the same type of notice. The notice will also almost certainly be in the same terms with broadly the same requirements, so that other than having benefitted from a bit of delay and having been able to make local authority A squirm the recipient is no better off and will have to fall into line and comply in the end.

2. The name and address of the party on whom the enforcement notice is served

Oh dear; the trouble that the words 'name and address' cause. I think that more than any other requirement 'name and address' appears to have the ability to cause even the most experienced enforcement officer to doubt themselves. I think it is easiest to consider the two elements separately.

Firstly, in order of appearance, the requirement to serve the notice *on someone*. That 'someone' need not be a person, it needs only be a party having a legal persona. 'Someone' can be a limited company, an unincorporated association, a charity, a partnership or a person. In most cases the legislation will tell the enforcement officer who the 'person' is. By way of example the Food Safety Act 1990 sec.11 identifies the relevant person as 'the proprietor of a food business'; the Environmental Protection Act 1990 sec. 80 goes further and says that the person on whom notice should be served is either 'the person responsible for the nuisance, the owner of the premises (if the nuisance alleged is a defect of a structural nature to a property) and if the person responsible cannot be identified, the owner or occupier of the premises'; sec187A of the Town and Country Planning Act 1990 identifies the person as being 'any person who is carrying out or who has carried out the development; or any person having control of the land.' None of these pieces of legislation tell the enforcement officer the identity of this person but they are clear about the capacity in which the person acts. The legislation therefore directs the enforcement officer to the party who is to be named on the notice; the next question is how to describe them on the face of the notice.

Quite obviously the potential recipient of the notice will be less than thrilled at the prospect of receiving it, therefore any excuse to distance himself from it will be embraced with enthusiasm. If the potential recipient can look at the name on the face of the notice and honestly say 'That's not me' he is justified in ignoring it. He can sometimes justify doing that if the enforcement officer serving the notice is insufficiently specific in describing him e.g. spelling his name wrongly or using nicknames or shortened versions of names. People using names other than the one their mother gave them are more common than you might think, and very often even their closest friends don't know what their 'real 'name is. By way of example; my father was christened Clive, which he hated; his middle name was Robert, so he called himself Bob and my mother, but only my mother, called him Mick (after the Hollywood mouse, since you ask). My brother is named Michael and ever since he could talk, he, and everyone but my mother who gave him his name, called him Mike. Most people could work out that my brother's name was Michael; very few would have worked out that my father's name was Clive. My father would be able to mount an argument that he was entirely justified in ignoring an enforcement notice addressed to him as Bob, Robert or Mick since none of them were addressed to him in his proper name.

Would there be a counter-argument that as my father called himself Bob and used that name in his daily life that he should know that the notice was intended for him and that therefore the notice was valid? Yes there would, but why have the argument when you don't need to? If you get the recipient's name right you can never be wrong. Accuracy is key.

Where the party is an individual they should be described by name. The individual's full name should be used; Rob Jones should be named as Robert Jones, not the informal shortened version Rob, and not by his initial R. Jones. If the officer knows that Robert Jones has a middle name and knows what it is so much the better, that middle name should also be included. The objective is to make sure that the Robert Jones named as the person who should undertake whatever action the notice demands is clearly identified and any possibility of confusing him with any other Roberts or Mr Joneses is avoided.

If the party to be cited is a limited company, it is the company that is to be served with the notice, not any of the individuals who work for it. On the face of the enforcement notice the party named should be cited as 'Big Bad Company Limited'. How Big Bad Company Limited goes about achieving compliance is a matter for the company; the Chief Executive can do the work, the tea lady can do it or a team of external contractors can do it, it doesn't matter and neither realistically does the enforcement officer care. In a similar vein, a local authority is cited by the name of the authority, 'Cautious County Borough Council' or 'Reckless District Council, not by the name of the Chief Executive, Leader of the Council or Mayor.

Enforcement officers often ask me what name they should put on the face of an enforcement notice when dealing with unincorporated associations, sporting and workingmen's clubs and similar which are run by managing committees of volunteers. There appear to be a number of schools of thought; one that every member of the committee should be individually named on the notice, another that the Chair of the managing committee should be cited as an individual by name or by describing him as Robert Jones, Chair of the Middlewich Ferret Fanciers Association; a further suggestion is that the notice should just name 'The Middlewich Ferret Fanciers Association' without reference to a post holder. Partnerships also cause problems. I am asked if all of the partners to a partnership should be sent an individual copy of the enforcement notice naming them personally as a partner in the partnership or can a notice be addressed to just one of them?

My advice is that enforcement officers must look at the organisation to which they are sending the notice. What is it, i.e. what is the legal persona on which the notice is to be served? Ignore the individuals concerned and park any concerns about what should appear on the envelope containing the notice. Just focus on the group or club or partnership. Irrespective of how many people make up the group or club or partnership there will only be one legal persona and that is the name that should appear on the face of the notice. Therefore, in my ferret fancier's example above the enforcement officer should use the 'Middlewich Ferret Fanciers Association' as the name on the face of the notice. In the case of a partnership, the notice is addressed, on its face, to 'Jones and Jones (a partnership)' or 'The Jones Partnership' or however it describes itself, without reference to the individual partners. Glascoed Rugby Club would be named on the face of a notice, as would Henllys Workingmen's Club, since those names are the titles of the clubs' legal personas.

Causing almost as much concern are churches and other religious buildings. Enforcement officers tend to tip toe around serving enforcement notices on religious buildings, not because they don't want to or don't think they should but because they are not sure who should be named on the face of the notice. Putting to one side the flippant answers, the answer is actually easier than most people tend to think, it just requires a bit of research. The church, or the religious building, is owned by a body that has a legal persona. It may be a Diocesan Board or Muslim Council or Board of Deputies, but whoever it is, it will have a legal persona and it is that name that should appear on the face of the notice at the address at which it is based.

The capacity of the recipient

Everything I have said about recipients to this point has been based on the assumption that the recipient is of full capacity, that is the recipient is capable of dealing with his own affairs. As many enforcement officers will only be too aware that is not always the case. Some proposed recipients will have learning difficulties, or may be suffering from mental illness, or may be incapable of dealing with their own affairs due to physical infirmity. In such circumstances the enforcement officer is in a difficult position. He has an obligation to the complainant to deal with whatever the issue happens to be, but he cannot unleash the full enforcement regime on someone who is either incapable of understanding or incapable of responding. As ever there is no do-nothing option, but the what to do question is not easily answered.

The first inquiry should be whether there is another person acting for the proposed recipient by virtue of a power of attorney. That person steps into the shoes of the proposed recipient and acts on his behalf and in his interest. He should be named on the face of the notice as A N Other (as the representative of X Y Recipient). X Y Recipient should not be named personally as the primary recipient since he will not be capable of doing the work necessary to achieve compliance and hence should not be required to do so. In the event of the person having the Power of Attorney failing to comply with the requirements of the notice he can be prosecuted in the same way as any other non-compliant notice recipient.

What about the person who is incapable of handling their own affairs but has no one acting for them? The example I have in mind is someone of extreme age, who is in residential or nursing care and who is the owner of a property that is falling into disrepair and adversely affecting neighbours. A notice could be served on them as the property owner but it is more than a little unrealistic to expect them to be able to do anything by way of compliance and there is no obligation on the care provider to step in and assist. What then should the enforcement officer do in such circumstances? I think the answer is that the enforcement officer has to play the game. He has to serve the enforcement notice on the property owner knowing compliance will not be achieved. At the end of the compliance period he should take a view on what action should then be taken. Prosecution of the notice recipient is hardly in the public interest but the option to do works in default presents itself. The local authority can carry out such works as are necessary, pursuing the costs incurred by registering a charge against the property. It's not ideal and it is probably not the course of action that the local authority would sign up to for given the choice, but realistically it has no alternative other than to bite the bullet and get on with it.

Once the enforcement officer has sorted out the party to be named and established their correct name, the second element has to be added, being the address of the party named. Again, this causes problems. It is important to bear in mind that the address at which the activity that provokes the notice occurs may not be the one that is to appear on the face of the notice. Clearly if the matter that causes the service of the notice occurs on land owned by its occupier everything is quite straight forward, but often this is not the case. The notice must show on its face the address at which the party named has its main address. Therefore notices served on limited companies are addressed to the company at its registered office address, irrespective of where the unlawful activity occurs. If the notice is addressed to a local authority the address of the civic headquarters, whether it is called the Town Hall, Civic Centre or County Hall must be used. It is not the sub-office, district office or one-stop shop address. Notices addressed on their face to charities must show the registered office of the charity. Notices addressed to partnerships must use the main address from which the partnership operates. Notices to religious groups must use the address at which the group has its main base, not the address of the religious building that is the cause for concern.

Enforcement officers tend to get confused between what to put on the face of the notice and what to put on the face of the envelope in which it is delivered. As I said let's park the envelope until the next chapter and concentrate solely on the face of the notice. The name of the party is the name of its legal persona. The address is the main address of that party, whether described as registered office, headquarters or main place of business. As long as officers just focus on those simple rules when completing the name and address requirement on an enforcement notice they shouldn't go wrong.

For a relatively simple requirement, getting the name and address of the party on whom the notice is served right, there are plenty of opportunities to get it wrong. Be that as it may, the responsibility for getting the name of the person on whom the notice is served right lies with the enforcement officer it is not for the person on whom it should be served to come forward and provide all the necessary details. There are ways of making sure the details that are relied on are correct; the obvious ones being the use of an Inquisitorial notice, inquiries at Companies House and the interrogation of Articles of Association or club rules. Given the potential for error what happens if the enforcement officer does get something wrong?

Getting the name or the address wrong

There are two forms of 'wrong' to consider. The first is when the
enforcement officer thinks they have identified the right person; the
party they name on the notice and the address on which the notice
is served accurately reflect the officer's intentions but the party
served claims that they are not the party on whom notice should be
served. Basically the 'Not me Guv' ground of appeal. In such cases
the party served with the notice must appeal against it, his ground of
appeal being that he is not the correct party and therefore the notice
should be quashed. He says nothing about the reasonableness or
otherwise of the requirements of the notice or of the compliance
period, just that it is nothing to do with him. This can occur where
there is a complete misidentification of the responsible party or
where the enforcement officer directs the notice wrongly, for
example addressing it to the Company Secretary of a limited
company (who is an individual and a post holder), rather than to the
limited company by name. In such cases the tribunal to whom the
appeal is made can quash the notice. This is a bit of a blow, but the
enforcement officer is not precluded from serving the enforcement
notice again, this time naming the correct party.

The other form of 'wrong' is more problematic. In this form the
enforcement officer accurately identifies both the right person and
where they live or work from, but there is some error in the way in
which the recipient is named in the notice or the address that is
used. As I said my father's name was Clive although no one called
him that, in fact most people didn't know he wasn't called Bob or
more correctly, Robert. Even though he was known as Bob to all
and sundry he would have been able to mount an argument that he
was justified in ignoring an enforcement notice that named him on
its face as Bob Barratt, however accurate the rest of the notice may
have been, simply because he was not Bob Barratt, therefore it was
not addressed to him. The fact that he would have known it was
meant for him is irrelevant. In practical terms how could an
enforcement officer prove that my father knew a notice not
addressed to him was meant for him, but had deliberately
disregarded it? It didn't name him by his proper name so he could
with complete justification say it was not for him. And what about
the circumstances where it turns out that the name used in the
notice is not a genuine, alternative name but just a nickname used by

some people but not others? Where do you draw the line? It is an argument you do not want to have because as I said you can always lose an argument. If you get the details correct there is nowhere for the recipient to go.

The problem for the enforcement officer serving the notice in these circumstances is that unlike the first type of wrong the recipient will almost certainly not appeal against the notice.   Only a fool would get in touch with the local authority to advise them that they have served him with a notice, that they have made a bit of a hash of it but he thinks that it is probably meant for him and would they be so good as to confirm that? The sensible wrongly named recipient just ignores the notice on the grounds it is not meant for them; if it was, it would say so, and it doesn't. Unfortunately to the blissfully unaware enforcement officer the recipient ignoring the notice looks very like the recipient not complying with it, and as with void notices discussed at (1) above, the reality of the situation may not come to light until a long way down the track. And as I said, that's not good.

3.   Clearly identifying the issue that the notice addresses and the statute under which the requirement arises

As far as the recipient of the enforcement notice is concerned this is the meat of it. This is where the enforcement officer says what it is that the recipient is doing or not doing and why he should stop or start, as the case may be. In the case of Inquisitorial and Assertive notices this is relatively straight forward; in the case of an Inquisitorial notice it is simply a matter of stating what information is required from the recipient and in the case of an Assertive notice what it is alleged that the recipient is or in not doing and then advising what action he must take to comply, citing the legislation, chapter and verse, that says so.

In the case of Permissive and Prohibitive notices it is more complicated because the enforcement officer is required to put his cards on the table and say what it is, in his opinion, that the recipient is doing or failing to do that has caused him to intervene, and to cite that part of the relevant statute that he says supports him.

It is here he also says where the breach is taking place, i.e. at what address. At 2 above, I pointed out that the notice has to be addressed, on its face, to a party at an address, but that the address used for service may be different from the address at which the matter complained of is occurring. In my limited company example the enforcement officer has already told Big Bad Company Limited, at their registered office, that this notice is for them: he now tells them that the reason it is for them is because of the something that is happening at their premises at 63 High Street, Smalltown. In some cases the address of the recipient of the notice and the address at which the alleged breach is taking place will be one and the same; a small butcher may have only one premises, in which case the same address will be used in sections (2) and (3) of the notice, but care must be taken to ensure that the correct address is used in the correct section of the enforcement notice.

Returning to the issue of what the notice addresses and the statute under which the requirement arises, the best way to demonstrate this in practical terms is using an example. Taking the Food Safety and Hygiene (England) Regulations 2013 and Regulation 6(1) Hygiene improvement notices:

6.—*(1) If an authorised officer of an enforcement authority has reasonable grounds for believing that a food business operator is failing to comply with the Hygiene Regulations, the officer may by a notice served on that person (in these Regulations referred to as a "hygiene improvement notice") —*
(a) state the officer's grounds for believing that the food business operator is failing to comply with the Hygiene Regulations [1]
(b) specify the matters which constitute the food business operator's failure to comply [2]

The regulation requires that two things must be done in the notice. In the first [1] the officer must state his grounds for believing that the operator is failing to comply with regulations and in the second [2] he must say how in practise terms this is being done. The form of words therefore will be

Regulation 5 of the XYZ Regulations 2014 requires a food business operator to protect food from risk of attack by weasels [2]. In the opinion of A N Officer, William Butcher, being a food business operator is breaching Regulation

5 by storing raw meat in the back yard of the premises at (address) an area A N Officer knows to be populated by weasels [1].

Doubtless we could bicker for hours about the exact form of words to be used, but the essential requirements are satisfied in that the notice states at [2] what the requirement of the regulation is and at [1] how it is in the opinion of the enforcement officer that the requirement is being breached.

The requirement that the notice should state what the legislation actually demands and be specific as to how the recipient is failing to comply means that firstly the recipient can acquaint himself with what the law actually requires him to do or not do, and can secondly measure what he is actually doing or not doing against what is required of him. The notice also tells him what the enforcement officer's opinion is, with his justification for that view. How nice it would be if the recipient of the notice shared the enforcement officer's view and would just quietly roll over and get on with the steps to achieve compliance, but life isn't always like that. This particular requirement is the element of enforcement notices that generates the greatest number of appeals after those based on the reasonableness or otherwise of the steps prescribed to achieve compliance.

Appeals

The recipient may appeal against an enforcement notice in the terms above by arguing that the officer's opinion is wrong. This is not a flat denial that that the activity alleged to be happening, or not as the case may be, is occurring or otherwise, but a claim that it is not such as to be a breach of the regulation or Act. To put this into context; in my example above the recipient of the notice, William Butcher, may concede entirely that he does store raw meat in the back yard of his premises and further that it is crammed with ferociously hungry weasels but may argue that his raw meat is protected in such a way as to make it invulnerable to attack so that the enforcement officer's opinion is wrong and there is no breach of the regulation. The issue between the parties is the difference in opinion between the enforcement officer and William Butcher and it will be for the appeal tribunal to decide whose opinion it prefers, based on the evidence it hears.

There is a second ground of appeal against this requirement and that is that the breach alleged is not one known to law. Basically, this means that in the view of the recipient of the notice the issue that the enforcement officer has identified as a breach is happening but is not unlawful.

This is certainly a less commonly used ground of appeal but tends to come into its own when enforcement officers are trying to help someone, usually a complainant with whom they have a certain degree of sympathy by squeezing the facts until they squeak to make them fit the legislation. Call it thinking outside the box or pushing the boundaries or whatever you like, but sometimes you can be too far outside the box or too far over the boundaries and this ground of appeal kicks in. My favourite example arises out of advice I gave to a local authority tussling with their local police force about responsibility for dealing with horses straying out of a badly fenced field and onto the highway where they ran about in front of moving vehicles generally causing traffic chaos. The police had originally dealt with the matter but with little success and the novelty of doing so soon wore thin. Searching therefore for a better and more expedient way to deal with the issue they stumbled on the statutory nuisance provisions of the Environmental Protection Act 1990 and specifically sec 79(f) which designates 'any animal kept in such a state as to be prejudicial to health or a nuisance' to be a statutory nuisance.

The apparently happy consequence of discovering this section was that responsibility for dealing with the issue could be passed to the local authority as the enforcing authority for the Environmental Protection Act and the police could go back to dealing with non-equine criminals. From the local authority point of view there were however certain difficulties. To successfully claim that the poorly fenced horses were a statutory nuisance they would have to show that they were kept in such a state as either to be prejudicial to health or a nuisance. The definitions of 'prejudicial to health' and of 'nuisance' are well defined and a raft of case law has evolved around both. It is clear that horses escaping from poorly fenced fields and marauding about being a menace to traffic fits within neither. Had the local authority served a notice alleging that the horses were a statutory nuisance it would have been vulnerable to being quashed on appeal, as the nuisance alleged was 'not one known to law'.

Basically, the recipient of the notice would have looked at the terms of the statute – the wording of sec 79 of the Environmental Protection Act 1990 and specifically sec 79(f) and looked at what the enforcement officer, in his opinion, considered to be the nuisance and said 'Just hang on a minute, that isn't right – what the officer says is a nuisance is not a nuisance as per the definition in law, I'm going to appeal'. And he would have succeeded. The requirement to specifically state what the legislation requires, as well as what the enforcement officer considers the recipient of the notice is doing that beaches the requirement, allows the recipient to work out whether it is the strict letter or the spirit of the law that is being enforced, and, where anything other than the strict letter is being enforced, to appeal against the notice.

In summary there are two grounds of appeal; the first that the recipient of the notice is not doing what the notice alleges that he is, the second being that he is doing what he is alleged to be doing but it's not a breach of the law because the law doesn't say that it is.

Unlike the situation where the recipient of the notice could just sit back and let nature take its course in the case of either of the two grounds of appeal cited here he must actively do something; he must actually appeal. As we will see later in the chapter covering appeals, failing to appeal when there are valid grounds for doing so can have very dangerous consequences, therefore where the recipient of a notice believes he has a valid appeal under either of the two grounds discussed he must actively prosecute the appeal. For the local authority concerned this means that they will be required to defend the notice at an appeal hearing, where it will either be quashed or upheld but this does at least have the advantage of ensuring some progress in the matter is being made.

4. The steps that are required to achieve compliance with the notice

Having identified that there is, in his opinion, a breach of the law and having said what that is the enforcement officer is required to specify what steps must be taken by the recipient of the notice to satisfy the requirements of the notice and comply with the legislation. These are of course the steps that *the officer* considers to be necessary as there is no list of 'standard remedial solutions' which he can cut and paste into the enforcement notice; no compendium from which the officer can take a neatly defined remedy that is agreed by everyone, has been tested and has withstood the rigours of the appeal process. It is either for the officer to define what must be done to satisfy the requirements of the enforcement notice or for the officer to say what must be achieved and leave it to the recipient of the notice to decide how to achieve that end.

I will consider both cases, starting firstly with those notices where the officer is required to specify what the recipient of the notice must do to achieve compliance. The wording of the requirements differs in the case of each piece of legislation, but the thrust is generally the same.

A Hygiene Improvement notice arising under the Food Hygiene and Safety Regulations 2013 requires the enforcing officer under reg.6 (1) I to specify the measures which, in the officer's opinion, the food business operator must take in order to secure compliance; the Town and Country Planning Act 1990 sec 173(3) states that *"An enforcement notice shall specify the steps which the authority require to be taken, or the activities which the authority require to cease, in order to achieve, wholly or partly, any of the following purposes…. "*

The enforcement officer must therefore nail his colours to the mast and say what it is that the recipient of the notice has to do to achieve compliance. It's fair to say that the enforcement officer should know exactly what needs to be done; he has after all identified what the problem is and he will have a pretty shrewd idea of what the solution needs to be and, for the purposes of the notice, he is required to articulate that. However before the enforcement officer launches into a list of requirements as long as his arm of the things, which in an ideal world, would make the premises to which the notice relates quite the finest example of its type in the local authority's area, he has to be aware of the restricting words in the legislation. The legislation does not talk in terms of works required to achieve the local authority's ambitions or of works necessary to make the business the best that it can be. It talks in terms of 'achieving compliance' or uses limiting words such as those in sec 173 of the Town and Country Planning Act 1990. The sky is not the limit; the limit is the bare minimum necessary to achieve compliance. Whilst it is acceptable for local authorities to work with, encourage and cajole businesses to be better that the minimum standards required to be compliant e.g. by using rating schemes such as the Food Hygiene or Tattoo Hygiene Rating Schemes they cannot force the issue by use of enforcement notices. If a business wants to bump along the bottom line of compliance or tread the fine line of control that is a matter for them and that is the most the local authority can require. Enforcement officers therefore have to be careful to ensure that when specifying what needs to be done to achieve compliance they go no further than that, because to do otherwise would be to exceed their power and make the excessive requirements *ultra vires* and void.

What if the notice recipient decides to appeal? What will he, now the appellant, want to achieve by appealing? As he is appealing under this head rather than that discussed in (3) above we have to assume one of two options; either he does not dispute the allegation contained in the notice but does dispute the steps demanded to achieve compliance, or he has unsuccessfully disputed the allegation and now he wishes to dispute the steps to compliance prescribed in the enforcement notice. To be clear, he cannot just dispute them because he doesn't like them. It was always difficult when I was in practice to explain to someone who had just been convicted that he could not appeal against a finding of guilt on the grounds that he didn't agree with it; he had to have some reason on which to base his appeal and his nose being out of joint didn't suffice for that purpose. So it is with appeals against requirements in notices, there has to be some justification for them; the appellant will have to make an argument such as the requirements are excessive in nature and scope or they go beyond what is reasonably necessary for the purposes of securing compliance with the legislation. He will have to offer his own ideas of what is reasonable and appropriate by way of actions to achieve compliance and he will have to persuade the magistrates that his view is to be preferred to that of the local authority. The local authority will be able to put its own case, arguing for the requirements in the notice as well as arguing against those put forward by the appellant. Ultimately it is for the magistrates to take a view as to what they think is right, having heard the arguments. The local authority may not succeed in getting everything it wanted by way of actions to achieve compliance but on the other hand it is assured of getting something, and is therefore on the way to resolving the matter of which complaint was made.

Perhaps more tricky are those forms of requirement that do not specify what is to be done but merely say what is to be achieved and leave it to the recipient of the notice to decide how he achieves compliance. A case in point is the abatement of statutory nuisances. The wording of the Environmental Protection Act 1990 sec 80 (1) is as follows:

(1) Where a local authority is satisfied that a nuisance exists …. (it) shall serve a notice imposing all or any of the following requirements-

    a.   requiring the abatement of the nuisance or prohibiting or restricting its occurrence or recurrence,

    b.   requiring the execution of such works, and the taking of such other steps, as may be necessary for those purposes.

Effectively the enforcement officer says what the end point will be, and the recipient of the notice decides how to get there. This means that where the nuisance has been described earlier in the notice the requirement for compliance can be as simple as ' Abate the nuisance', or can be extended to say ' Abate the nuisance and ensure that it does not recur'. The requirement is usually slightly more specific than that, but it doesn't need to be. What the notice cannot do is direct the recipient as to exactly how he must comply. If there are alternative ways he can use, the choice is a matter for him. He can gild the lily if he wishes or he can do the bare minimum, as long as he complies.

You might wonder what there is to appeal about when the recipient of the notice can do pretty much what he likes, as long as he achieves compliance within the prescribed time. There are two grounds of appeal; the first being that the works required by the notice are unreasonable in character or extent or are unnecessary; the second is that the local authority has unreasonably refused to agree alternative works which would have the same effect as those specified. There is not a great deal to say about the second ground of appeal, except to note that there is no dispute between the appellant and the local authority about what needs to be done, just how it is to be done, and each side has its own view and won't shift from it.

The first ground of appeal is more interesting because it is effectively two separate grounds. The first is that the works demanded are unnecessary in character or extent; that is not to say that the works are unnecessary, it is to say that their character or extent is unnecessary. It is a challenge about how and to what degree the works are necessary, not whether they are necessary at all, and the appeal will come down to the two parties arguing their respective cases. The second part of this appeal is that the works are unnecessary, full stop. It will generally be teamed with an appeal made under (3) above, where the appellant disputes that there is a nuisance and therefore disputes that there needs to be a remedy. Again, it will be for the magistrates to hear the parties and to make a decision as to whose evidence they prefer.

The legalities of the grounds of appeal are fairly straight forward; the appellant must bring an appeal based on one of the grounds of appeal and the tribunal of fact, usually the magistrates court, will decide whose view is to be preferred. From the point of view of the lawyer representing the local authority this element of the appeal is relatively easy; all that has to be checked is that the proposed appeal is properly made, in that it is an appeal based on one of the grounds of appeal; the merits of the argument not being a matter for the lawyer. From the professional enforcement officer's point of view it is much more difficult because he is going to have to make the case for that works he has required are essential in the form he has prescribed them. Being realistic, I am fully aware that enforcement officers don't just write a wish list of compliance requirements on the basis that if they get them all that is a bonus and that some are just there to be shot at and lost if needs be. I know that requirements are usually carefully considered and are not included unless they are considered to be essential. Where the local authority stands its ground and the appellant will not move there is a Mexican standoff that can only be resolved by each side making their case to a third party who will rule on its findings. As a lawyer I can advise on the legalities of the appeal process but the argument to be made is a professional argument for the officer in the case and all I can do is showcase what he says at the appeal hearing.

5.   The time period for compliance to be achieved

It is critical that the recipient of a notice knows how long he has to comply with its requirements. Before I get involved in talking at length about compliance periods I want to make a side point about the starting point for achieving compliance. Where there is a right of appeal attached to an enforcement notice there will be an appeal period, being the period laid down in the legislation during which the appeal must be brought. Depending on the legislation this may be as little as 14 days or as long as 28 days but whatever the period the enforcement notice does not take effect until the appeal period has ended. It is only at the end of the appeal period that the compliance period starts to run and that is the period the enforcement officer has inserted into the notice. If the recipient of the notice appeals the notice goes into abeyance until the appeal is either heard or is withdrawn, at which point the compliance period starts to run. The answer to the question, 'When does the compliance period end?' is therefore, 'It depends on when it starts'. Enforcement officers know that of course, but it is rather more difficult for complainants to understand that they can't be given a hard and fast finish date until the start date is known, and that date is a movable feast.

It is also instructive to consider what the compliance period actually is. It is the period during which compliance must be achieved, when all of the works required by the enforcement notice must be completed. That is, completed. Not started or nearly finished, but completed. That might seem a bit of a self-evident statement but it is important to bear it in mind because it should be a major factor for the enforcement officer when he comes to consider what the compliance period or periods should be.

Although the strict wording may be different in most cases the ground of appeal against a compliance period will be to the effect that the time within which the works are to be executed is not reasonably sufficient for the purpose (Public Health Act 1936). From my point of view as a lawyer it is always a bit of a disappointment when the only issue between the parties is the time period for compliance. I always take the view that if all else is agreed there is much to be said for a bit of horse trading around the period for compliance because once that is agreed the works needed to achieve compliance can be started. If it cannot be agreed everything is on hold until the appeal hearing when the issue is thrashed out and the court takes a view as to what the compliance period should be. Nonetheless I accept there are occasions when the local authority says compliance can be achieved in 4 weeks and the notice recipient says it will take 2 years, and that in such cases there is never going to be a reasonable coming together of minds. In such cases an appeal on the grounds that the period for compliance is unreasonable is the only way forward.

In order to progress to full compliance as quickly and as smoothly as possible the calculation of the time scale in which works are to be carried out is of considerable importance. A compliance period that is too short will provoke an appeal which will delay the notice until the appeal is determined. Even if the magistrates uphold the notice and the original compliance period, achieving compliance will almost certainly take longer owing to the delay occasioned by the appeal.

Dwelling, as we do, in the real world it is probably safe to say that it is a rare enforcement notice recipient who will want to appeal on the grounds that the period for compliance is too long. Even the legislation doesn't envisage this, as it cites as the ground of appeal that the time period is not reasonably sufficient but makes no mention of its being overgenerous. From a practical point of view however, a compliance period that is too long is not a good thing. It may ensure that the risk of an appeal on the grounds of an unreasonably short compliance period is avoided but it will not fill the recipient with any sense of urgency, and it will also mean that the persons suffering because of the nuisance or whose health or wellbeing may be at risk from the circumstances giving rise to service of the notice will have to suffer for an unnecessarily long period.

I do bang on about officers writing down their thinking, but I think it is vital that officers should record their thinking regarding the time periods they require for compliance, at the time they draft the enforcement notice. If there is an appeal against an enforcement notice based on time for compliance or if there is a trial based on failure to comply with the requirements within the compliance period prescribed, it is likely that the officer will be asked to justify his thinking regarding the compliance period. If this happens it will be helpful for him to have evidence of his thought process, recorded at the time at which the process was undertaken. It will enable him to demonstrate firstly that there was a thought process, secondly that it was reasonable and took account of the appropriate things and thirdly that it took place at the proper time, rather than the officer giving the appearance of justifying the compliance period prescribed in retrospect and when under pressure. If some elements that were considered e.g. availability of specialist contractors or potential periods of good weather have changed between the original thinking and the appeal hearing it will be easier to demonstrate this if the original thinking and its time of consideration are recorded.

Calculating compliance periods is not a black art. The enforcement officer will know exactly what has to be done, and where necessary can take some advice about how long it will take from someone with more knowledge in the specific field. Some things will take longer than others, for example repairing a tiled roof can be done much more quickly that repairing a thatched roof because tilers are much more readily available than thatchers. Nothing involving listed buildings is ever achieved quickly and specialist processes will require specialist intervention to make them compliant, but in many cases compliance can be achieved as quickly as the recipient of the notice is minded to achieve it. Local knowledge will be important. Enforcement officers will be aware of particular local issues such as the fact that a carpenter cannot be had for love nor money but plumbers at a loose end are hanging round every street corner. The thought process is important but just as important is recording it.

I was occasionally been asked by enforcement officers whether I considered the compliance period they had selected to be appropriate. My answer was always that I had no idea but that if they felt the need to ask me, they were questioning their own judgement and they might like to consider why that was. I cannot say what a reasonable compliance period is, but I can give some idea of what I expect enforcement officers to have considered in calculating the one they have prescribed.

Considerations when calculating compliance periods.

- Consider the nature of the remedy required - can it be quickly achieved or is it likely to be complex?
- How many persons/bodies will be involved in achieving the remedy – e.g. will general builders have to be engaged, is the work of a particularly complex nature needing specialist input?

- If contractors or specialists are required how readily available are they? E.g. if thatchers or specialist builders are required are there any locally? Do they have long waiting lists? Is their work seasonal?
- In the case of staged works - at what point do different parties get involved, and are all of them on site at the same time?
- If compliance requires a specialist fix, e.g. the purchase of specialist equipment or the making of a bespoke solution how long will this take? Does the solution have to be sourced from abroad? Does it need particular permits? What is the waiting time?
- If the works have considerable financial consequences is the recipient likely to have to raise funds? If so, should the fundraising period be taken into account?
- Will the complainant or any other party who may be affected by the works co-operate with the recipient? For example, will a tenant decamp during works? If not, should the period be extended to take account of this?
- Are consents or approvals from other agencies required, e.g. planning permission or listed building consent? How long will this take?

My thoughts are not exclusive or exhaustive, but they do give an indication of the sort of thought process I expect an enforcement officer to have engaged in, and as importantly, to demonstrate if they want to argue that they have been reasonable in calculating compliance periods.

While I am on the subject of calculation of compliance periods I would like to make a suggestion as to the form of words that should be used. When an enforcement officer calculates a compliance period he recognises that the recipient isn't obliged by the terms of the notice to wait until the last minute of the last hour of the last day of the period before achieving compliance. Ideally the enforcement officer, and certainly most complainants or persons affected, would like compliance to be achieved sooner than the dying seconds of the compliance period, the operative word being 'sooner'. What enforcement officers actually want is compliance as soon as possible, but certainly no later than the final day of the compliance period. In order to underline that compliance is desirable as soon as possible, I suggest that the wording should be that compliance be achieved 'On or before (date)'. The recipient of the notice knows the exact date by which compliance is to be achieved but is also aware that he could complete the works before that date. It is worth noting that this form of words only applies where compliance is calculated to a specific date; it can't be used where e.g. compliance is required 'within 3 months'.

Finally I think I should make a comment about what happens if for some reason the enforcement officer accidentally forgets to put a compliance period on the notice. To describe such an oversight as unfortunate rather undersells it, but it does happen. In one case with which I had the misfortune to be involved it came about when the officer in the case over-typed a previous notice of a similar kind on the computer and, having deleted the compliance period used by the creator of the original notice, forgot to add his own. I did inquire as to how such an error has slipped through the checking procedure net, but it seemed no-one could come up with an answer. The consequence in law of such an unfortunate omission is that the recipient of the notice can never be prosecuted for failing to comply with its requirements. It hardly needs to be said that the recipient of such a notice is highly unlikely to appeal against it, since to do so would invite the court to quash it and open the door to service of another notice. Far better to say nothing, make a few token gestures that look for all the world like preparatory works for compliance and then sit back and see what happens. What certainly can't happen is that he will be prosecuted for failing to comply with the notice. What might happen is that the local authority will realise the error of its ways, withdraw the notice and serve another with all the necessary elements included. The recipient will then have to consider how he wishes to deal with the 'proper' notice.

    6.   The consequences of failing to comply.

As I said in Chapter 4, the recipient of the notice must be told the consequences of failing to comply with its requirements so that he can make an informed decision about whether or not to comply with it. The consequences of failing to comply with the various Assertive and Prohibitive notices are set out in the legislation that creates them, but in general terms the consequences are that the recipient of the notice can be prosecuted, usually in the magistrates' court and if convicted, fined. This information must appear on the face of the enforcement notice and must be in clear and readily understood language. This includes telling the recipient how much he could be fined if convicted; how much in figures rather than in the shorthand of 'up to a maximum of Level 4 on the standard scale'. Whilst that information about the standard scale may be true it doesn't tell someone who has no idea that there even was a standard scale how much he may be fined if convicted. He needs to know if he will get change out of a tenner or if he is looking a fine of £10,000 in the face. There may be other consequences of which the recipient should also be made aware, for example in some cases a fine handed down on the date of conviction is by no means the end of the story and the legislation allows for the imposition of a continuing penalty, to be imposed for every day that the non-compliance continues after conviction. In most cases this is a relatively small amount, between £2 - £10, but when it accrues on a daily basis it soon mounts up and it needs to be factored into the recipient's compliance plan. He must be told about the risk of a daily penalty being imposed before he starts thinking, rather than finding out about it as the sting in the tail of a conviction.

7. Information about any right of appeal that may exist, including how to appeal, to whom to appeal and the time period for the appeal to be lodged

It is not entirely inconceivable that by the time the recipient of the notice has read it as far down as the bits about what might happen if he doesn't comply with it, he might just be hopping mad. He may be filled with righteous indignation or blind fury or just a bout of full on intransigence. Or he might just accept the requirements of the enforcement notice as appropriate and reasonable but have some doubts about whether he can do all of the necessary works in the time he has been given. Whichever is the case he may feel compelled to appeal against the notice.

In anticipation of this the notice must contain, on its face, in clear and understandable language, information about any right to appeal that exists and it must tell the recipient how he must go about making his appeal. If the appeal has to be in writing this must be clear; if it has to be in triplicate and served on three different parties this must be clear; and if there is a fee attached to the appeal this must also be clearly set out.

Given that in the matter of an appeal the ball is squarely in the recipient's court he must be told how long he has to get on with it and actually file his appeal. This may need to be explained carefully because it may require some calculation on his part. If the appeal period is 21 days after service of the notice it will need to be made clear to the recipient how to work out on what date the notice was served. He needs to know if Sundays do or don't count when calculating number of days for making an appeal and the status of Bank Holidays and so on. This information should be put at his fingertips, on the face of the notice, to ensure that his position is not prejudiced and his right to appeal adversely affected.

Finally, the recipient must be told where he should go to go to file his appeal. In most cases it will be the local magistrates' court, so the address and post code of that building should be on the face of the notice. Of course this is information that the recipient could readily find out by doing a swift Google search or looking it up in the Yellow Pages, but that is not the point. As I said, all the information he needs must be at his fingertips, and the address of the premises where he should file his appeal is information he needs, so it must appear on the face of the notice.

None of these requirements are difficult. The information will be known to the local authority and can readily be put onto a standard document template, subject of course to my earlier comments about making sure it is correct and kept up to date. The important thing is to make sure that this information is on the notice. It's dry, deadly dull and generally an enforcement officer would be able to tell you this sort of detail off the top of his head but the recipient cannot be expected to know it, may need to know it and must therefore be told it.

What happens if the detail required to satisfy (6) (the consequences of failing to comply) or (7) (the details relating to making an appeal) are missing off the face of the notice? The answer is quite simple; the notice is flawed and is null and void. It will not contain the information that it is required by statute and therefore it is fatally flawed. Maybe the recipient of the notice will not know this and will try to battle his way through the process, or he may take the notice to a solicitor and ask for advice, but once the omission comes to light the court will quash the notice or the local authority, on discovering that it is flawed, will have to advise the recipient to that effect and tell him that he can ignore it with impunity. The notice cannot be withdrawn because it was never a proper notice in the first place and if I were advising the recipient I would certainly insist that the local authority write to my client advising him of the error and telling him that he was at no risk by ignoring it.

Having completed all of the requirements necessary to ensure that the content of the enforcement notice is as required by statute there remains one formal requirement. An enforcement notice is not a notice proper until it is signed on behalf of the local authority that serves it; and to that I would add the requirement to date it as well.

Who should sign the notice depends on the wording of the statute that creates it. In most cases the notice is signed by an authorised officer on behalf of the local authority but in the case of notices under the Health and Safety at Work etc. Act 1984 the notices are signed by 'the inspector', since that is what the legislation says. It is not necessary for the authorised officer to actually sign the notice by hand, it is acceptable for a facsimile of his signature to be used; a rubber stamp or electronically generated signature (Local Government Act 1972 sec 234 (3)). Once the enforcement notice is signed and dated it is good to go and can be served on the proposed recipient.

10 Top Tips for getting it right!

1. Check that all of the essential elements of the enforcement notice appear on its face. If they don't, change it to ensure that they do.
2. Make sure any details contained in the notice are correct and up to date.
3. Ensure your notice is clear and the language understandable. The recipient needs to understand what it means and what he must do.
4. Before you serve a notice make sure you have identified the correct party on whom it should be served. Use an

Inquisitorial notice to ascertain details about interests in land etc. if necessary.

5. Be careful about getting the name of an individual right. Do not use shortened forms, nicknames or initials.

6. Remember you can only require the recipient of the enforcement notice to do the minimum necessary to achieve compliance with the requirements of the legislation. Don't try to gild the lily.

7. Record your reasons for requiring the particular steps needed to achieve compliance; you may be required to justify them at appeal.

8. Calculate the time period for compliance with care, taking account of local conditions. Record your reasons for selecting the compliance period/s that you do.

9. If there is some horse trading to be done with the recipient that may avoid the enforcement notice going to appeal ,do it. It may make sense to make a few changes and then achieve compliance sooner than to slug it out in court and incur delay.

10. When you have drafted your notice check it carefully. Then check it again. It is better to find and correct a mistake before the notice is served than have to withdraw it and go through the process again.

Chapter 6

Serving the notice

Having drafted the enforcement notice, checked it and made sure it is signed and dated the next step for the enforcement officer is to serve it. By 'serve it' I mean getting it into the hands of the person or party for whom it is intended. We know who that party is, their name appears on the face of the enforcement notice but as we know there is many a slip 'twixt cup and lip and there are plenty of things that can go wrong in the process of serving the enforcement notice. It is not enough to just serve it; it is also necessary to prove that it has been served. In all cases the burden of proving service is on the party who claims to have served it. If a party on whom the local authority claims to have served an enforcement notice alleges that he did not receive it, it is for the local authority to establish that service was effected unless the authority is relying on sec 7 of the Interpretation Act 1978 (the rule of posting). Where there is any doubt as to whether an enforcement notice was served the alleged recipient will be entitled to the benefit of the doubt; hence the importance of being able to prove service.

The general rules relating to service

Service of enforcement notices, or indeed any legal document, by a local authority is part of the legal process, and as you might expect is governed by legislation. In general, the rules of service are contained in sec 233 of the Local Government Act 1972, entitled Service of notices by local authorities.

Sec 233 states that

(2) Any such document may be given to or served on the person in question either by delivering it to him, or by leaving it at his proper address, or by sending it by post to him at that address.

(3) Any such document may—

> *(a) in the case of a body corporate, be given to or served on the secretary or clerk of that body;*

> *(b) in the case of a partnership, be given to or served on a partner or a person having the control or management of the partnership business.*

(4) For the purposes of this section and of section 26 of the Interpretation Act 1889 (service of documents by post) (as amended by section 7 of the Interpretation Act 1978) in its application to this section, the proper address of any person to or on whom a document is to be given or served shall be his last known address, except that—

> *(a) in the case of a body corporate or their secretary or clerk, it shall be the address of the registered or principal office of that body;*

> *(b) in the case of a partnership or a person having the control or management of the partnership business, it shall be that of the principal office of the partnership;*

and for the purposes of this subsection the principal office of a company registered outside the United Kingdom or of a partnership carrying on business outside the United Kingdom shall be their principal office within the United Kingdom.

This is a very useful section because it effectively tells the enforcement officer how effective service of an enforcement notice is to be achieved in just about every case.

It is to be read alongside sec 7 of the Interpretation Act 1978 which describes the rule of posting:

> *7. References to service by post.*

> *(1)Where an Act authorises or requires any document to be served by post (whether the expression "serve" or the expression "give" or "send" or any other expression is used) then, unless the contrary intention appears, the service is deemed to be effected by properly addressing, pre-paying and posting a letter containing the document and, unless the contrary is proved, to have been effected at the time at which the letter would be delivered in the ordinary course of post.*

Serving individuals

These are the relevant sections of the legislation and it is instructive to see what they tell us in practical terms. Take by way of example an enforcement notice that is to be served on an individual. Working through the list of alternatives offered by Sec 233(2) we see that the first is delivering the notice directly to the recipient, what most of us know as hand delivery. In simple terms the enforcement officer hands the notice to the recipient who takes it from him. In some cases it is as simple as that, in others it is more complicated. Many proposed recipients will be only too aware of what is in the brown envelope and will be none too willing to just reach out their hand to take it, quite the reverse. They may go to some lengths not to receive the notice. 'Deliver' however has a somewhat wider meaning that the everyday use of the word would suggest.

If a document is to be hand delivered but the recipient refuses to take it because he suspects that what the envelope contains will not be to his advantage, all is not lost. There does not have to be a formal handing over and receiving of the notice; all that is required is that the enforcement officer ensures that the recipient knows what is going on; knows that the server of the notice is trying to give him something and only failing because he (the recipient) is either refusing to take it or deliberately preventing the server getting close enough to hand it over. If you have to, you can tell him what it is and drop it on the floor as close to him as possible; if you can get closer it is a better idea to touch the recipient with the notice and *then* let go of it. If it falls to the floor so be it. All that is required is for the recipient to be aware that the enforcement officer has touched him with the envelope. Awareness is critical, enforcement officers cannot sneak up unseen behind a prospective recipient, pat him gently as a fairy's kiss with it and then run away; either there has to be some acknowledgement on the part of the recipient that he knows what is going on or the circumstances must be such that he can be deemed to have known. Pretending it has not happened won't work. I have fond memories of attending on site with a colleague to serve an enforcement notice on a particularly difficult individual who knew my colleague but had never met me. When we arrived on site the gentlemen was up a ladder fixing the guttering on his property. As my colleague stood to one side looking innocently about him I asked the gentlemen to come down to speak to me, which with some reluctance he did. As he got within arms' reach I advised him that we had something for him, touched him on the foot with the notice and we both took off like rabbits while the recipient shouted abuse at our departing backs. It wasn't exactly textbook service, but it was effective, and we dined out on the story for weeks.

Important as touching the recipient with the notice is, there is a further requirement of equal importance. After the enforcement officer has touched the recipient with the notice and has let go of it, or has dropped it sufficiently close to him having advised him that he is doing so under no circumstances must he pick it up again; to do so would be to resume control of it and that is not the plan at all. Once he has touched the recipient with the enforcement notice and let go of it the enforcement officer has no further interest in the notice. It is up to the recipient what he does with it. He can leave it on the ground and walk away, he can put it in a nearby litter bin or he can tear it into a million pieces and throw them to the four winds because from that point on he will have to live with the consequences of doing so.

Sec 233 (2) next offers the alternative of either leaving the notice at the recipient's proper address or posting it there. To further illuminate the issue Sec 233 (4) helpfully notes that the 'proper address' is the proposed recipient's last known address, being the last address known to the local authority. In some cases this will be a domestic property where a notice can be posted through the door without any difficulty. In others the 'last known address' may be a somewhat trickier proposition. It may be that the property is now vacant and very clearly so, it may be derelict or burned out or it may be that the proposed recipient has moved on and someone else has moved into the property, someone who is very willing to advise the enforcement officer to that effect. Bizarre as it may seem, it doesn't matter. As long as the address on both the enforcement notice and the envelope in which it is delivered is the recipient's last address as known to the local authority, good service is achieved. I know of one case where the local authority achieved good service by putting a number of notices that it needed to serve on one recipient into a clear plastic wallet and hung them on a field gate. The gentleman they sought had previously lived in the field in a caravan but had decamped and they had no idea where he had gone. The field however was his last known address and for the purposes of sec 233 good service was achieved.

'Posting' is an interesting word. I have included the wording of sec 7 of the Interpretation Act 1978 because so few enforcement officers seem to be aware of it or of how useful a tool it is. The section says that where an act authorises or requires any document to be served by post, regardless of how the term 'served' is described; service of the document can be achieved by putting it in an envelope that is properly addressed to the proposed recipient, putting the correct postage on it and putting it in the post. It is then deemed by a rebuttable presumption of law to have been delivered on the date that it would have arrived in the normal course of posting. If the envelope carried stamps or was franked with a sum amounting to first class postage rate it is deemed to have been successfully delivered two working days later, weekends and bank holidays permitting. Happy days! What could be simpler?

There are a couple of riders I need to add to this apparently fool proof method of getting a notice into the hands of the proposed recipient. The first is that the presumption of service is a rebuttable one. If the proposed recipient can prove that the notice was not delivered to the address on the envelope then service is not deemed to have been achieved. The burden of proof is the civil one i.e. on the balance of probabilities. The second rider is that the letter has to be posted. It has to be put into the postal system. Not into an out tray from which it is collected and taken to a post room where it is put in a bag and collected by a post man; not delivered to a central point where it is collected and taken away. It has to be posted. In a pillar box or at a post office. That may seem pedantic and ridiculous, but if the enforcement officer is to take advantage of this rule he has to show that the envelope containing the notice did enter the postal system, and if he wants to calculate when it should have arrived he needs to know exactly when it entered the postal system. He cannot say either of these things if he just drops the envelope into an out tray from which it disappears, hopefully into the hand of someone else, to go somewhere else and from there into the postal system. Given the ease of achieving service using this presumption of delivery it is hardly an onerous requirement to just post a letter; once it is posted the enforcement officer can sit back and let the post office get on with doing the job of delivering the notice.

I know that some authorities are deeply wedded to using the Recorded Delivery postal system, but I have never been sure why. I know that if I was anticipating the arrival of something in the post and I didn't want to receive it, I certainly wouldn't agree to accept and sign for anything that came recorded delivery. I would politely decline and let the post man keep it. Back in the day when I was a practising Environmental Health Officer we did use the Recorded Delivery postal system, but back then the post office used to send us a post card to confirm whether or not the letter had been delivered so that we knew whether service had been achieved. Unfortunately, that system no longer operates and those who use the Recorded Delivery system, internet tracking notwithstanding may only find out that their efforts to get their notice delivered has failed when some weeks later it arrives back on their desk. If you want my advice, I would say don't bother with Recorded Delivery, use the presumption of delivery in Sec 7 of the Interpretation Act 1978.

Serving bodies corporate or partnerships

Moving on from serving notices on individuals to serving notices on a body corporate or a partnership, sec 233 spells out for the enforcement officer both the identity of the party to whom the envelope containing the notice should be addressed and the address to which it should be delivered or posted. Where the business is a limited company the envelope should be addressed to the Company Secretary and should be served at the registered office of the company. This should be readily discernible from the company particulars that must be displayed at each premises of the company. Unlike limited companies since the Companies Act 2006 came into force, private companies are not obliged to have a company secretary but they are obliged to register the names of their directors, or where there is only one to register the name of that person. The director who is nominated to receive documents on behalf of the company must be identified and his address must also be registered Enforcement notices must be served on the named director at the registered address.

I suspect most enforcement officers have experienced the frustration of trying to deal with someone who unexpectedly has to leave the county and is not expected back in the immediate future. In this context it's worth noting that some individuals on such occasions authorise others, usually their solicitor or accountant, to receive documents on their behalf. Such people would typically be landlords or business people who may be out of the country for periods of time but whose business requires them to be contactable, if not available. Where this arrangement is in place the local authority may serve enforcement notices on the authorised person in lieu of the person named on the face of the notice by using any of the methods prescribed. The authorised recipient cannot decline to accept the enforcement notice as he has to accept all correspondence on behalf of his client. Importantly the local authority has to prove that the existence of this arrangement.

Specific rules of service

The rules above are the general rules regarding the service of documents, including enforcement notices. In many cases however the specific statute creating an enforcement notice will also contain rules for the service of the notice and it follows that the rules to be followed are those laid down in the specific legislation. Hence if a Planning Enforcement officer wishes to serve a notice arising under the Town and Country Planning Act 1990 he must follow the rules of service as described in sec 329 of that Act; if a Food Safety Officer wishes to serve a notice arising under the Food Safety and Hygiene Regulations 2013 the rules as laid down in reg. 30 must be followed. In such cases there are usually particular refinements or additional requirements that must be followed. Take as an example the provisions of sec 329 of the Town and Country Planning Act 1990; in addition to the methods of service described in the Local Government Act 1972 there are additional provisions covering the service of notices on persons who have an interest in the property to which the notice relates but whose names cannot be ascertained by the local authority. Provided that the authority has made what are described as "reasonable inquiries" the notice can be served by addressing it to 'the owner' or 'the occupier' and fixing it conspicuously to the premises. The Planning Enforcement Officer is also required to mark the face of the envelope containing the enforcement notice to the effect that the contents are important, so that anyone observing it will recognise it as a significant piece of correspondence. There is an additional requirement that copies of the enforcement notice shall be served on all parties having an interest in the property, which would necessarily include mortgagees and those holding a charge over the property. There is a similar requirement in the Housing Act 2004 and since e.g. mortgagees have an interest, albeit passive, which may be adversely affected by the requirements of the notice they should be made aware of both its existence and content.

The fact that a particular piece of legislation contains its own specific rules of service should alert the enforcement officer to the need to ensure that the rules of service it lays down are followed, and followed to the letter. The rules of service are designed to ensure that all the parties who need to be aware of the existence and the content of an enforcement notice are made aware of both so that they can take whatever action they consider to be necessary and appropriate. In most cases it is only the central character who will actively engage with the notice and with the local authority. He will be the named party on the notice and he will have to ensure that compliance is achieved. There are cases however where others may be very interested in what is happening, notably those where property, whether its use or condition, is the subject of the notice. Mortgagees or charge holders may be very engaged with the notice and its requirements, not least because the value of the property against which they have loaned money may be adversely affected by the way in which the recipient of the notice is using it and they will wish to protect their investment. Galling as it may be for the enforcement officer, in such cases the recipient of the notice may be more concerned that the mortgagee may call in the loan made against the property than about anything the local authority may be able to do by enforcing the provisions of the notice.

Service by electronic communication – fax or email

None of the methods of service described are what you would call cutting edge technology at a time when most of us rely on electronic communication for most things. Occasionally the legislation has caught up with the pace of progress and service of documents by electronic communication is recognised and approved. Electronic communication means either email or fax, but realistically in most cases it is likely to mean email. Before electronic service can be used the local authority is required to check that the proposed recipient is willing to accept service of documents by electronic mail. Many businesses will accept service in this way, but in order to avoid arguments about the validity or otherwise of service, it is wise to ask first and have evidence of the answer. As with everything there are rules around service of documents by electronic means. The first is that if a business or individual accepts service of any documents by electronic mail they are deemed to accept service of all documents, from any party, by electronic mail. Just as a property owner cannot tell the post office he will accept delivery of post addressed to him from everyone but HM Customs and Revenue, the owner of an electronic mail box cannot decide who may and who may not serve documents on him using his electronic address nor is he allowed to 'block' incoming emails from specific electronic addresses. It's all or nothing.

Proving that the notice has been served

As I said at the start of this chapter, except in cases where the Interpretation Act 1978 sec 7 rule of posting is relied upon, it is incumbent on the local authority serving the enforcement notice to prove that good service was effected; this accords entirely with the usual legal maxim that he who asserts must prove. The recipient of a notice may be put to considerable expense and inconvenience by the requirement to comply with its contents and there may be much to be gained from his point of view by denying that he ever received it and that he was unaware of its existence or requirements. If he is prosecuted for failing to comply with the requirements of the notice and claims in his defence that he did not comply with it because he did not receive it the local authority will be put to strict proof that good service was effected.

Given that service of the notice is of such importance I would always advise enforcement officers to record the way in which service was effected and to do so in a way that can be used in evidence. To my mind the best way to do this is to produce a witness statement that just addresses the issue of service of the notice. I think there is much to be said for separating the issue of service from the issue of non- compliance. A short sharp witness statement that crisply addresses service of a notice not only closes the door on arguments about knowledge of the existence of the notice but more, it demonstrates that the enforcement officer is aware of the importance of the enforcement notice being properly served and has made sure that this was achieved.

If the enforcement notice was served by hand I would expect the officer who served it to make a witness statement describing on whom he served it, where and when and the recipient's reaction to it being served on him. The date and time of service is important because if there is an appeal against the notice, the appeal period starts to run from the date of service; if there is no appeal the compliance period starts to run immediately after the appeal period expires. A record of the response of the recipient to being served with the notice serves a number of purposes. If he ripped the enforcement notice up and threw it over his shoulder the officer's witness statement not only proves that service was achieved it also helps to explain the absence of an appeal against the notice and further explains why compliance has not been achieved. In the alternative if he thanked the officer warmly and advised that he would get straight in with whatever action was required a record of his words is helpful if he needs to be challenged at a later point about a change of attitude; alternatively it can be factored into a decision about further action if complete compliance is not achieved within the compliance period.

It will hardly come as a surprise, given my comments about using the rule of posting, when I suggest that officers who rely on it need to make sure that they can evidence what they did. Careful reading of sec 7 of the Interpretation Act 1978 makes it clear that the rule of posting can be relied on by local authorities when posting any document *unless the contrary intention appears*. For an enforcement officer contemplating which method of service to use the first step is to look at the sections of the statute under which the notice arises and check whether there are specific rules of service that apply. If there are rules of service included in the act those are the ones he must use, although obviously he can select which of the methods of service contained within the section of the act he chooses to use. In the absence of specific rules of service the officer is free to run to the rules of service in the Local Government Act 1972, as discussed, and to the rule of posting.

Having decided to use the rule of posting the officer must ensure that he can evidence its use as he will be relying on the act of posting for a number of reasons. It will be used to prove delivery, to calculate the presumed date of deliver, to calculate the end of the appeal period and the end of the compliance period. My advice to the enforcement officer who elects to use sec 7 is to make a photocopy of the enforcement notice and the envelope in which it is posted. He can then either post the notice in a post box, recording which box and the date and time of posting or hand it over the counter of a post office and asking for a certificate of posting. I accept the certificate of posting is a bit of belt and braces approach, but it costs nothing so why not? Finally he should make a witness statement in which he explains simply that he prepared a notice, a copy of which is exhibit 1; put it in a pre-stamped and addressed envelope, of which a photocopy is exhibit 2; and posted it by either putting it in a post box, at location, date and time or by handing it over the counter at a post office, at location date and time securing a certificate of service, exhibit 3, if obtained. He should then finish with a flourish by saying that according to the rule of posting contained in sec 7 of the Interpretation Act 1978, delivery of the notice would have been achieved on the date that the notice would have been delivered in the 'ordinary course of post', i.e. the time that the post office says it will arrive depending on the class of postage used.

There is no need at this stage to start making calculations about when the appeal period ends and when compliance should be achieved because there is no suggestion that either will be relevant. If there is a need to take further action the officer can make a second witness statement in which he references his first statement and the dates in it using them as the basis of his calculations. I think a good witness statement that covers all of the bases through a thorough explanation and the use of exhibits is extremely useful. The first reaction of many people when told they have been sent something through the post is to claim that they didn't receive it. Only they know whether they did or didn't, but the fact is that it is for them to prove that they didn't get it, and that is extremely difficult to do. Even though they only have to prove it on the balance of probabilities they will still have to come up with something stunning to convince the court that the notice did not arrive. Provided you follow the procedure for using it the rule of posting is a very useful tool indeed. That is why police forces use it to send out Notices of Intended Prosecution for speeding offences.......

In addition to the above there are a couple of practical evidential points that can usefully be made. The first is to note that an enforcement notice will usually be served in a sealed envelope. The enforcement officer who hands it over, sticks it through the letter box, sticks it to a conspicuous point on a building or slides it into the pillar box must ensure that he can say what was inside the sealed envelope as he will need to be definitive on the point in his witness statement. He must have seen the enforcement notice and ideally have made a copy of it, so that he can credibly say that the envelope contained an enforcement notice, a copy of which is exhibited to his statement. If he has not seen the enforcement notice all he can say is that he handed over an envelope the contents of which were not known to him. Equally if the legislation requires that the envelope in which the notice is served should be clearly marked to the effect that the contents of the envelope are important, it is sensible to make a photocopy of the envelope to prove that it was so marked and exhibit it to the officer's statement. Finally, if service if achieved by sticking the notice to a prominent part of a building or structure, a photograph of it *in situ* is a good idea as it establishes that the notice was stuck to the building as claimed. This is particularly important given the potential for people who have no interest in the issue taking the notice down or destroying it once the enforcement officer has left the site.

I noted earlier in this chapter that practise is catching up with progress and that some statutes now allow for service of enforcement notices by electronic means. In these cases certain questions logically follow. When was the notice actually served? How do you prove it? Is an enforcement notice, served by fax or email, served when it is sent by the enforcement officer or when it whirrs and grinds out through the fax machine in the office of the recipient or pops up in his inbox? This is a question that has engaged the courts, and to which there is the court has provided the answer. The answer is that it is served when the send key is pressed or the fax is sent. (*R v Pontypridd Juvenile Court ex p B and Others [1988] Crim LR 842*). The enforcement officer does not need evidence of receipt but I would suggest it is good practice to evidence that the enforcement notice was sent. If it was served by email a screen shot of the sent box showing the document with date and time of sending is helpful, along with a copy of the enforcement notice; both can be exhibited to a witness statement. Faxed documents are generally marked on their face by the fax machine that sends them and should be exhibited to a witness statement which records date and time of sending. In both cases it is helpful if the witness statement addresses the fact that the recipient has agreed to accept service of documents by electronic means and, where possible, how this has been ascertained.

The final point I want to make about service of the enforcement notice concerns parties who have an interest in the property but are not the party required to carry out works to achieve compliance. As I have noted, in some cases, notably those concerned with town and country planning and housing notices, it is a requirement that copies of the enforcement notices must be served on all parties having an interest in the land, hence mortgagees and charge holders have to be served with copies of the notice. However, in apparently similar cases there is no such requirement. In the case of property related statutory nuisance abatement notices even where there are parties other than the one to whom the notice is directed who have an interest in the property that is the subject of the notice there is no such requirement. The fact that there is no statutory obligation to serve a copy of the notice on other parties having an interest does not mean that the enforcement officer cannot send a copy to those other parties for their information and edification. They may not care one way or the other, but equally they may be concerned and consider that the breach alleged is also a breach of a condition of a mortgage or loan and will therefore be just as keen as the enforcement officer to see remedial works put in hand. They have access to screws that the enforcement officer does not, and it may be that the turning of those particular screws is a more effective way of achieving compliance than the enforcement officer waiting for compliance with the requirements on his notice. There is nothing wrong with using all the tools at your disposal, the ones you can use as well as the ones you are obliged to use.

The consequences of failing to achieve good service

There are a number of ways in which the enforcement officer can fail to serve the notice properly. He can serve the notice at the wrong address or he can give it to the wrong person. In either case the notice will simply not taken effect. There may be nothing wrong with it, but it will be of no effect because the person to whom it is addressed or the one on whom it should have been served will know nothing about it. It is incumbent on the officer who claims that he served the enforcement notice to prove that he did and if he cannot, the conclusion must be that the enforcement notice was not served, and there the matter ends. Thankfully there is nothing to stop the officer from re-serving the notice in the same terms, with amended dates, on the correct person or at the correct address.

What about cases where the notice has to be served on several parties but not everyone has been served? We saw above what happens when the notice is not served on those required to do the work to achieve compliance, but what if you fail to serve those with a less immediate interest in the property such as mortgagees or charge holders? In such cases it depends on how the omission arose. If the enforcement officer just overlooked serving the enforcement notice on the mortgagee, such was his rush to get on with it, good service is not achieved. If however he has made appropriate inquiries with the Land Registry to establish ownership details and the registered title to the property shows no other parties having an interest, maybe because it has not been updated, he will be able to rely on that to show that no other party was revealed as having an interest at the time the enforcement notice was served. Conversely good service is achieved even if the enforcement notice is served on a party whose interest in the property has lapsed if he is still shown as having an interest on the face of the registered title. He will not be prejudiced by being served with a copy of the notice and if he has passed his interest on to another party he will be alerted to the fact that the registered title has not been updated. He may then pass on the information to the party succeeding him or perhaps advise the local authority of the identity of that party. The local authority would then be able to serve a copy of the enforcement notice on the previously unknown party. It is worth noting that it does so as a courtesy and no more. Whether it chooses to do so or not the service of the original notice is in no way prejudiced. It was properly served on all those parties who at the time the authority knew or believed to have an interest.

The proposed recipient who was not properly served with an enforcement notice has a compete defence to an allegation that he failed to comply with its requirements. Clearly he cannot be expected to comply with something he has never seen and knows nothing about. As I have said, other than in cases where the rule of posting has been used, the recipient does not have to prove that he did not receive the enforcement notice, that burden lies with the enforcement officer to prove that good service was effected. When I was defending clients who were alleged to have failed to comply with enforcement notices my first line of inquiry was always to see whether the prosecutor could prove that the notice had been properly served. If he could not, I would try to lean on him to see if he could be encouraged to withdraw the matter, and if he would not, I would run a defence based on the failure to serve my client with the notice, cross examining the enforcement officer on the point. If the prosecution could not prove that service had been effectively achieved, or conceded it had not, my client would inevitably succeed. Even if we both knew he had indeed got the notice in his hot little hand we would win because the prosecutor would have failed to prove his case. The enforcement officer who has prepared a witness statement that addresses the how, where and when of the service of the notice closes the door very firmly on such tactics.

Completing the legalities

After selecting the appropriate type of notice, drafting it carefully and effecting good service it may be tempting to sit back and start crossing off the days on the appeal or compliance period calendar. In some cases that is an appropriate thing to do and the enforcement officer will be free to get on with his life until such time as the relevant date is reached. Not in all cases though. In some cases there are legalities to be completed. The Town and Country Planning Act 1990 sec 188 requires that a public register of enforcement notices be kept in which details of enforcement notices served within their area are recorded. Under the Housing Act 2004, subject to certain conditions, Improvement and Prohibition notices are registerable as local land charges and need to be registered.

Enforcement officers should check the provisions of the statute authorising the specific enforcement notice they have served and make sure that they satisfy any post service technical requirements that there may be. They should also ensure that if circumstances change e.g. should a notice be withdrawn, that any relevant details in the public register or the Local Land Charges Register are removed in the interests of both accuracy and fairness to the recipient of the original notice.

Key points of note

1. For a notice to take effect it must be served on the recipient. It is for the local authority to prove that good service of a notice was effected.

2. If the particular statute under which the enforcement notice arises has its own rules regarding service of the notice the enforcement officer should follow them

3. If the particular statute under which the enforcement notice arises does not contain its own rules of service the general rules in sec 233 of the Local Government Act 1972 should be followed.

4. Whichever form of service is used, it is important that the enforcement officer who serves the enforcement notice evidences that he has done so.

5. Electronic methods of service may only be used where the proposed recipient has indicated that he is willing to accept documents electronically.

6. Where there are technical requirements to be completed post service of the enforcement notice it is important to ensure that they are completed.

Chapter 7

All about Appeals

Once the enforcement officer has served a Permissive or Prohibitive notice on a recipient he should be able to sit back and wait to see what happens. The ball is in the recipient's court and he makes the next move. In the ideal world the recipient will read the notice, agree with it in its entirety and fall over himself in his urgency to comply with all of its requirements. Well yes. But sadly, that isn't always how it goes. Sometimes the recipient is not at all delighted to be at the sharp end of an enforcement notice and does not feel an overwhelming desire to fall in with the enforcement officer's request; what's more he declines to do so. He exercises his right to appeal.

There are a number of reasons for appealing. I think we can overlook the recipient who appeals because he just doesn't understand what is going on, and just concentrate on the two that most concern enforcement officers. The first and probably the one that interests us most arises when the recipient is genuinely aggrieved by the requirements of the notice and wants to argue his case and have the requirements considered by a third party who could if persuaded by the strength of his argument amend or quash them. The second, and extremely annoying reason, occurs when the recipient knows he will have to comply but wants to delay the inevitable. Following the pattern that has evolved in this book, let's start with the technicalities; the appeal period, the grounds for appeal and appeals being properly made.

The appeal period

The recipient of the notice will know what the appeal period is because the notice will tell him. As I discussed in chapter 5 the local authority is required to tell the recipient how long he has to appeal against the notice, and how and where he can do so. How to appeal against the notice and where to go to file the appeal are matters of fact; all the recipient has to do is read the information on the notice. Then he only has to do a bit of simple mathematics to work out how long he has to file his appeal. He should know when he received the notice and the notice itself tells him how many days he has to appeal so he can work out when the cut-off date is and make sure he hot foots it off to the magistrate's court or else gets his appeal into the appropriate tribunal in good time.

Grounds of appeal – failing to get the technicalities right

The grounds of appeal have the potential to be more difficult. There are two routes an appellant can go down when appealing against an enforcement notice. He can appeal on the basis that one of the necessary technicalities has not been completed or he can appeal against the merits of the requirements. I will deal first with an appeal based on the fact that the technical requirements of the notice have not been completed. This is variously described in the different statues that give rise to enforcement notices, but generally is described along the lines that *'there has been some informality, defect or error in, or in connection with, the abatement notice" The Statutory Nuisance (Appeals) Regulations 1995 (reg.2(2)(b)).* I would freely admit that I tend to be a pragmatic lawyer. I don't see the point in thrashing things out in court if they can be sorted out more quickly in some other arena to the mutual satisfaction of the parties. I would strongly urge any local authority that has served an enforcement notice that is appealed on the basis on an *"informality, defect or error in connection…"* to scrutinize their process with a very fine tooth comb to see if they can identify any error that could give rise to the appeal. If that does not throw any light on the matter the authority should ask the appellant or his advisors what they consider the error, defect or informality to be. Once the error is identified the authority can consider if the appeal has real merit. If it does the sensible thing to do is to withdraw the enforcement notice and re-serve it, this time ironing out the glitch that was the downfall of the original version. There is no need to wait for the appeal hearing. In the interests of making progress I suggest that a pragmatic view should be taken and the enforcement officer should go back to square one. If the local authority decides that it is appropriate to withdraw an enforcement notice they are required to serve copies of the notice of withdrawal on all the parties that were served with the original notice and to remove the notice from any public register of enforcement notices.

Grounds of appeal – the legalities

We need now to move on to consider the legalities surrounding the proposed appeal. Let's be clear, there is no scope for invention or creative thinking in respect of grounds of appeal. The grounds upon which an appeal can be made are contained in the statute and they are the only grounds that can be used to found an appeal. That has to be the case otherwise recipients could appeal on any weird and wonderful ground that they dreamt up and which the local authority could not conceivably second guess. The theory underpinning the grounds of appeal is that they are the grounds that parliament considered to be both necessary and potentially arguable and hence appropriately included in the statute. As they are critical to the recipient's understanding of his right to appeal they should appear on the enforcement notice. He can then compare his grievance regarding the notice with them and check whether his grievance amounts to a legitimate ground of appeal. Let's assume that the recipient does accept that the local authority is justified in its complaint but considers that the requirements for compliance are excessive or unreasonable. He can check his complaint against the grounds of appeal and, if they fit, he knows he can appeal based on the ground that the requirements are excessive, unreasonable or both. If he is upset that the local authority are engaging with his property or land and just wants to be left alone he can check to see whether ' I should be allowed to do what I like, it's a free country' is a ground of appeal. Just to be quite clear, it's not.

There are a number of ways in which potential appellants can be helped to appeal. In addition to the fact that the grounds of appeal, the method, the place and time scale are provided for them they may, if they wish, engage someone to help them such as a solicitor or a planning agent or other specialist. In addition to checking that all of the technical requirements of the enforcement notice have been satisfied the expert will advise them whether their proposed ground of appeal is in fact one on which they can legitimately appeal. They may also draft and file the grounds of appeal and, in some cases, will attend the hearing and represent the appellant. Solicitors and agents should filter out the more exotic of the proposed appeals, but it should be remembered that they are bound by their client's instructions. If, despite their best advice, their client still wants to appeal and they can bring the proposed grounds of appeal within the legitimate grounds the solicitor or agent must follow their client's instructions even if it means bringing an idiotic appeal or one with no reasonable prospect of success; thereafter they are obliged to represent him to the best of their ability. The proposed appellant can also seek advice from the tribunal to which the appeal is to be made. The Justices Clerk's office in the Magistrates Court or the administrative staff at the Planning Inspectorate will advise a proposed appellant whether he can appeal on the ground or grounds which he wishes to use. They do not advise on the merits of the appeal, that is a matter for the tribunal that ultimately hears it, but they can advise on whether the proposed appeal can legitimately be made. Upping the ante somewhat, they must refuse to accept an appeal that is not made on legitimate grounds as an appeal without a lawful basis.

Grounds of appeal – is the appeal properly made?

It usually takes a while for the enforcement officer who served an enforcement notice to discover whether there has been appeal. Firstly the appellant must file his appeal with the tribunal; occasionally he may be compelled to simultaneously serve a copy of his appeal on the local authority but in other cases this is done by the court. Where an appeal is made to the magistrate's court the court will serve a summons on the local authority instructing the authority to attend and defend the appeal. This summons will not be served on the enforcement officer who served the enforcement notice but will be served on the officer authorised to receive documents on behalf of local authority; the Head of Paid Services or the Chief Legal Officer. It may therefore be a while before it percolates its way down to the enforcement officer who will be the one required to attend and defend the appeal.

I would strongly urge the enforcement officer to look at the appeal documents in forensic detail. An appeal has to be properly made. That means it has to be made in time; it has to be founded on proper grounds; and if there is a fee to be paid, it must have been paid. The Justices Clerk, the administrative officer at the Planning Inspectorate or whoever the person accepting the appeal documents happens to be, has no legitimate authority to amend or bend the rules for appealing but on occasion things slip through the net. Appeals are sometimes accepted 'out of time' i.e. appeals filed after the appeal period has ended. Sometimes this is just an administrative glitch, sometimes it is a Justices Clerk or an administrative officer trying to be helpful to an appellant who does not know the system and has been too slow off the mark. Whichever of these is the case the appeal is unlawful and the local authority should resist it on the grounds that it is not an appeal properly made. Technically such appeals do not have to be resisted, they are void. This may seem a bit harsh, particularly where the appellant appears to have good grounds to appeal, but we should not lose sight of the purpose of the appeal period. It is a finite period at the end of which the local authority is entitled to believe that the issue of appeal is closed. It need no longer consider the prospect of appeal and is entitled to take the view that the requirements of the enforcement notice and the time periods for compliance are unchallenged. If there is a complainant or person affected by the issue that is addressed by the notice, they can also sit back and wait for compliance with the requirements of the notice. It cannot be right that at some unknowable point after the appeal period has ended that all the cards can be thrown into the air and that issues believed to be closed suddenly become live again. The appeal period is finite for a reason and local authorities should not acquiesce to informal extensions to them. To do so opens up an appeal process that should be closed, is unfair to complainants and may cause the Local Government Ombudsman to raise his eyebrows.

The next thing to check is whether the grounds on which the appellant proposes to appeal are actually lawful grounds of appeal. As I have said, the grounds on which an appeal can be founded appear in the statute that creates the enforcement notice and they are the only legitimate grounds of appeal. Without wishing to appear critical of the administrative staff that accept and process appeal documents, too often they do not check that the appeal is made on lawful grounds. They will rightly be very conscious of the fact that the merits of any appeal are not matters for them but are for the Inspector or the Magistrates. Nonetheless they are the gate keepers for the lawfulness of the proposed grounds of appeal and they should refuse to accept appeals that are not made on lawful grounds. A colleague of mine who dealt primarily with licensing issues was constantly at odds with his local Justices Clerk whose attitude to appeals appeared to be to accept them all and let the

Magistrates sort it out at the hearing. This sort of suck it and see attitude will not do with enforcement notice appeals.

Appeals made out of time and appeals made on unlawful grounds both have the same effect; they put the enforcement notice into abeyance and delay compliance with its requirements. The enforcement officer, more than anyone else, knows when the enforcement notice was served and therefore knows when the appeal period ends. He also knows what the grounds of appeal against the notice are and therefore is probably the best placed person at the local authority to check that the proposed appeal is lawfully made. If it is not, he should immediately advise the local authority lawyer and instruct the lawyer to bring the matter to the attention of the Justices Clerk or the administrative officer to the tribunal, asking that the appeal be rejected, If it is not rejected he should instruct that representations be made when the 'appeal' hearing is opened, but before the hearing of the appeal proper, inviting the tribunal to throw out the appeal. To do so is not acting in an oppressive way or playing hard ball, it is playing by the rules. I have talked at length during the chapters that precede this one about the need for the local authority to comply with the rules for creating notices, drafting and serving them. The requirement to play by the rules is not a one-way street and applies equally to the appellant. If he does not comply with the rules the local authority is within its rights and should take issue with him and resist the proposed, but unlawfully made, appeal. Some might go further and say it is the authority's duty to do so. The authority represents the broader interests of the public and has no interest beyond that and arguably it can only appropriately discharge this duty by ensuring a proper adherence to the rules as laid down by Parliament.

The final element of an appeal lawfully made is that any fee required should have been paid in full. I accept that it is rather more difficult to check this; it is something that initially will only be known to the tribunal and the appellant. You might wonder why I would care about this element of the requirements but to my mind it is as important as the two I have already discussed. I accept that finding the fee for appealing might be difficult for some appellants and that there can be a delay between the appeal being filed and the appeal being heard. I also accept that if the appellant files and pays for an appeal but then chooses not to proceed with it his money will not be refunded. It is also the case that if the appellant is successful in the prosecution of his appeal he will get his money back, but none of these things are reasons for the appellant not paying the appeal fee in full before the hearing of the appeal. I know from discussion with Justices Clerks that some of them are content to accept payment on the day of the hearing on the grounds that there is less administrative hassle involved in doing so. The alternative is to take the money before the day and then refund it if the appeal is successful. Courts also dislike taking the appeal fee and then having to tell the appellant he is not getting it back if the appeal does not proceed. I have no sympathy with either argument because their effect is to allow the appeal to be made out of time. The date of the hearing of the appeal is going to be some time after the close of the appeal period; hence payment on the day of the hearing means that the appeal is not properly made during the appeal period. I won't repeat my comments about the local authority acquiescing in such matters and I accept, as I said, that the issue of when and whether payment in full has been made is rather more difficult to check, but it is an inquiry that can and should be made. If the answer is in the negative the local authority has grounds on which it could and should resist the proposed appeal. Trust me on this, it is not an inquiry that a local authority would have to make very often before the tribunal got the message and adopted a less 'flexible' approach to payment of appeal fees.

The merits of the appeal

I said at the beginning of this chapter that once the enforcement officer had served the enforcement notice he could sit back, kick off his shoes and wait for the recipient of the notice to make the next move. Unfortunately, once the appeal papers are received he is required to sit back up, put his shoes back on and consider what the appeal papers contain. Suppose that the papers show that the appeal is not against technical defects and that the appeal is properly made on appropriate grounds. All we are left with is an appeal against the merits of the notice. These are problematic as they pitch the subjective view of the enforcement officer against the subjective view of the appellant and it is quite possible that the two will be poles apart. It is of course quite possible that the enforcement officer will be fully aware of the appellant's view. The service of an enforcement notice is quite often the last stage in a negotiation process that has failed to achieve what the enforcement officer wanted and is seen as the only way to make progress. In such cases there is very little prospect of identifying any middle ground and the only way to resolve the matter is to thrash it out in front of a neutral third party who will determine what the requirements should be. Where that is the case, the best advice I can offer if for the enforcement officer to get on with preparing his case for the appeal and making sure that his file is in order.

On the other hand, it may be that the enforcement officer looks at the grounds on which the appeal is made and sees some merit in them. If for example he has said that compliance is to be achieved in 60 days and the appellant in his grounds of appeal suggests that 72 days is more reasonable, the casual observer is bound to come to the view that there isn't that much between the parties; surely with a bit of give and take they can resolve this? If the enforcement officer wants bells and whistles and the appellant considers bells and horns to be more reasonable does it really matter as long as some sort of noise can be made? As I said, I tend to the pragmatic view. Achieving something that is as near as damn it what is wanted and achieves the same outcome in a 'no risk and no delay way', seems to me to be a better option than going to court to slug it out over the width of a shirt button. Not only is progress made more quickly but the working relationship between the appellant and the enforcement officer is preserved. Given that the two will have an ongoing relationship, at least until compliance is achieved and possibly longer, that may be no bad thing.

I have to admit that on occasions when I have suggested a bit of give and take to enforcement officers in this sort of situation the suggestion has not always been met with universal acclaim. A number of views have been expressed; that I am undermining their professional judgement; that the appellant will have 'won'; that I am 'afraid' to go to court and fight it out being amongst them. None are true. If the officer has asked for bells and whistles and considers, in his professional view, that they and only they are what is required I am in no position to argue. I fully accept that if beads and feathers are offered as an alternative they may not be quite what is required and the appeal should be resisted, but I don't think there is any harm in exploring why bells and horns won't do the job. It is a question that will have to be answered at the appeal hearing so giving it some consideration sooner rather than later is no bad thing. I struggle with the 'appellant has won' argument too. Even if were talking in terms if winning and losing, which we are not, giving a couple of inches in a battle that is a mile long does not constitute a loss. What we are talking about is progressing a matter to a satisfactory conclusion, and even if we do give a couple of inches the appellant is still going to have to have to comply with the requirements within the prescribed time. It's hardly a crushing victory; it's a minor giving of ground to gain a greater advantage. As for not wanting a fight, for me as for most lawyers, nothing could be further from the truth. I am always happy to fight, if a fight is necessary, but I do like to have something to fight with. I am not keen on facing down heavy weapons with water balloons, that's all. The trick is not to take appeals personally but to look to see whether there is any advantage to be had from resolving the now crystallised differences before the hearing. If there is not then so be it, but if there is, it is probably in the interests of the local authority and the complainants or persons affected to see what can be achieved.

The appeal hearing and attempts to delay

If the view of the enforcement officer is that the appeal is to be resisted, and there is nothing to be gained by give and take the appeal proceeds to a hearing.

In some cases 'hearing' is not necessarily the right word. In town and country planning cases the appellant can opt to be heard by way of written representations where both parties reduce their view to writing. The Planning Inspector then considers the matters on the papers and gives a written judgement. Where this mechanism is available it has its own rules and time limits and the most I would say about them is that officers should check the rules carefully and make sure that they comply with them. Generally, such procedures do not require the input of lawyers, which I suspect is one of their attractions for all parties concerned.

Of more concern to enforcement officers are what they consider to be 'real' appeals, appeals that are heard by magistrates or an inspector, where examination in chief and cross examination are part of the process and where a decision is handed down based on the view that the magistrate or inspector forms on the day.

Where the appellant is convinced of the righteousness of his cause he will be keen to progress the appeal and to argue his corner. To that end he will want to have the matter heard as soon as possible. He will seek to get on with things and will be as keen as the local authority to see the matter resolved quickly without any unnecessary delay. Other than to note that, as the appellant, he has the benefit of proving what he says to the civil standard of proof, (on the balance of probabilities) rather than the standard we more usually associate with such matters, the criminal standard, (beyond reasonable doubt) I do not intend to talk about the procedure of the hearing. Readers who wish to acquaint themselves with the procedure should refer to the companion volume to this book (Investigation and Prosecution: practical guidance for local authority enforcement officers) or to other standard criminal procedure texts.

Having considered the appellant who has what he considers to be meritorious grounds of appeal and wishes to pursue them, what about the other sort of appellant? The one whose grounds of appeal are legitimate but of dubious merit and which he employs purely to buy time for himself and to frustrate the ambitions of the enforcement officer? The one, in short, who uses the appeal process as a delay process. To put this form of delay in context we need to consider its timing and its potential impact. Suppose by way of example, that a local authority environmental health department receives a complaint about some issue that turns out, upon investigation, to be a statutory nuisance. The complainants may have suffered from the nuisance for a while before they complained or may have complained immediately, but either way the Environmental Health Officer will have to undertake an investigation to determine that the nuisance exists. That investigation, with all of the necessary evidence gathering that goes with it, will take time. Having determined that a statutory nuisance does exist the Environmental Health Officer will then have to go through the process of serving an abatement notice. Depending on the procedure of the council for which he works this could be a slick and speedy process or it could be long and drawn out requiring both a consideration of the evidence and approval at a higher, or heaven forbid, political level. Once the necessary hoops have been jumped through the notice can be drafted and served. Even at this point there is the further delay of the appeal period, which must elapse before the abatement notice actually takes effect. Then comes the compliance period and it is only at the end of that period that the matter will be resolved. Or won't be, depending on the attitude of the recipient.

The uncooperative individual served with the abatement notice will now start to play the delay game. Fully aware that they will eventually have to comply with requirements of the notice, as they have no reasonable excuse for not doing so beyond their overwhelming desire not to co-operate with the local authority, they will wait until just before the expiry of the appeal period before issuing their appeal notice knowing that it will necessarily drags things out. The date of the first hearing and the subsequent hearing of the appeal proper has to come and go before the compliance period starts to run.

The rules of the delay game are straightforward. Nothing should be done until the very last minute and every opportunity for further delay should be taken. The appeal should be lodged on the last day of the appeal period. At the first hearing the unrepresented appellant will request that a long adjournment of the matter be granted for the purpose of, for example, instructing a solicitor or some such; at the next hearing an early date for the hearing proper will be resisted for whatever reason can be dreamt up so that the appeal is listed as far into the future as possible. There are then a variety of wild cards that can be played to promote further delay – the note from the doctor saying the appellant is ill and cannot attend; the funeral of a late lamented relative; the failure to turn up at all, so the matter has to be relisted; the change of solicitor and consequent need give further instructions. All will require a further adjournment and promote further delay.

So what you might say? As long as the enforcement officer and any other local authority staff required are all present, correct and good to go what does this matter? More pertinently, how can you stop it? The short answer is you cannot. If the appellant wants to try his hand at all, or any of these stunts, he is entitled to do so however reprehensible we may consider his behaviour. More important is the reaction of the council. It is important not to lose sight of the fact that all this started because a member of the public was suffering from the impact of a statutory nuisance. As far as they are concerned nothing has changed. The nuisance is ongoing. While the local authority is using its best endeavours, objecting to applications for adjournments to keep the matter moving along, the complainant has no legitimate cause for complaint. He may however if the local authority meekly acquiesces in the various attempts of the appellant to delay the hearing of the appeal. In order to protect the health of the complainant and, perhaps as importantly, keep the Ombudsman from the door, the local authority team must be seen to actively resist applications for adjournments. They should inform the court that they are ready to proceed and explain the consequences of the delay on the complainant. It's probably right to recognise that this may make no difference at all, the court may feel it is in the interests of justice to grant an adjournment, but at least the local authority will be seen trying to progress the issue and the court record will show that. As important as doing something, is doing it with due expedition and that includes not going along with the delaying tactics of the reluctant appellant. An objection made and denied at least demonstrates the local authority's intent; acquiescence says nothing but can be interpreted as a lack of engagement with the problem. In such cases being seen to object to delay is as important as not causing it.

The result

There are three possible outcomes at an appeal against a Permissive or Prohibitive notice. In order of descending horror they are that the tribunal can quash the notice, uphold but amend it or uphold it.

The worst case scenario for the local authority is that the tribunal will quash the notice. This can occur for a variety of reasons. The notice may be flawed in its content, missing one of the key pieces of information; there may be an administrative error, such as a miscalculation of the appeal or compliance periods. Alternatively, the notice may have been served on the wrong person. There may be no objection to its form or content but the fact that it is was served on the wrong person, even if the local authority thought at the time of serving that it was correctly targeted, will be fatal and the notice will be quashed. The local authority should be fully cognisant of what it should do when drafting and serving the enforcement notice so it cannot would not be right if it could make a glorious mess of drafting or serving a notice and then be able to correct it at the hearing of the appeal. Whether an error is sufficiently serious as to justify quashing a notice will depend on the error. The acid test is whether the informality, defect or error was a material one, and that is a question of fact and degree. The wrong person or wrong premises is a material defect, as are citing incorrect appeal or compliance periods. A misspelling of the recipient's name where the error is a minor one, for example describing the recipient as Ann when she is properly named Anne or Thomas when he properly called Tomos, but where otherwise the identity of the person is readily identifiable, is probably not a material defect and can be corrected by the court. Where the defect is a material one the tribunal must quash the notice as it would be an injustice to the recipient to allow it to stand.

To describe the notice being quashed as a bit of a blow is probably understating it. It is much more than that. It means that the local authority has to go right back to the starting point and consider its position. It should consider whether the reason for serving the notice remains, and if so, whether it should re-serve the notice with the correct details. Things may have changed and the position may have moved on, so a knee jerk 'just bang it out again' response may not be appropriate, and a new notice, if appropriate at all, will have to take account of what changes have occurred and reflect them. It is also likely that the complainant or the persons affected by whatever circumstance caused the quashing of the original notice will be less than impressed to find that after a period of suffering, evidence collecting and waiting for the notice to take effect that nothing is going to happen and to all intents and purposes things are as they ever were. In such circumstances the idea that to err is human and to forgive divine is not one that is readily embraced, and a request for details of the local authority's complaint procedure is the more likely outcome. To add injury to insult the tribunal has the discretion to award costs against the local authority. The appellant whose appeal is upheld will see the notice quashed and be entitled to claim costs against the authority. The appellant will have to calculate how much dealing with the appeal has cost him and make an application for that sum; the court will try and put him back in the financial position he would have been had he not had to address the appeal. The discretion to award costs is a wide one and the appeal court is reluctant to interfere with its use, even where the error that brought down the notice was not made recklessly. I don't suppose the day that an enforcement officer leaves the magistrates court with his enforcement notice quashed, an award for costs against him in his pocket, to find on his return to the office a message from the complainant asking for the local authority's complaints procedure would be the highlight of his career; there is a lot to be said for not being that officer.

The second possible outcome of an appeal is that the notice is upheld in principle but is amended by the tribunal. In such cases the tribunal is persuaded of the need to serve the notice but not persuaded of the need for the requirements as outlined in the notice. It may be persuaded by the appellant that a requirement should be altered, for example by extending the compliance period, or that it should be deleted altogether. I have already said that I tend towards the pragmatic when dealing with proposed appeals and if the only issue between the local authority and the appellant is a slight tweak to the wording, the time period for compliance or some other requirement I would urge them to sort it out rather than go all the way to a full blown appeal. I would only advise going to appeal if the local authority considers that there is no room to move as far as their requirements are concerned.

Insofar as both these outcomes are concerned I think there is a second consequence that is often overlooked by enforcement officers, but which lives on long after the hearing is over. It is the loss of credibility suffered by the enforcement officer, in the eyes of both the appellant and of the tribunal. The tribunal issue may not be one that causes him to lose much sleep, he may never have cause to appear before that particular bench of magistrates or Planning Inspector again, but the loss of credibility in the eyes of the appellant and possibly his agent or solicitor should be of more concern. The officer will be required to engage with them during the life of the instant notice and possibly beyond. Credibility is hard won; it shouldn't be discarded lightly.

If the appellant approaches the local authority and makes suggestions about amending the requirements of the notice the local authority is well advised to give those proposed amendments detailed consideration and, if it decides to reject them, to ensure that it is able to justify the decision. The court's discretion to award costs should be a factor in the considerations; costs can be awarded where the local authority has unreasonably refused to consider the proposals of the appellant. However deeply wedded the officer is to the requirements in the notice he is very well advised to consider the proposals in detail as a rejection that amounts to just digging in his toes is not going to commend itself to anyone.

The final potential outcome, and the one to which every enforcement officer in this situation must aspire, is that the enforcement notice is upheld without amendment. Unfortunately the local authority in such cases is unlikely to be awarded costs unless the appellant's grounds of appeal were so ludicrous as to be farcical and, given the filters that they have to go through to get before the tribunal, which is somewhat unlikely. Other than in such circumstances there is no reason for the appellant having to pay costs; after all he has the right to appeal, has paid to exercise it and should not be punished again for being unsuccessful.

There is one final comment to make on the issue of appeals where the notice is upheld, whether amended or otherwise. The date of the hearing of the appeal becomes day 1 of the compliance period, the requirement for compliance beginning to run immediately upon the notice being upheld.

The effect of failing to appeal

Given that I have spent the best part of this chapter talking about the process of appealing you might think that it is the obvious step to take for anyone served with an enforcement notice with a right of appeal attached. It's not. The recipient of the enforcement notice is not obliged to appeal, and many do not. Some take the view that they are bang to rights and will just have to get on with complying with whatever the requirements of the notice happen to be. Others may have agreed that they will do the works necessary but may need evidence that they are obliged to do so for reasons such as to access finance or to move tenants out of property or similar. Others may just not get round to it and may miss the appeal time period boat which will have sailed by the time they think about boarding. As far as the enforcement officer is concerned the reasons for failing to appeal are not a matter of concern; he can content himself by resuming the seat back position and counting the days to the end of the compliance period.

The consequences of failing to appeal

There are consequences for the recipient of the notice who chooses not to appeal and because they have an impact on the local authority they are worthy of consideration. The first consequence is that all avenues of appeal are closed other than one; a claim that the enforcement notice was never a proper notice as it was so flawed as never to have been valid; in legal terms it was *void ab initio*. This argument would be used as a defence to an action brought by the local authority alleging non-compliance with an enforcement notice, the defendant saying effectively 'Why should I comply with something that is so bad I didn't recognise it as being an enforcement notice?' It's a high risk strategy since failure of the argument means that conviction is inevitable.

The second consequence is that the defendant will not be able to argue anything in his defence which he could have raised as a ground of appeal. The time for that argument has gone; the defendant knew of his right to appeal and argue his case and should have done it in the appeal arena. He cannot be allowed to have two bites of the cherry; the local authority must be entitled at the end of the appeal period to take the view that there is no challenge to the notice and to proceed accordingly.

The third consequence is a comfort for local authorities that have relied on the absence of activity from the recipient of the notice, have undertaken works in default of compliance and then seek to recover the costs from the recipient. For the same reasons as in the second consequence above the recipient cannot raise as an objection to the works in default anything that could have been raised as a ground of appeal to the notice. I suggest that in this case it is more important to the local authority that he should be unable to do so, since it has expended public money in the belief that the requirements of the enforcement notice were unchallenged.

Notes about appeals

1. Grounds of appeal appear in the statute that creates the enforcement notice. Appellants cannot create their own grounds to suit their own purposes.

2. Appeals must be properly made. They must be within the appeal period, based on legitimate grounds of appeal and the fee must be paid in full before the end of the appeal period.

3. Local authorities should object to appeals that are not properly made. Their duty to the complainant and the wider public demands that they should.

4. It is always worth considering whether there is merit in the appellant's grounds of appeal – and if there is withdrawing the enforcement notice and serving an amended version.

5. If the grounds of appeal are communicated to the local authority by the appellant but rejected by the local authority the reasons for rejection should be recorded as it may be necessary to justify the refusal to compromise at a later date.

6. Costs can be awarded against a local authority where a notice is quashed or amended because of the local authority's unreasonableness in refusing to amend the notice.

7. Grounds of appeal may not be used once the appeal period is over. Anything that could have been argued as a ground of appeal cannot be used as a defence to an allegation of non-compliance with the requirements of a notice.

Chapter 8

Compliance and non-compliance

Whichever of the four types of notice is served by an enforcement officer the ambition is the same; to achieve compliance. More than that, the ambition is to achieve compliance as quickly as possible, and in doing so either solve the problem that had been suffered by the complainant or protect the land or building. Achieving compliance should be the end of the matter, effectively being a job done and a solution achieved. If only life was that simple.

The end of the compliance period

There are a number of scenarios that can present themselves at the end of the compliance period. The first is that compliance in full is achieved; if it is the enforcement officer can make the necessary annotation on the file, close it and file it away, affording himself a moment of quiet pride before getting on with whatever else he has to occupy his day. The second is much as the first, except that once compliance has been achieved there is an ongoing element of monitoring to ensure that compliance continues to be achieved. The third scenario is that compliance is achieved in part by the time the end of the compliance period rolls around, but works that are necessary to achieve full compliance remain to be undertaken. Strictly speaking, in this scenario, compliance has not been achieved, although the recipient of the notice has made some effort to comply with the requirements of the notice. The fourth and final scenario is that nothing has been done. At all. Everything remains as it was before the service of the notice, other than time, which will have moved on, and the attitude of the complainant which will have hardened considerably. Each of the scenarios merits consideration as each has consequences for the enforcement officer.

Ascertaining the compliance position

At this stage can I please make a plea on behalf of local authority lawyers who may be called upon to prosecute allegations of non-compliance with enforcement notices, whether in part or at all? As soon as the end of the compliance period beckons please go and check whether compliance has been achieved. Immediately. Or send a student or ask a colleague to check, but please check. Let me explain why this is important. Assume that the local authority has decided to instigate legal proceedings alleging that the recipient of the notice has failed to comply with its requirements within the compliance period. The prosecuting lawyer should explain to the court, in forensic detail, either himself or through a witness, why the enforcement notice was served; the conditions that were found on inspection; what the risk, actual or potential, from the conditions was; and what the local authority has done. What the local authority will have done is to serve an enforcement notice, which will be produced with a flourish, as an exhibit, and waved about. The lawyer may talk expansively about the requirements and their reasonableness; he should certainly talk about the time in which the specified works had to be carried out. He will tell the court that upon the expiry of the compliance period there was a revisit when it was discovered that the works, either in whole or in part, had not been carried out. He may give evidence about the ongoing risk to health, land or property condition that will be occasioned by the failure to comply. Properly presented, the case can be compelling listening and the Magistrates can be persuaded to impose an appropriate sentence. But this isn't always what happens.

Why is it that some local authorities fail to take their own cases seriously? I come across examples of cases where the procedure has been undertaken well. The properly authorised and delegated officer has identified a nuisance or breach, served an enforcement notice with reasonable and appropriate remedial actions specified, has given an appropriate period for compliance and has served the notice on the correct party. No room for complaint in the way in which the complaint and its investigation were handled or in the way in which the enforcement officer sought to achieve a remedy. Where it all falls down is what happens when the compliance period ends. From the lawyer's point of view this is the point where he should be able to tell the court that at the end of the compliance period the officer had rushed back to the site to find to his shock and horror that the work had not been done, that the risk to health or the detriment to the land or building was persisting and hence the case had been brought before the Justices. All too often however the lawyer is put in the position of having to say that some weeks after the compliance period had ended the officer found a moment to pop along, discovered that the works had not been completed, perhaps allowed another couple of weeks to elapse for whatever reason, went back, saw that things were still not completed and hence decided to bring proceedings. Heaven knows it happens but it is hard to make a case about the current risks arising from the continuation of the peril, if it has continued unabated for a number of weeks with the knowledge of the enforcement officer and without any real action being taken.

We all know that going to court does not resolve the non-compliance issues – the non-compliance persists even after conviction of the offender, but that is not the point. If the local authority is trying to impress on the court the importance and urgency of tackling the matter that gave rise to the serving of the notice, it will also have to demonstrate that it acted expeditiously throughout. This means that the enforcement officer has to go to back to the site as soon as the compliance period ends to check for completion of works. Anything less risks giving the impression that the matter had ceased to be important; in effect, that service of the notice, rather than compliance with its requirements, has resolved the issue. My plea therefore is that at the end of the compliance period enforcement officers should go back to the site and assess the state of compliance. If a matter is important enough to warrant action it is important enough to follow through. If the local authority doesn't think it is important, why should the court?

Full compliance

Oh happy day! At the end of the compliance period the enforcement officer breezes up to the land or premises which is the subject of the notice and finds that every requirement of the notice has been satisfied in full. It may be, at the end of a period of many months, considerable works of renovation and improvement have been completed, or perhaps after a few hours or days, something, whether a process or an unauthorised redevelopment, has stopped. What more could an enforcement officer want? In some cases, nothing at all. The achievement of full compliance will draw a line under the matter, the issue will have been resolved and everyone, enforcement officer, complainant and recipient can move on with their respective lives.

Surprising as this may seem this scenario is not actually as good as it gets. Compliance by the end of the compliance period is as much as the enforcement officer can ask for, but it may not be as much as he can get. Sometimes he can get more than he wants. This rarest of birds is seen when compliance is achieved before the end of the compliance period. For whatever reason, the recipient of the notice gets his finger out and delivers full compliance before the compliance period ends. This may be for one of two reasons. The first is because the recipient just wants to achieve compliance and moves heaven and earth to do so quickly. The second, and less edifying reason, is because the compliance period on the notice was too long. The recipient had all the time he needed and more so he was not required to make a focused effort to do whatever the notice required, rather he could drag his feet and still get all of the necessary work completed in time. I say nothing about the first outcome; the second is not wholly a cause for celebration.

As I keep saying we need to remember that at the start of the process was a complainant or someone adversely affected by the activity the subject of notice, or land or a building adversely affected. The ambition of the enforcement officer was to deliver a solution or remedy as quickly as he could; not at some point between the serving of the enforcement notice and the end of time. Complainants, perhaps not unreasonably, believe that the enforcement officer will be keen to achieve compliance in the shortest possible time rather than languidly hoping it may happen, given a fair wind. As we saw in the previous chapter, the recipient of the notice can appeal if in his view the period for compliance is too short, and if he does the tribunal hearing the appeal has the discretion to extend the period. However there is no similar right for third parties, such as the complainant or any person affected by matter that is the subject of the notice, to appeal against it on the grounds that the compliance period is too long; as I noted it is highly unlikely that the recipient of the notice would make such a case. The third party just has to sit back, albeit somewhat aggrieved, because they cannot get involved in either the requirements of, or time for, compliance on the face of the notice. That is not however to say that there is nothing he can do. If the complainant considers that if he availed himself of a hammer and some nails or a bucket of hot water and a cloth, or whatever is required, he could have achieved compliance in half the time specified by the enforcement notice, he may feel he has a new but nonetheless justified grievance. He might just decide to avail himself of the council's complaints procedure and complain that the enforcement officer has not done as much as he reasonably could to achieve a speedy resolution of the matter and has caused him to be prejudiced for longer than was necessary. If he gets no satisfaction he may take the matter up with the Local Government Ombudsman and the enforcement officer may find that he is forced to justify the length of compliance period on the enforcement notice. Mere compliance is not enough. Compliance within a period that is reasonable but not excessive is the order of the day.

As I noted above, achieving full compliance within or by the end of the compliance period may not always be the end of the story. In some cases compliance may be achieved by doing something that once done cannot, or is highly unlikely, to be undone, and in such cases the file can probably be archived. In other cases compliance is achieved by stopping an activity or a form of behaviour. Either explicitly stated or implicit in the requirement to stop is the requirement not to start up again. Ensuring that the activity or behaviour does not restart, or if it does is stopped again quickly, requires either ongoing monitoring beyond the end of the compliance period, or, if the compliance period is open ended, monitoring for as long and as often as is necessary to ensure ongoing compliance.

Partial compliance

'Partial' is an interesting word in the context of compliance. For a start it quite obviously means that 100% compliance has not been achieved, but it doesn't tell us what has actually been achieved. It can mean 99% compliance, or it can mean 5% compliance and there is a world of difference between the two. Technically of course it means that an offence has been committed because compliance has not been achieved on or before the end of the requisite period, and therefore the local authority would be justified in commencing proceedings alleging failure to comply with the requirements of the enforcement notice.

Partial compliance creates further investigative work for the enforcement officer and requires him to make and justify a decision, or series of decisions, regarding how to deal with the matter. Before I consider the decisions to be made and what should influence them, I want to just put down a bit of a marker. Up to this point in this book I have talked almost exclusively about the serving of enforcement notices and the process and procedures that are involved in doing so. It is only now, almost in the final chapter, that we have to think about a different form of enforcement; the prosecution of the recipient who does not comply with the requirements of the enforcement notice. I think it is important not to lose sight of the fact that mere failure to comply with all of the requirements of a notice, within the compliance period, does not necessarily mean that prosecution should follow as the sun rises in the east. It doesn't. The enforcement officer who finds at the end of the compliance period that only partial compliance has been achieved has to ascertain what percentage of compliance has been delivered and why full compliance has not been achieved. Having armed himself with that information he must consider what is the most appropriate way to proceed. It may be prosecution, and if it is he must apply the full rigour of the two limbed Prosecutor's Test to his decision. It may be that prosecution, though an option, is not the best way forward and cutting the recipient a bit of slack may be the most pragmatic route to achieving full compliance.

The first line of inquiry for the enforcement officer in the case of partial compliance, is just how much of the required work has been completed? Following closely on the heels of that question is why has this been the case? What has prevented a greater degree of, or even full compliance, being achieved? There is a range of potential reasons. They run from the recipient who really doesn't care one way or the other about the requirements of the notice, and makes only the most token of token gestures towards compliance, to the recipient who has moved heaven and earth to achieve compliance but has been frustrated in doing so through no fault of his own. There are questions to be answered. Did the recipient make a start towards compliance as soon as he got the enforcement notice but proceeded at snail's pace and therefore has run out of time? Did he do nothing for three quarters of the compliance period and then went at the requirements like a whirling dervish with absolutely no chance of finishing in time? Was he a man with a plan which has fallen apart through no fault of his own? Maybe funds ran out, or parts or specialist skills were not available, and he is as frustrated as the enforcement officer. Whatever the reason, and whatever the attitude of the recipient of the notice, both are important

128

intelligence for the enforcement officer because they will inform his decision about what action should be taken next.

Having raised the issue of the Prosecutor's Test it is helpful to elucidate what the test requires. The test is set out in the Code for Crown Prosecutors and comes in two parts. Each part must be addressed separately and in the right order. The first part is the evidential test; is there is a realistic prospect of conviction?: secondly comes the public interest test; is it in the public interest to prosecute? If there is insufficient evidence to provide a realistic prospect of conviction there should not be a prosecution and so the public interest test becomes irrelevant. In the case of partial compliance there is no difficulty with the first limb of the test, there is a prosecutable case; full compliance was required and full compliance has not been delivered. As is so often the case it is the second limb of the test, the public interest test, that poses the harder questions and requires the more detailed consideration. For enforcement officers it is not the only matter that needs to be considered. The enforcement officer will also have to consider the local authority's enforcement policy and factor that into his decision making process.

It is also helpful to consider the realities of the situation. Theory on its own is relatively straightforward, but unfortunately the real world is more complicated. The enforcement officer will have to inject into his inquiries his experience and knowledge of the situation and the parties to it. If the recipient of the notice tells the enforcement officer that, through no fault of his own, he has been frustrated at every turn, is he telling the truth, the whole truth and nothing but the truth or is he lying through his teeth? Do their earlier encounters suggest that he will resist every inch of the way, that he will have to be dragged kicking and screaming towards compliance, that anything he says about being willing but unable, can be discounted? Is he, in the view of the enforcement officer, as trustworthy as a penitent nun and if he says that circumstances have conspired to prevent his achieving compliance, that is how it is? This sort of information is what a colleague of mine used to call 'soft intelligence' and it's hard to put a price on its value. To the soft intelligence we can add experience, the experience that the local authority has from its previous dealings with the recipient. Maybe it has never dealt with him before, in which case there is nothing to consider. On the other hand, the local authority may have long and bitter experience in dealing with the recipient and know that it can prosecute him all day, every day and he still will not comply. Alternatively, the local authority may know that the recipient talks a good game but if the whiff of prosecution is in the air he will fall in and comply. Enforcement officers should not underestimate the value of this sort of information; it is only by throwing it all into the mix that the most appropriate decision in a particular set of circumstances can be made.

Partial compliance – the options

I'll start by putting a marker down. There is no "do nothing" option. Once an enforcement officer has established that compliance has not been achieved he has to do something. There are a number of options; doing nothing and hope it all turns out well in the end is not one of them. What are the options? There is the extension of the compliance period, whether done on an informal or formal basis or the formal legal option, offering a simple caution or instigating legal proceedings. The choice of which option to use will be informed by the considerations previously discussed.

Partial compliance – extending the period

An extension of the compliance period may be appropriate where compliance has all but been achieved or where the enforcement officer accepts the reasons offered by the recipient of the notice for his failure to achieve compliance. The enforcement officer has to have reasonable cause to believe not only that that the extension will give the recipient of the notice enough time to achieve compliance but that he will not find himself at the end of the extension period wondering whether or not to give a another extension. Other than in very exceptional circumstances an extension should be a one shot deal. Extensions are not to be thrown about lightly. Enforcement officers must first check whether the legislation under which the original notice arose makes provision for an extension to the compliance period. If there is, the legislation will prescribe how this is to be done, whether in writing or by the use of a prescribed form of extension notice. Where there is a prescribed form the strict requirements of the legislation must be followed, as they were in the drafting of the original notice, and the same rules apply to service of the extension as applied to service of the notice.

Where no formal provision is made in the legislation for an extension to the compliance period we are forced to assume that the legislator did not intend that the compliance period should be extended. That is not to say however that an extension cannot be allowed, just that it cannot be done within the confines of the legislation. If the enforcement officer is minded to allow an extension of the compliance period in such circumstances, he is well advised to ensure that his decision has the support of his line manager since he is now going off piste. There are two ways to give an extension. The first is to serve another notice on the recipient which should contain just those parts of the work that remain outstanding. This will not be possible in all cases. The matter that gave rise to the original complaint may no longer exist in the way that justified the service of the original enforcement notice and those parts that remain may not justify the service of another notice. In such a case a new notice is not appropriate and to serve one would be an abuse of process. To be realistic, the recipient is hardly going to appeal against it on the basis that it is unjustified as he will be getting what he wants, but nonetheless it would be inappropriate for the local authority to act in this way. Where the works required to achieve compliance can legitimately form the basis of another notice, the local authority should remember that an appeal period attaches to the 'new' notice. As I said the recipient of this new notice is not likely to appeal against it, but the local authority is well advised to remember that there is nothing it can do to stop him if he chooses to do so and if the wrong call has been made, considerable further delay could ensue.

Perhaps the simplest way to give the recipient a short extension of time is to do so informally by writing to him and advising him that he has a further period of X weeks or days in which to finish the work. It would be sensible, before setting the extension period, for the enforcement officer to discuss with the recipient how long he considers he will need and to satisfy himself that the outstanding works can be finished within the extension period. Pragmatic as I am, I do get a bit twitchy about informal extensions. As a prosecuting lawyer I was never sure whether what I was looking at was a real informal extension or a neat way of describing a failure by the local authority to do anything about non-compliance at the end of the compliance period. The informality also concerned me as it had consequences if compliance was not achieved at the end of the extension period and the local authority decided to prosecute for non-compliance. The problem was, and remains, that the non-compliance does not occur at end of the extension of time, it occurs at the end of the compliance period on the face of the notice. If a local authority has granted an informal extension of 6 weeks, and two weeks after the end of the extension period determines that compliance has not been achieved, even if it leaps into action immediately to get an information laid alleging non-compliance it is already 8 weeks after the event. And that is if they leap straight into action...... Informal extensions can be used, but used with care. I strongly suggest that they are only used where the enforcement officer knows and trusts the recipient and is satisfied that at the end of the extension the works required for compliance will be completed. When they work they are very effective. They achieve the desired result and save time and money for the local authority in not going through the legal process. They may also build up a fund of goodwill with the recipient, which may be important if the local authority expects further dealings with him in the future.

Partial compliance – the legal options

Having considered extensions, formal or informal we move to the formal legal options. Both a simple caution and a prosecution alleging non-compliance start at the same point; the local authority must be satisfied that it has enough evidence to prosecute for non-compliance. All too often I hear local authority officers telling me that as they did not have enough evidence to bring proceedings they offered the party a simple caution. It doesn't work like that. A local authority may offer a simple caution instead of taking someone to court, but it must be both able and prepared to proceed to court if the proposed defendant declines to accept the caution. A simple caution is not the 'fall short' option; the threshold for a simple caution is exactly the same as for prosecution, and the adequacy of the evidence should be determined before a decision as to disposal is made.

When a simple caution is offered, the recipient must be explicitly told that firstly he must admit that he is guilty of committing an offence i.e. non-compliance, and secondly that he must understand that the caution has the same effect as a conviction, in that it can be cited in court if the defendant is charged in the future with a substantially similar offence. He should then be asked to sign a document confirming this which should then be signed by a representative of the local authority. For a simple caution to have any value the defendant must be aware that he could have been prosecuted and that a caution is not, in effect, getting off with it. The advantage for the local authority is that it achieves a result without the requirement to go to Court. The defendant, similarly, is spared the expense and the adverse publicity of a court hearing. Simple cautions should be offered judiciously. If there is any suggestion that the defendant may believe that he has got away with it a simple caution would not be the proper course and formal proceedings should be considered. The value of the simple caution is in the effect that it has on the defendant and any devaluing of it as a procedure should be avoided.

The final option is to prosecute the recipient, alleging non-compliance with the requirements of the notice. It's not the purpose of this book to discuss the procedure in court; all I note is that the local authority must be satisfied that it is in the public interest to proceed to prosecution. Where the percentage of compliance achieved is very small I would argue the public interest is well served by prosecution; enforcement notice recipients cannot be allowed to ignore their requirements with impunity. It is less certain that the public interest is well served if compliance has been all but achieved, but equally, the recipient cannot be allowed to determine at what point enough effort has been made towards achieving compliance and down tools.

Where partial compliance has been achieved it is a professional call for the enforcement team when deciding the way in which the matter is to be progressed. The legal options are as described but, subject to the evidential requirements being satisfied, the call is one for the enforcement team. They will have to deal with the notice recipient and ultimately it will be for them to justify the decisions that they take. Whatever decision is taken, I cannot urge strongly enough the need to record the decision and the reasons for it, and where necessary, to ensure that it is signed off by a senior officer.

Non-compliance

Where 100% non-compliance is found the local authority has little option but to take action. The reasons for non-compliance should be ascertained and should be factored into the disposal decision. There are in reality two possible reasons. The first is that the recipient of the notice has just point blank refused to do the necessary work. The second is that the recipient of the notice considers that the enforcement notice is so flawed as not to be a notice at all and has chosen to disregard it.

As I noted above, where a matter is sufficiently serious to warrant the serving of a notice it must also be sufficiently serious to warrant legal action in the event of non-compliance. This is particularly the case where no effort at all has been made to achieve compliance. If it does not take a robust stance the credibility of the local authority as an enforcement agency will be called into doubt and its failure to act may be challenged by the Local Government Ombudsman. It should be remembered however that prosecution will not achieve compliance with the requirements of the notice. Prosecution will result in the imposition of a penalty on the defendant, whether financial or community, but the court has no power to require the defendant to complete the works.

The effect of a prosecution lies in its publicity value. If the local authority succeeds in its case, and the penalty is one of significance e.g. a considerable fine, the publicity such a case attracts will act as a warning to others who might consider ignoring the requirements of notices. It will tell them that the local authority will take the same robust stance with them as it has in the instant case, and that they can expect to be treated in the same way. It should however be noted that in the event of a small fine or a conditional discharge being handed down the best recourse may be not to issue a press release. The effect may be exactly the opposite of what is wanted.

Works in Default

I have noted, on more than one occasion, throughout this text that serving an enforcement notice may cause the recipient to comply with the local authority's wishes and carry out the prescribed works but that this is by no means guaranteed. Most enforcement officers are all too aware that, out there in the real world, there are characters that will do pretty much anything rather than comply with the wishes of the local authority, whether communicated as a request or required through an enforcement notice. These death or glory merchants are quite happy to play the 'serve a notice, let the compliance period lapse and then be prosecuted' game over and over, but will not lift a finger to carry out the necessary action to comply with the enforcement notice. The local authority will have to play along with this game and whilst the fines and the costs may mount up, compliance will be no nearer.

Sadly in such situations the local authority cannot shrug its shoulders and tell the complainant or persons affected that it is 'doing everything it can', because that may well not be true. It may have the nuclear option of doing works in default. Speaking as a lawyer, my view is that where the recipient of an enforcement notice has not complied with its requirements and there appears to be no realistic prospect of him doing so and there is the statutory power to do so, the council must consider undertaking works in default. It would be invidious to suggest that if the defendant does not do the works they should be left undone. Speaking as an enforcement officer however I am all too aware that the financial consequences for the local authority in undertaking works in default can be considerable. The recipient of the notice may have no financial resources and the local authority may find itself paying for significant works with little chance of recovering the money in the short term. Taking the wider view this should not be a problem as in most cases the cost of works carried out in default can be registered as a land charge and recovered on the sale of the property or land. Taking the realistic view, this is cold comfort indeed as the costs of the works may be significant and the land or property may not change hands for many a long year, leaving a cash strapped local authority waiting for a long time to see the money coming back into its coffers.

The view is not quite so gloomy where the legislation puts in place a specific money recovery mechanism. The Environmental Protection Act 1990 allows a local authority to serve a notice under sec 81A of the Environmental Protection Act 1990 where it believes that the recipient has the resources to pay for works carried out in default. A defendant who receives a notice under section 81A can appeal to the County Court, where the notice may be upheld, dismissed or upheld in amended form. Once the debt is established it may be pursued through the normal debt recovery processes and interest is chargeable on the outstanding debt. Such mechanisms allow for money to be recovered from those notice recipients who can pay but have dug their toes in over compliance. They cannot unfortunately magic up money from those who do not have it, and the local authority will still be left to pick up the bill. The local authority that has played this particular hand out does at least have the comfort of being able to tell its auditors that it has done as much as it can to recover the public money it has expended on works in default; but that is probably cold comfort.

Limitations on Works in Default

It is probably true to say that a local authority that ends up with no other recourse available to it than to embark on works in default is usually heartily sick of the property or land that is the subject of its actions; it would like to just sort it out once and for all. It may well take the view that if it has to do the work it may as well get in there and sort out anything and everything that is a problem now, or may be in the future, so that at the end of the work programme it can shut the door on the problem once and for all. It's a nice idea but works in default don't work like that. They are more akin to triage than complete cure. There are limits to what can be done through works in default and local authorities carrying them out need to be aware of them.

The first is that the local authority can only do as much by way of works in default as it required the recipient of the enforcement notice to do. However desirable it may be to do additional works (e.g. to paint woodwork when replacing guttering etc.), if the additional works did not form part of the notice requirements they should not be undertaken by the local authority. That is not to say they cannot be done, but if they are, they will be regarded as having been done gratuitously and costs may not be recovered in respect of them. In a similar vein, the local authority, in the course of carrying out works in default, may discover other necessary works which had they known about them would have formed part of the requirements of the enforcement notice. If this happens they should not carry out the additional works. They must serve a further enforcement notice requiring their completion which will be subject to the same appeal period and compliance period procedures as the original notice. This may seem counter intuitive. The local authority is fully aware that the requirements of the first notice were not complied with and serving a further notice will almost certainly cause considerable delay to works currently being done by the authority and may require some elements of the original work to be undone when carrying out works in default phase 2. It is a real dilemma for the local authority. To just patch it up and walk away is to prime a ticking bomb which will go off at some point in the future, although arguably that the local authority is forewarned about it and may be better placed to deal with any problems that arise in the future. Conversely to stop the works in default in order to serve a notice to legitimise the carrying on of the unforeseen works injects a healthy portion of delay and has the deeply undesirable effect of ramping up the costs of the works. If there was an easy legal answer I would be happy to share it, but there isn't. The decision as to which way to jump is a professional shout for the officers in the case, or more likely their Head of Service. Whichever decisions is made it is crucial to record it and the supporting thought processes that led to it, because in a rock and hard place scenario such as this, there is a very real likelihood that the decision will come back to haunt its maker.

The second limitation arises from the duty of fiscal care that the local authority carrying out the works owes to the owner of the land or property that is the subject of the works. Not only must the local authority restrict its activities to those works it required of the recipient of the notice, it must also do so for best value. It may not call up artisan craftsmen and crack out the gold leaf. There is no punitive element to works in default and best value must be obtained for monies expended. Practically, this is usually achieved by a competitive tender process for the works so that achievement of best value can be demonstrated; the process also protects a local authority from claims that it just awards all such contracts to an in-house team, where it has one. By way of a small crumb of comfort, the costs of engaging in a tendering process can be added to the costs of the works in default.

The third requirement, which is not really a limitation, is the requirement to share benefit. It may be that in some circumstances there is benefit to the local authority or another party, as a result of works in default being under taken, e.g. scaffolding erected to carry out works in default may allow a neighbouring property owner to make repairs or inspect their property. In such cases the benefit of access must be shared; the neighbouring property owner must chip in and make a contribution to the costs, reducing the costs to the notice recipient to represent that shared benefit. In such cases the local authority has a fiscal duty of care to the recipient of the notice and must take such opportunities on his behalf should they arise.

Recording decisions

As important as making decisions about works in default, is ensuring that decisions made are recorded properly and lawfully. Prior to the switch to 'cabinet' style local government most decision making powers were delegated by the council to the Environmental Health Committee or Planning Committee, where decisions were made in public and then recorded in the Committee minutes, which were approved by members and signed by the Chair of the Committee as a true record. The switch to cabinet style local government means that decisions are not made by committee in open session, rather they are often made, in private, by the Executive Member, an individual to whom the power to make the decision is delegated. Because decisions that had been made in open committee were being removed from public scrutiny there was a requirement for safeguards to ensure that government remained open and publically accountable.

In England the safeguard is found in the Local Authorities (Executive Arrangements) (Meetings and Access to Information) (England) Regulations 2012. These regulations put in place requirements as to how executive decisions are to be recorded and publicised. It should be noted that the requirements of the regulations are mandatory and executive decisions that are not recorded and publicised as prescribed are void, as are any actions taken in reliance on the decision. At the time of writing similar legislative provisions did not apply in Wales or Northern Ireland.

The Regulations require local authority executives to keep written records of prescribed decisions made at meetings of the executive or their committees or sub-committees and of prescribed decisions made by individual members. The Regulations also prescribe the circumstances in which such meetings may be held in private and set out the circumstances in which written records relating to executive decisions are to be made and when those records are to be open to the public

What constitutes an Executive Decision is outlined in Reg 2

"executive decision" *means a decision made or to be made by a decision maker in connection with the discharge of a function which is the responsibility of the executive of a local authority;*

To determine whether the regulations apply it is necessary to consider whether the function being discharged is one for which the executive of the local authority is responsible. This will require consideration of the constitution of the council and is likely to include decisions to carry out Works in Default in respect of notices served e.g. in respect of Statutory Nuisance and contaminated land remediation.

The process of recording executive decisions is outlined in the regulations. It is prescriptive, and worth consideration.

Recording of executive decisions made by individuals

13. *(1) As soon as reasonably practicable after an individual member has made an executive decision, that member must produce or instruct the proper officer to produce a written statement of that executive decision which includes the information specified in paragraph (2).*

(2) The statement referred to in paragraph (1) must include—

> *(a) a record of the decision including the date it was made;*
> *(b) a record of the reasons for the decision;*
> *(c) details of any alternative options considered and rejected by the member when making the decision;*
> *(d) a record of any conflict of interest declared by any executive member who is consulted by the member which relates to the decision, and*
> *(e) in respect of any declared conflict of interest, a note of dispensation granted by the relevant local authority's head of paid service.*

(3) Executive decisions made by individual members of local authority executives are prescribed decisions for the purposes of section 9G(4) of the 2000

Act (duty to keep a written record of decisions made by individual members of local authority executives).

(4) As soon as reasonably practicable after an officer has made a decision which is an executive decision, the officer must produce a written statement which must include—

> *(a) a record of the decision including the date it was made;*
> *(b) a record of the reasons for the decision;*
> *(c) details of any alternative options considered and rejected by the officer when making the decision;*
> *(d) a record of any conflict of interest declared by any executive member who is consulted by the officer which relates to the decision; and*
> *(e) in respect of any declared conflict of interest, a note of dispensation granted by the relevant local authority's head of paid service.*

The implications of a failure to record and publicise decisions are considerable. If a decision is not recorded as required, it is not a decision properly made and therefore any action that flows from it is null and void. In the worst case scenario this may result in a local authority being unable to reclaim costs for works carried out in default of compliance with a notice served.

Take for example, an executive decision to serve an Environmental Protection Act 1990 sec 79 (Statutory Nuisance) notice taken, but not recorded and publicised as required by the Local Authority (Executive Arrangements) (Meetings and Access to Information)(England) Regulations 2012. There is no requirement for a recipient who is aware of the omission to appeal against the notice because it is null and void and as such it does not exist in law and he may ignore it with impunity. The local authority serving the notice will almost certainly conclude that the notice took effect at the end of the appeal period and that compliance was not achieved. They may carry out works in default of compliance and then seek to recover their costs. As all of the actions taken flow from the void decision the local authority could neither recover the costs of the works in default nor succeed if it was to prosecute the recipient of the notice. I would not expect an enforcement officer to concern themselves overly with this technical requirement but I would expect someone somewhere higher up the food chain to know about it and to ensure that the relevant requirements have been met before the local authority embark on the path of active enforcement for non-compliance.

Final Thoughts on Compliance

1. The end of the compliance period is by no means the end of the enforcement process. Compliance achieved may require ongoing monitoring; non-compliance will need to be addressed.
2. As soon as the compliance period ends, check whether compliance has been achieved; in full, in part or at all.
3. If the recipient has not complied with the enforcement notice it is worth considering why he has not done so. Is there a procedural flaw that has made the notice void? Check everything before embarking on further action.
4. Prosecution for non-compliance may be necessary, but it will not achieve compliance.
5. Where the power to carry out works in default exists local authorities must consider using the power. Where they decide not to use the power the reasons for their decision must be recorded.
6. The limitations on works in default must be respected to protect the local authority from incurring irrecoverable costs.
7. Local authorities should do as much as is practically possible to recover any costs they have incurred through carrying on works in default, whether by actively converting them to a civil debt, where the law allows, or by recording them as a charge against land or property.

Chapter 9

Fixed Penalty Notices – Legalities and Technicalities

In the first 8 chapters of this book I have considered in some detail the rationale underpinning enforcement notices and the processes involved in drafting, serving and enforcing them. I talked in chapter 1 about the myths surrounding them and specifically the myth that they are a quick, easy and cheap way of dealing with issues. I think that particular myth has been well and truly busted by the chapters that followed. Whatever else may be said for enforcement notices, it can't be said that they are a quick and dirty way of resolving issues. That is not necessarily a criticism; some matters cannot be dealt with by a 'dash in, do a bit and dash off intervention', they need careful consideration and the crafting of a finely tuned solution that will have a lasting impact. No one can dispute that some issues merit the sort of long and drawn out process that follows the decision to serve an enforcement notice, but it is also fair to say that some environmental crimes certainly don't merit that sort of process. I do not want, in any way, to belittle environmental crimes such as litter dropping, failing to put out household waste in accordance with the local authority's scheme, graffiti, dog fouling and a whole raft of other crimes at the lower end of the criminality scale, but they do not merit an enforcement notice to prevent their occurrence or recurrence; neither do they justify prosecution as a first resort. All of which by way of a preamble brings me to Fixed Penalty Notices.

Origins and developments

Although Fixed Penalty Notices are a fairly recent weapon in the local government armoury they have been around since the 1950s when they were introduced to deal with minor road traffic offences. As motor vehicle ownership increased dramatically it was recognised that prosecuting every offending motorist through the magistrates' court would bring the whole system to a standstill very quickly. It was also recognised that while it was inappropriate to criminalise an individual for a little light parking on a double yellow line, there had to be a mechanism for penalising them and making sure that road traffic legislation was both respected and effectively self-enforcing. A speedy way of dealing with the more trivial motoring and parking offences was required and Fixed Penalty Notices was the answer.

Moving to the present day, Fixed Penalty Notices are an enforcement option in more and more legislation enforced by local authorities. From enforcing the ban on smoking in enclosed public places, dropping litter, failing to produce a transfer note when transporting controlled waste to various types of anti-social behaviour they provide a quick, easy and cheap way of dealing with offences. As an alternative to prosecution they are swift, visible and transparent. They provide an effective way of dealing with criminal behaviour without the offender engaging with the traditional criminal justice system and emerging with a criminal record; a record that might have very damaging consequences, and which is in no way proportionate to the original offending behaviour. A Fixed Penalty is an interesting hybrid. It is not a conviction, neither is it a fine. The recipient who pays the financial penalty imposed by a Fixed Penalty Notice does not concede that they are guilty of the offence alleged but payment of the penalty does preclude the possibility of prosecution for the offence, and in consequence the possibility of a criminal record. To these advantages can be added the benefit of paying a penalty rather than going through the horrors of the criminal justice process. There are also a number of advantages for the enforcement authority in being able to deal with offenders through this quick, easy and cheap enforcement mechanism. In recent years Fixed Penalties have become the go-to enforcement method of first choice for legislators in the UK, particularly in matters that are the enforcement responsibility of local authorities. In part, this is a response to the UK government policy of rationalising magistrates' courts, where rationalisation is a euphemism for closing a considerable number of them, and thereby reducing the capacity in the court system. In part it is also a response to the fact that many of the offences created are personal offences for which the offender, on conviction, would be liable to a financial penalty at the lower end of the standard scale.

Fixed Penalty Notices are not without their critics. They have been criticised as a revenue generating mechanism, as a license for enforcement officers to throw their weight around and as a mechanism for offenders to buy their way out of trouble. In some cases they are seen as an almost inevitable consequence of certain types of behaviour. For many motorists it is not a question of *will* they get a fixed penalty ticket for speeding, it is more a matter of *when* will they get one, as Fixed Penalty Tickets, whether for exceeding the speed limit or for some other traffic violation, are seen as an occupational hazard of driving. There is no social disgrace attached to speeding or being caught in a box junction and so common are speed and traffic enforcement cameras that the motorist who hasn't had a Fixed Penalty Ticket is the exception rather than the rule. More importantly the Fixed Penalty mechanism has been criticised on the grounds that it undermines justice. It is claimed that individuals who believe they have not committed the offence alleged are discouraged from fighting their corner in the magistrates' court, and the discount for early payment of some Fixed Penalties is said to undermine justice further. The jurisprudence is a side issue as far as enforcement officers are concerned. The fact is, that more and more legislation is enforced by local government enforcement officers using Fixed Penalty Tickets as a sanction and therefore it is essential that they get the legalities, technicalities and practicalities of serving them right.

Service - The need to be authorised

Those enforcement officers who started this book at Chapter 1 must please forgive me for repeating myself; those who have just joined us because their only interest is in Fixed Penalty Tickets will have missed the stuff in Chapter 3 about the importance of authorisation and therefore I need to re-iterate its importance. Enforcement officers who serve Fixed Penalty Notices have to be properly authorised and that is made clear in the statutes that give them the power to do so.

Examples of the specific requirement for officers to be authorised appear in various statutes. Sec 9 of the Health Act 2006 states;

> *(1)   An authorised officer of an enforcement authority who has reason to believe that a person has committed an offence under section 6(5) or 7(2) on premises, or in a place or vehicle, in relation to which the* **authorised** *officer has functions may give him a penalty notice in respect of the offence.*

Sec 47ZA of the Environmental Protection Act 1990 states;

> *(1)   This section applies where on any occasion an* **authorised** *officer of a waste collection authority has reason to believe that a person has*

committed an offence under section 46 or 47 above in the area of that authority.......

As I said, the clue is in the legislative provisions.

There are a couple of mantraps here into which the unwary can plunge. The first is the issue of basic authorisation and the need to ensure that all officers who serve, or may serve, Fixed Penalty Notices are authorised to do so. There are, for these purposes, two sorts of officers; those whose job is only to focus on one specific area of work and those whose field of operation is much wider. An example of the first is someone whose specific area of work is domestic waste collection and recycling and who will therefore only be authorised to serve Fixed Penalty Tickets under secs 46 and 47 of the Environmental Protection Act 1990 which relate to that specific area. Their authorisation will necessarily be limited and will not stray outside secs 46 and 47. The second sort of officer is, for example, an Environmental Health Officer who may enforce the whole range of environmental and public health related legislation, or a Trading Standards Officer who may similarly enforce a vast array of legislative provisions. In my view it is worth such officers ensuring that they are duly authorised to serve Fixed Penalty Notices before they embark on doing so. The reason for my saying this is because on occasions the legislation that permits the serving of Fixed Penalty Tickets creeps in under the radar. By way of example, the Environmental Protection Act 1990 made no mention of Fixed Penalty Tickets back in the day when it came onto the statute book. It has however been subject to many and various amendments and now bears only a passing resemblance to the mother act as it first saw the light of day. Fixed Penalty Notices, and the use thereof, in relation to domestic waste and recycling do not appear until the Environmental Protection Act was amended by the Clean Neighbourhoods and Environment Act 2005 and we see how far down the list of amendments the provisions come as they appear in section 47ZA ; in simpler notation, section 47, amendment 27. Getting to the point, those enforcement officers who were authorised to enforce the Environmental Protection Act 1990 and 'any amendments made thereto', or similar words to the same effect, need not worry; their authorisation extends to take account of the amendments and all the consequences that flow from it. Those who are authorised simply to enforce the Environmental Protection Act 1990 might just like to spend a moment considering whether that means the Environmental Protection Act 1990, as it was originally laid down, or that Act and the many amendments to it that have followed. Powers, as I have said, are to be read narrowly, therefore in my view the former, rather than the latter, view should prevail. If that is the case, they are not authorised to serve Fixed Penalty Notices under sec 47ZA. This is hardly the end of the world and the matter is easily rectified by amending the authorisations, but it is better to make the necessary amendment proactively before it matters, than attempt to do it reactively, by which point it is too late.

Before a notice can be served - the preliminaries

I said in opening this chapter that a Fixed Penalty is neither a conviction nor is it a fine. It is a financial penalty, a form of administrative justice administered without recourse to a third party who forms a judgement in the matter. Basically the enforcement officer tells the offender that they have offended, the offender, without necessarily agreeing, accepts and pays the penalty and avoids the necessity to attend at court and slug it out with the authority that issued the Fixed Penalty Notice. Both parties are aware that if the individual declines the Fixed Penalty Notice option they will go to court, so the enforcing authority must have sufficient admissible evidence to support its case and the individual must be satisfied that he can either deny or diminish the evidence to the point that he will be successful.

In some cases the offender will not know what evidence the enforcement officer has. He is entitled to see it to satisfy himself that it would be sufficient to convict him. I always advise anyone who is sent a Notice of Intended Prosecution for exceeding the speed limit to ask for the Calibration Certificate for the device used to measure their speed and also to ask for the photograph. If the device used had not been calibrated properly, pointed questions about how the constabulary can be certain of its accuracy can be raised; if the photograph does not clearly show the driver of the vehicle, the alleged driver will have to be certain that he was indeed driving before he makes any admissions to that effect. I used to call this good advice, but I was told by a colleague of mine that he had passed it to a friend of his who found himself the unfortunate recipient of a Notice of Intended Prosecution. Following my helpful advice he asked to see the photograph. Unhelpfully it showed clearly that not only was he the driver but that he was also on his mobile phone at the time.

The point I am making is that in most cases there are preliminary requirements to be satisfied before enforcement officers can start issuing Fixed Penalty Tickets. Very often the preliminary issues will not be matters in which they have any involvement; they may be administrative or may require resolutions of the Council. Let me revert to my use of sec 46 of the Environmental Protection Act 1990 as an example. The power to serve Fixed Penalty Notices that arises under section 47ZA does not arise as a free-standing power. A duly authorised enforcement office cannot just hand out Fixed Penalty tickets to those whose recycling methods are beyond the pale or whose domestic waste disposal does not pass muster. There is a preliminary requirement; the person must first be served with a notice under sec 46(1)B in which the local authority tells them what they must do in respect of their waste and how they must do it. The notice may, for example, tell the recipient what sort of waste should be put in what sort of receptacle; when, where and what time it should be placed out for collection; how certain waste should be treated, broken glass to be wrapped and food waste to be contained in a food caddy; and such similar requirements.

The point of serving the notice is that the recipient is effectively on notice; he has been told what to do and when to do it. This will not be the first time he has been told this by any means; there will have been campaigns and leaflet drops and photo opportunities for elected members with unfortunate members of staff dressed up as tin cans, and so on, but these are community wide initiatives and may have passed over the heads of those who do not read local newspapers or engage with the local authority web site. The service of a notice makes the requirement specific to the individual on whom it is served so he cannot thereafter deny that he knew what he had to do or how or when. More than that, he is at risk since section 46(6) makes it an offence to breach any of the requirements without reasonable excuse, an offence that can make him liable on summary conviction to a fine not exceeding level 3 on the standard scale. It is at this point that the option of a Fixed Penalty raises its head. Section 47ZA states;

(1) This section applies where on any occasion an authorised officer of a waste collection authority has reason to believe that a person has committed an offence under section 46 or 47 above in the area of that authority.
(2) The authorised officer <u>may</u> give that person a notice offering him the opportunity of discharging any liability to conviction for the offence by payment of a fixed penalty to the waste collection authority.

The net effect of this is to make issuing a Fixed Penalty Ticket for an offence relating to either the disposal or recycling of domestic waste a three stage process. There must firstly be some offending behaviour; there must then be the service of a sec 46 notice on the offender which must be followed by a breach of the requirements of the notice. Only then can he be offered a Fixed Penalty Ticket in respect of that second incident of offending behaviour.

As a final comment on this particular example it is worth noting that the local authority is not obliged to offer a Fixed Penalty to the offender. The inserted section of the legislation shows a deliberate underlining in (2) which says the authorised officer *may* give the person the opportunity to accept a fixed penalty rather than *must* do so. The discretion as to how to deal with the matter is the enforcement officer's. He can decide to do nothing at all, to offer a fixed penalty or to instigate proceedings but the offender can do nothing; he cannot, for example, demand to be offered a fixed penalty disposal. It is for the enforcement officer to decide how to proceed, and he may in his discretion, offer a fixed penalty but he is by no means obliged to do so. Importantly, as with all discretionary powers, he must exercise his discretion responsibly, fairly and equitably and can be challenged in the courts if he does not.

The preliminary issue identified above is clear and straightforward; it is the service of the notice under sec 46(1)B. Subject to it being properly served, the recipient will know of it and be unable to complain if he transgresses and is caught in the future. Sometimes however the preliminary issues are both technical and extremely pedantic. Anyone who has had any experience of making Road Traffic Orders will be only too aware of the steps that have to be taken before an order can take effect. The Order must be drafted, signed, published for consultation and then a defined period allowed for objections, which must normally be made in a prescribed way. After any objections have been heard and resolved, or if there are none, the order must be confirmed and then published again as a confirmed order before it takes effect. No-one can be convicted of breaching the order until it is made and confirmed and, if it is not properly made; no-one can ever be convicted of breaching it. Some lawyers make a living poring over the process by which road traffic orders were made to find flaws, glitches and slips to prevent their client being convicted. Taking a step back, most of us would agree that this is just as it should be; no-one should be convicted if a law is not properly made, as it is not, and never was, the law. You might think that I am obsessing over nothing but you would be surprised how often administrative errors happen, and more than that, how long ago some of these errors happened and how long it takes for the spotlight to fall on them.

Getting the details right – what happens if you don't

Moving back to Fixed Penalties, it is usually the case that the interaction occurs between two parties; the enforcement officer and the transgressor. In accepting the Fixed Penalty the transgressor accepts that it has been validly issued and that all the technicalities demanded by the law have been complied with. In most careful and conscientious councils this will be the case, but where it is not there is the potential for serious consequences. If the transgressor decides to 'ask for the calibration certificate', in manner of speaking, he may root about in the legislation to see what the council should have done before it could lawfully offer Fixed Penalties to those who acted as he did. If he finds that something that should have been done has not or has not been done in accordance with the specified procedure, he not only does not have to accept the offer of a Fixed Penalty but he cannot be prosecuted for the offence. Additionally, all those who have gone before him and who have been offered and have paid Fixed Penalties are entitled to have their money back, and all those who were convicted are entitled to ask for their conviction to be quashed. I say this to enforcement officers, who look at me kindly and explain in words of very few syllables that they have handed out hundreds of Fixed Penalties and that not only has no-one ever challenged the process that preceded the Fixed Penalty, but that no-one has ever asked if they are duly authorised. For the record, I'd like to say that I am pleased that the public in their area is so trusting and so confident in the local authority's ability to do things entirely properly. And I hope for their sakes that they continue to be, because it does happen; not often, but once is too often if it happens to you.

Fixed Penalty Enforcement Policies

In the course of researching this book I gathered up a collection of Fixed Penalty Enforcement policies to do a bit of comparing and contrasting. In order to get my hands on them I dropped 'Fixed Penalty Enforcement' into Google. I can confidently report that Fixed Penalty Enforcement Policies are not rare birds. Pretty much every local authority and most police forces have them and, in two clicks of a mouse, so can any member of the public who is sufficiently interested. Just in passing, I think it is worth commending whoever it was who wrote the first enforcement policy. Whether it is described as 'sharing', or 'partnership working' or out and out plagiarism, their enforcement colleagues all owe them a debt of gratitude; most of the enforcement policies are mirror images of each other. Up to a point that is to be expected; the legislation under which Fixed Penalties can be offered is the same, the way in which they should be handed out is the same, and the considerations about who should and who should not be given one, are the same. The unique bits tend to be the amount of slack that various authorities are prepared to give offenders before they get to the 'showing their teeth and deciding to do something formal about the offending behaviour' stage. Some cut straight to the chase and offer Fixed Penalties immediately; others give a first warning before moving on to formal options; and some seem prepared to do pretty much anything, up to and including offering counselling, before actually using the powers that the legislation gives them. It is not my place to criticise any local authority's policy and I do not seek to do so; from what I read it seems most of them have been through some form of cabinet or council scrutiny and sign off procedure, and that is how democracy works. Each local authority has the policy that those elected to represent the community are happy with and so be it.

More important, from a practical standpoint as far as the enforcement officer is concerned, is that these finely honed documents are public documents. They are out there to be found on the World Wide Web so that any member of the public with sufficient interest can find and read them. Most members of the public could not care less how many policies the local authority has nor what they say, but those who are directly affected may suddenly develop a deep interest, not just in what the policy says, but in making sure that they have been treated exactly as the policy demands. If the policy talks expansively about three warnings before formal action is taken, and the offender claims he was not warned by anyone, about anything, before he was offered the rock or hard place choice of a Fixed Penalty or prosecution, he has a right to be aggrieved and to complain. He will be even more aggrieved if it comes to his attention that his neighbour has been warned on one or more occasions for the same behaviour. All sorts of allegations about inequitable treatment, inconsistency and failure to apply stated policy can and will be made and with some justification. The purpose of a publically available policy is to tell the public how they can expect to be treated, and the consequence of telling the public how they should be treated is that they will have an expectation that this is indeed how they will be treated. Any deviation from the stated policy will lead to all sorts of allegations being bandied about and a general belief that the policy is not worth the paper on which it is written. Enforcement officers therefore need to know what the policy says and to make sure that they act in accordance with it. Whilst somewhere in the policy it will say that it is for guidance, and that officers are not bound to follow it slavishly, or words to that effect, it seems to me that there is much to be said for following the policy unless there are compelling reasons for not doing so. I fully accept that there will be occasions where the enforcement officer may feel that he should act other than as stated in the policy, but such incidents should be exceptional and, where they occur, the justification for acting outside the policy should be recorded for future reference and in case of challenge.

There is one final point to make about exceptions to enforcement policies. Periodically the senior officer managing the enforcement team should review the exceptions that have been recorded to determine whether or not any trends can be identified. It may be that one enforcement officer consistently records exceptions; it could be that all of the team record the same circumstance as an exception to the policy. If one enforcement officer is going his own merry way, as if the enforcement policy did not exist, that is a management issue, but if all of the enforcement officers are dealing with a particular set of facts or circumstances as an exception, there is an argument to be made that the enforcement policy needs to be reconsidered and amended. Any amendment should ensure that what was formerly the 'consistent exception' is now properly addressed by the new policy. Any policy that is honoured more in the breach than in the observance is probably not fit for purpose and needs a root and branch redraft.

Making the call

It is an over simplification to say that it is for the enforcement officer out on the street or on site to make the call about whether to offer a Fixed Penalty or not. Whilst it is true, it is not the whole truth. Before he makes any decisions about disposal of the matter the enforcement officer must be sure that the offence with which he is concerned has been committed and that he can prove it. Just as there is a myth that an offender can be offered a simple caution when there is not quite enough evidence to satisfy the evidential requirement for prosecution, there is a myth that an enforcement officer can offer someone a Fixed Penalty because he thinks, but can't actually prove, that they committed the offence in question. The view seems to have taken root that as a Fixed Penalty is not recorded as a conviction the evidence to support the offer does not have to be as rigorous as is necessary to support a prosecution. It is viewed as a watered down form of justice if you like. To be absolutely clear, just as the simple caution idea is a myth so is the Fixed Penalty idea. There is no difference in the amount of evidence required to justify the offer of a Fixed Penalty to that required for prosecution. The enforcement officer may offer a Fixed Penalty as an alternative option to prosecution, but he must be in a position to proceed to prosecution in the event of the offender declining to accept the offer.

Subject to the enforcement officer having enough evidence available to him to establish a realistic prospect of conviction for the offence he must consider what the local authority's enforcement policy says about the next step in the process. If the policy says that offenders are to be offered a Fixed Penalty or prosecuted for the first identified incident of offending, he has a call to make. If the policy requires that offenders be warned as a first step, or there is an escalation policy, he must go along with the requirements of the policy unless there are very compelling reasons not to do so. If there is an escalated policy requiring e.g. first warnings before the offer of a Fixed Penalty or a prosecution, there must be a method which tells enforcement officers whether the particular offender has been dealt with on an earlier occasion for a similar incident and if so how he was dealt with. It is a more than unfortunate situation where three different enforcement officers have all given the same individual a final warning for the same type of incident, and it brings the whole enforcement system into disrepute. It is important that all the members of an enforcement team are aware of the actions that their colleagues have taken, and that any subsequent action is incremental rather than identical. How this is done is a matter for the local authority. Whether it is done though red flagging files or by messages on hand held data collectors is for them, but it is essential that it is done, to ensure that the blushes of all concerned are spared and the credibility of the enforcement policy is maintained. Having reached the stage where warnings or final words are no longer appropriate the enforcement officer will have to decide whether to issue a Fixed Penalty or recommend that the transgressor be prosecuted. Even at this point it will not be a matter solely for him; it is likely that the enforcement policy will have something to say on the matter. Most enforcement policies require the enforcement officer to take a view about the likely attitude of the offender to the offer of a Fixed Penalty; if, in his judgement, the offender will take the view he has 'got off' with the offence it is unlikely that it will be appropriate to make the offer of a Fixed Penalty. Enforcement policies are consistent in the view that multiple Fixed Penalties should not be offered, and that the offender who has been offered and accepted one, should be prosecuted if he repeats the offending behaviour.

In reality the discretion vested in the enforcement officer to determine how to proceed is limited by evidential requirements and by the local authority's enforcement policy. Is that necessarily a bad thing? I am not sure that it is. As I have said, the decision of an enforcement officer to offer a Fixed Penalty, and the offender's decision to accept it and to discharge his liability to prosecution by making the necessary payment, is justice administered in a very short form. It is open to abuse whether through mistake or through megalomania on the part of the enforcement officer. For everyone to have confidence that the system is working in a fair and equitable way it has to be subject to safeguards and to be open and transparent.

The Fixed Penalty 'Ticket'

The local authority may have a certain amount of discretion about what their enforcement policy says but it has precious little discretion about what the Fixed Penalty Ticket will look like. Just as there are strict requirements about what must appear on the face of an enforcement notice there are requirements about what must appear on the face of a Fixed Penalty Ticket. In most cases the legislation that enables a local authority to offer a Fixed Penalty, as an alternative to prosecution, will prescribe the information to appear on the face of the Fixed Penalty Ticket. The Health Act 2006 is a case in point. Sec 9 of the Health Act reads;

(1) An authorised officer of an enforcement authority (see section 10) who has reason to believe that a person has committed an offence under section 6(5) or 7(2) on premises, or in a place or vehicle, in relation to which the authorised officer has functions may give him a penalty notice in respect of the offence.

(2) A penalty notice is a notice offering a person the opportunity to discharge any liability to conviction for the offence to which the notice relates by paying a penalty in accordance with this Chapter.

(3) Schedule 1 makes further provision about fixed penalties.

Schedule 1 certainly does make further provision about fixed penalties. It reads:

Contents of penalty notice

1 A penalty notice must—

    (a) state the alleged offence, and

    (b) give such particulars of the circumstances alleged to constitute it as are necessary for giving reasonable information about it.

    2 (1) A penalty notice must also state—

        (a) the name and address of the enforcement authority on whose behalf the authorised officer was acting when he gave the notice,

        (b) the amount of the penalty and the period for its payment,

(c) the discounted amount and the period for its payment,

(d) the consequences of not paying the penalty or the discounted amount before the end of the period mentioned in paragraph (b),

(e) the person to whom and the address at which payment may be made,

(f) by what method payment may be made,

(g) the person to whom and the address at which any representations relating to the notice may be made.

(2) The person mentioned in sub-paragraph (1)(e) and (g) must be the enforcement authority referred to in sub-paragraph (1)(a).

3 A penalty notice must also—
(a) inform the person to whom it is given of his right to be tried for the alleged offence, and

(b) explain how that right may be exercised.

4 A penalty notice must be in a form specified in regulations made by the appropriate national authority.

As was the case with enforcement notices there should be nothing that the recipient of a Fixed Penalty Notice needs to know about what it is, what it says he has done, what he has to do, when and by what date. This is just as it should be; if the system is to be simple and straightforward to administer and cheap for both the prosecutor and the offender, everything about it must be clear and transparent. Whilst the local authority can choose to personalise the Fixed Penalty Ticket with its logo and strap lines it is obliged to include all the prescribed information. This ensures that the recipient has all the information he needs to discharge his liability should he choose to comply with the legislation. If the Fixed Penalty Ticket does not include all of the elements prescribed in the legislation it will be invalid and unenforceable. Enforcement officers may shower them about like leaves in autumn, but it will all be to no effect. The recipients may ignore them with impunity and those who do not, but dutifully hand over their money, are entitled to have it returned to them. Given that the legislation tells a local authority what information must be on a Fixed Penalty Ticket there is no reason to get it wrong; given the consequences of getting it wrong there is a considerable incentive to get it right.

I will discuss the practicalities of issuing Fixed Penalty Tickets in the next chapter but now I want to move on to the legal and technical requirements of dealing with the response to Fixed Penalty Notices.

The response to Fixed Penalty Notices

In the ideal world a person offered a Fixed Penalty Ticket would immediately accept it, raid their piggy bank or look under their sofa cushions, find the money, rush off and pay it within the discount period. They might perhaps proceed more slowly but still manage to pay it within the period for payment. We could all then draw a line under the matter and move on. Sadly, most of us don't dwell in an ideal world and not all the recipients of Fixed Penalty Tickets, even those who are willing to accept them, are happy to just roll over and pay them. Some recipients, as the legislation coyly puts it, wish to 'make representations' about them. The word 'appeal' is not used, probably advisedly, since appeal has a formal meaning and tends to refer to a formalised process where both parties have the opportunity to make representations to an impartial third party who makes an adjudication.

The actual process by which the aggrieved recipient can make representations about the Fixed Penalty Notice can be whatever the local authority considers it should be. The time period for making the representations, to whom they should be made and how they should be made, can be prescribed by the local authority, as can the potential outcome of making the representations. These range from upholding the representations and quashing the ticket, to dismissing the representations and upholding the ticket. In the interests of fairness and transparency the local authority should publish how it will deal with representations made against Fixed Penalty Tickets, usually as part of its Fixed Penalty Enforcement Policy. As we saw, the fact that representations can be made against the Fixed Penalty Ticket, and the way this is to be done, should appear on the face of the ticket. The combination of the information on the ticket and the availability of the Enforcement Policy should ensure that the recipient who wishes to make representations is fully informed as to how this should be done, how his representations will be considered and what are the potential outcomes.

The recipient who does not wish to make representations and accepts that he will have to pay the ticket also has a choice; when to pay. Where the legislation allows a discount for early payment and the local authority has determined to apply it, the recipient must decide whether to take advantage of it. Whether he does so or not is a matter of indifference to the local authority; its interest is in the Fixed Penalty being paid, discounted or not.

Non-payment

There are a number of reasons for non-payment of Fixed Penalty Tickets. Firstly, there is the recipient of a Fixed Penalty Ticket who accepts it and then does nothing. It may be that he believes that the local authority will not follow it up and, so long as he kept his head down, it will quietly be forgotten. Secondly, it may be that the recipient has every intention of paying but leaves it too long and the payment period expires; thirdly, it may be that he just forgets all about it. Finally, there is the possibility that after accepting the Fixed Penalty Ticket, the recipient decides that he does not want to pay after all. It is not that he wants to make representations about the ticket or the way it was issued, rather he wants to take issue with the allegation that he has offended at all, so he advises the local authority that he wishes to have the matter heard by the Magistrates. As far as the local authority is concerned, it doesn't matter which of the reasons for non-compliance explains the failure to pay; the bottom line is that payment remains outstanding after the payment period has expired.

If payment has not been made the local authority makes the next move. A Fixed Penalty is offered as an alternative to prosecution and if it is not paid, all bets are off and the prosecution option comes back into play. The local authority *may*, in its discretion, prosecute the recipient who fails to pay, but to my mind there is not much thinking to be done about whether to prosecute or not. If the local authority is not prepared to pursue the offender who does not pay, it might as well stop issuing Fixed Penalty Tickets. Word will spread very quickly that non-payment of Fixed Penalty Tickets is not pursued and payment will dry up. I think there is also a question of fairness to be considered; it cannot be right that a local authority should acquiesce in a process whereby the law abiding pay and the non-law abiding do not. Fairness and equity demand that all parties are treated fairly and such a system is neither equitable nor fair.

Issuing proceedings –getting on with it

Clearly where prosecution is considered to be the appropriate way
forward the enforcement officer will know because he will have
been central to the decision making process. Where the recipient of
the Fixed Penalty has decided that he wants the matter heard in
court it is likely that the enforcement officer who served it will
know since it is probable that the recipient will have told him. What
is less certain is whether the enforcement officer who issued the
Fixed Penalty Ticket will know whether it has been paid, or more
importantly, whether it has not. In some cases payment will be
made to the department that issued the Fixed Penalty Ticket. Where
that is the case the department will know when the ticket was
issued, what date the discounted rate expires and the final date for
payment. It follows that if payment is not made before the payment
period expires the department will have active knowledge of that
and can immediately spring into action. It can lay an information in
the Magistrates' Court alleging non-payment or convert the
outstanding penalty to a civil debt and pursue it through debt
recovery procedures, whichever is appropriate to the legislation they
are enforcing. I say spring into action advisedly. Where the matter is
to be heard in the magistrates' court the local authority has 6
months after the date of the commission of the offence to lay its
information and the clock has already begun to tick.

Not all Fixed Penalties are paid directly to the department that
issued them. In some cases local authorities direct payment to their
general revenue collection systems; to one-stop shops or over the
counter payments at the council offices. The fact that a payment has
been made, and the date on which it was received, is information
that can readily be passed from the receiving department to the
department that generated the Fixed Penalty. Non-payment is more
difficult; the fact that payment has not been made is not
information that is going to be passed between departments.
Because of this the department that issued the Fixed Penalty must
ensure that it knows the last date on which payment should have
been made, and in the absence of evidence that it has been made,
makes inquiries of the revenue collecting department. If it is advised
that payment has not been received it should immediately spring
into action as described. Given that time is of the essence, the
inquiries need to be made as soon as the payment period expires

and the response needs to be immediate and accurate. Any delay will prejudice the position of the local authority in pursuing the non-payment and therefore the process of inquiry and response needs to be a slick one. The mechanism for making sure that the system works needs to be embedded and everyone needs to understand why it is important.

The legalities and the technicalities of issuing Fixed Penalties are important but they can be attended to in the calm of the office. The local authority that reads the legislation, learns what it has to do and how to do it properly, *before* it starts issuing Fixed Penalties, should get them right.

Aide Memoire

1. A Fixed Penalty Ticket may only be issued where the enforcement officer has reason to believe a person has committed an offence
2. A Fixed Penalty is not a fine. If the recipient pays the penalty he cannot be convicted of the offence to which the penalty relates.
3. Payment of the penalty is not an admission of guilt and the recipient will not get a criminal record.
4. An offender is not obliged to accept the offer of a Fixed Penalty. He may elect to proceed to trial of the issue
5. The essential elements of a Fixed Penalty Ticket appear in the legislation that creates it. They are essential because missing any of them off the Ticket renders it void.
6. Where recipients of Fixed Penalties do not make payment in full or at all local authorities should prosecute.

Chapter 10

Fixed Penalty Notices – Practicalities

In the preceding chapter I talked at some length about the legalities and technicalities of Fixed Penalties. The need for enforcement officers to be authorised and the fact that a duly authorised officer may, subject to the local authority's enforcement policy, use his discretion when deciding whether to offer the offender a Fixed Penalty or proceed to prosecution. For the purposes of this chapter can we please take it as read that the enforcement officer is duly authorised and is acting within the scope of his authorised powers? Can we also take it as read that any pre-requisites, such as the serving of notices, or publishing notices of intent in local papers, and such like, have been done and done correctly, so that everything is as it should be as the enforcement officer heads out of the office?

A chapter airily titled practicalities by someone who is not going to be out there pounding the streets, actually doing what she advocates, has the potential to cause those who are to grit their teeth and wonder whether she has any idea about the difficulty of doing all of the essential things she is writing about. Well yes, I do. I've done it myself and I have made a hash of things myself. I look back now on some of the things I did and got away with, and they make a light sweat form on my brow. I am fully aware of all the things you have to get right, of how difficult it is to get them all exactly spot on when you are out there dealing with a situation but, as a lawyer, I also know how critically important it is that enforcement officers do get everything right. That is not to say that if the enforcement officer doesn't get everything exactly right he will not get away with it; given a fair wind he might wing it. I certainly did on occasions, but I can't advocate blagging your way through the legal requirements in the hope that no-one will notice that the practise or procedure was less than perfect. Aim to get everything 100% right, and if something goes slightly askew, consider where that leaves you.

Know the law

Most enforcement officers know an offence when they see one. They work with the legislation day in and day out, know their way around it blindfolded and, if asked, could give anyone a brisk run down of what the law says and what it means in practical terms. That is to be expected. However when they are dealing with individuals who may have committed an offence, an Everyman's guide to the legislation is not enough. The enforcement officer needs a complete understanding of the requirements of the legislation he is enforcing. He will have to judge the realities of the situation, as he sees it, against the fixed requirements of the legislation and do some mental computation, to check that he has all the legal requirement ducks in a row, before he takes any action.

To explain what I mean in detail, I will take the prohibition on smoking in enclosed public places, outlawed by the Health Act 2006, as an example. It is helpful first to look at the limitations to serving a Fixed Penalty, which are explained in sec.9 of the Act.

9 (1) An authorised officer of an enforcement authority (see section 10) who has reason to believe that a person has committed an offence under section 6(5) or 7(2) on premises, or in a place or vehicle, in relation to which the authorised officer has functions may give him a penalty notice in respect of the offence.

Looking at the limitations in the section we see that a Fixed Penalty may only be given in respect of the offences described in sections 6(5) or 7(2) of the Act, and then, only where those offences are committed on premises, or in a place or in a vehicle.

It is not necessary to reproduce sections 6 and 7 the Health Act 2006 here. Section 6 concerns itself with signage relating to the prohibition of smoking in enclosed public places and vehicles; its positioning, size, content, design, wording and so on: section 7 concerns the offence of smoking in a designated smoke free place. For an individual to commit an offence under the legislation a number of elements have to be satisfied. He has to be smoking as defined in the legislation; he has to be in an enclosed public place or a vehicle, again as defined in the legislation; and none of the exceptions to the legislation must apply. Hence, by way of example, a person may be smoking in a hotel bedroom which as an enclosed space to which the public have access would, to all intents and purposes, appear to be in breach of the provisions of sec 6 the Health Act 2006 and consequently an offence, but if that bedroom had been designated as a room in which smoking was allowed no offence is committed. Conversely, if the same person were to go next door, to what seems to be an identical room, but one which had been designated a non-smoking bedroom, the same activity would be an offence. Similarly, an individual would be committing an offence if he was smoking in a wholly enclosed marquee, but if the sun came out and the sides of the marquee were rolled up, it would not be a wholly enclosed space so he would not be committing an offence. What appears, on the face of it, to be relatively straightforward, on closer examination is anything but. There is a raft of permutations; some result in offences and some do not. The same is true of any piece of legislation and lawyers and enforcement officers will crawl all over the wording to extract every ounce of meaning and intention from them.

This in-depth analysis of legislation is all well and good when it is done in the relative calm of the office; everyone can chip into the debate and hypothetical situations can be debated over cups of coffee and chocolate digestive biscuits. For the enforcement officer out on the street, it is very different; he has to make a snap determination as to whether what he has witnessed is an offence. Does it satisfy all of the requisite elements of the offence, or is it saved by being within one of the exceptions; does it fall short by one requirement? And more than that, if what he has witnessed constitutes an offence, can he prove, beyond reasonable doubt, that he saw what he thinks he saw, or is there some doubt about any of the elements? In some cases there will be no doubt at all. The enforcement officer who witnesses an individual, sitting in a wholly enclosed room, smoking a pipe and generating clouds of smoke that could be seen from the moon will have no difficulties at all in establishing that an offence has been committed; the same cannot be said for the enforcement officer who sees someone, apparently smoking, in a van that drives past him in the opposite direction at 30mph as he is sitting in his car. In the real world, the call as to whether an offence has been committed or not has to be made on the hoof and based on what the office saw and can clearly recall. That is an altogether different scenario from sitting round in the office debating the ins and outs of what is required. Having been an enforcement officer I know that. As a lawyer I also know that there is no allowance in law for the difficulty of actually doing the job versus hypothesising about it. The requirement is that the officer must be able to prove every element of the offence alleged, beyond reasonable doubt, and that is the bottom line. The practical implications are that the officer has to know the elements of the offence, know the exceptions and be sure of what he saw, so that if required he can prove what he says beyond reasonable doubt. And do all that when he is out on the street. No-one said it was easy.

Establishing the identity of the offender

Knowing that an offence has been committed, and believing that he can prove it, is only half of the story as far as the enforcement officer is concerned. He makes a decision as to whether the offence has been committed based on what he witnesses and what he knows about the law. There are however a number of unknowns and he has to determine the answers to them before he can do anything with the evidence of offending behaviour. He has to know who committed the offence, because he cannot offer a nameless person a Fixed Penalty, just as he could not bring proceedings against A. N. Other (name unknown). He also has to know that the person who committed the offence is a person against whom proceedings can be brought and, therefore, one to whom a Fixed Penalty can be offered.

A Fixed Penalty has to be directly addressed to the person to whom it is issued as that person, and that person only, has to accept it. It is because of this that they should only be issued where the enforcement officer is sure of the name and address of the offender; they cannot be posted through the door of a house or slipped through a car window. That sounds straightforward enough, but it must be remembered that a local authority enforcement officer has no right to demand to see identification. There is no doubt that being able to do so would make life considerably easier but the most the enforcement officer can do is ask if the offender has any form of identification that can confirm his identity. If he says he has not the officer must accept what he is told. I know from discussions with colleagues, who work in areas which are popular holiday destinations, and who issue Fixed Penalties to non-residents for littering offences, that they are given false names and addresses on a regular basis; it is an ongoing source of frustration. I think we all accept that Duck, Donald of Hollywood Boulevard, Hollywood, is likely to be a false name, but offenders who give a false, but plausible name, and a fictional, but feasible address, are hard to spot and can't be detained while the enforcement officer makes the necessary checks to establish the accuracy of their claim.

I often get asked by enforcement officers what they should do when someone either refuses to give their name and address, or gives a name and address they believe to be wholly false. The same problem arises when the identity and address seem authentic but not that of the person who gives it. They are difficult questions to answer. In the case of some legislation, for example littering contrary to sec 87 of the Environmental Protection Act 1990, there is a specific offence of obstruction; a person who gives a false name and address to an enforcement officer who offers him a Fixed Penalty Ticket could be prosecuted for obstructing the officer. This however requires the officer to know that the name and address is false, and quite obviously that information may not be available to him as he hands over the ticket. Equally, it would be obstruction were the offender to give an authentic identity and address but that of another person, rather than his own; again the officer cannot make the necessary checks as he stands on the street corner. Clearly, if the local police are willing to assist life gets very much easier, but police officers are not always just on hand or in a position to drop everything and come rushing in to assist, and the local authority enforcement officer has no powers to detain or arrest individuals until such time as the police turn up. On occasions a bit of high profile enforcement, in partnership with the police, can work wonders, but as a police officer of my acquaintance pithily remarked, he very often has better things to do that go rushing out because some old boy is smoking his pipe in the wrong place or someone has put their recycling in the wrong box. If there was an easy answer to the question I would happily give it, but there isn't. It is very much a case that the enforcement officer is required to do the best he can; getting proof of identity where he can; occasionally taking things on trust; occasionally being lied to; accepting that a Fixed Penalty might not be paid and recognising that it is the way it is. Without wishing, in any way, to diminish the importance of the enforcement roles to which Fixed Penalties attach or to be over philosophical about what is in fact hard edged enforcement, we have to recognise that we will win some and we will lose some, and that's the way it goes.

Is a Fixed Penalty appropriate?

It is important to recognise that there are some people or groups of people to whom Fixed Penalties should not be offered. They may not understand the process and their acceptance or rejection may not be properly informed, or they may be classed as vulnerable and be unable understand that they have offended through their behaviour. Most local authorities consider such persons or groups in their Enforcement Polices and advise how they should be dealt with, but generally, I think there are 6 groups to whom special regard should be given.

I have said that a person who is offered a Fixed Penalty Ticket has to understand that they have offended and has to accept the ticket. Where a person has learning difficulties or a mental disorder they may not understand that they have breached a legislative provision and that their behaviour is unacceptable. It is also true that their acceptance of a Fixed Penalty may not be true acceptance since they may be unable to understand the consequences of their actions. In such circumstances prosecution as an alternative to the acceptance of a Fixed Penalty would also be unacceptable, and, to my mind, would not be in the public interest. Enforcement in such circumstances has the potential to lay the local authority open to considerable criticism in the local media, which realistically, will be a consideration. In such cases, where the offending behaviour is a one-off, I suggest it is best dealt with by way of a conversation; where it is repeated, there is an argument for working with the individual and those who care for him or her, to stop the offending behaviour. What is in the public interest is a very important consideration in such cases. Someone evidently thought that that the public interest was best served by threatening to prosecute a group of individuals with learning difficulties who were living as a household in the community and were fanatically keen on the idea of recycling but not very good at separating out recyclables in line with the local authority's policy. I can't say I agreed with the decision, and after one or two memos containing blunt truths, were exchanged, happily, they drew in their horns. Understanding and acceptance are key and where they cannot be guaranteed neither a Fixed Penalty nor prosecution is appropriate.

A fixed penalty is also inappropriate where the person to whom it is offered does not *understand* what they are being offered. This may be the case where the person is deaf or has hearing difficulties or cannot understand the language used by the enforcement officer. Where the offender is deaf or has hearing difficulties the enforcement officer should make every effort to ensure that he is understood, and that the acceptance of the Fixed Penalty is based on a proper understanding. If he is in doubt he should not offer a Fixed Penalty and, as with persons with learning difficulties, should give serious consideration to whether prosecution is appropriate. Where the offender does not understand English there are further considerations. If the offender lives in the UK they may have someone who can translate for them or in the alternative, and subject to the offender's name and address being known, the local authority may consider prosecution as a more suitable alternative, since the offender will have time to access translation and legal advice. Where the offender is a foreign visitor there are different considerations. It is a well rehearsed truism that ignorance of the law is no defence, but I suspect it is a fairly rare visitor to any country that bones up on every piece of that country's extant legislation before arrival. Even if the officer can make himself understood, and the foreign offender accepts the Fixed Penalty with full knowledge of what it is and its requirements, it is hard to see how the local authority can take enforcement action if he skips back off to his country of origin without troubling himself to pay. It is also true that the sorts of offences that attract Fixed Penalties are not the sort, even if unsatisfied, that will cause Immigration Officers to deny re-entry to the country. If the enforcement officer is sure that the offender can understand, or can be made to understand that he has offended; can understand what the Fixed Penalty Ticket is and give an informed acceptance he should be issued with one, but if he does not pay I think some deep philosophical sighing and moving on is the order of the day.

The third group to whom Fixed Penalties should not be offered are those who are of no fixed abode, such as rough sleepers or homeless persons. Practically, it is not possible to serve a summons on someone who does not have an address for service so prosecution is effectively out of the question, and realistically it is often, unfortunately, the case that such people have other problems such as mental health issues or dependency on alcohol or drugs.

Pragmatically, it is also unlikely that they will have any money to pay a Fixed Penalty. In such cases the enforcement officer will have to take a view about whether meaningful enforcement is possible, and if it is not, he should use his discretion not to pursue the matter through an enforcement route.

The next group is those offenders who not only understand that they have offended but also what it means to be given a Fixed Penalty, because they have been given one on a previous occasion. If the enforcement officer finds that it is Groundhog Day, in that the individual has offended in the same way before, there is a compelling argument that he has not learned anything at all from the previous interaction and that issuing another Fixed Penalty will achieve nothing. In such cases, unless the circumstances of the offence are materially different, I suggest that there is little merit in issuing a further Fixed Penalty, regardless of any professed enthusiasm on the part of the offender to accept one. In such cases prosecution would appear to be a more appropriate disposal.

The fifth group that I suggest should not be offered Fixed Penalties are those who are abusive, threatening or violent towards the enforcement officer. In such cases, the enforcement officer's own safety should be his first consideration and he should withdraw. That is not to say he should do nothing, but he certainly should not hang around to be further abused or threatened. He should seek the assistance of the police, with a request that the offender be arrested if necessary, not for the originating offence, which is unlikely to carry a power of arrest, but for their abusive, threatening or violent behaviour towards the enforcement officer. I suggest, in such circumstances, that prosecution is the only appropriate disposal, not only for the originating offence, but also for the behaviour towards the enforcing officer.

This takes us off the point a little bit, but I think it is worth taking the diversion. Whenever I say to enforcement officers that they should always pursue proceedings against offenders who have abused, threatened or, heaven forbid, assaulted them I am told the same things. Either the police don't consider it important enough or else it goes with the territory. What the police think is a matter for them, but it most certainly does not go with the territory or anywhere near to it. Enforcement officers must be able to do their job as public servants without fear of being assaulted, physically or verbally, and where they are assaulted the local authority has the power to prosecute the alleged assault. Section 222 of the Local Government Act 1972 states that local authorities can instigate proceedings where they consider it expedient for the promotion or protection of the interests of the inhabitants of their area. It cannot be other than for the promotion or protection of the interests of the inhabitants that local authority officers be free to do their job, without fear of being abused or assaulted, and they should be safe in the knowledge that their employer will take strong action in the event that they are so treated. There are various alternatives. The Public Order Act 1986 contains, amongst others, the offence of affray i.e. using or threatening unlawful violence towards another, and the offence of using threatening words and behaviour, both of which carry, on summary conviction, the maximum penalty of a fine of up to £5,000 and/or up to 6 months imprisonment (affray carries a maximum penalty of 3 years imprisonment or an unlimited fine in the Crown Court). Moving on up the scale, the offence of common assault, which does not need physical contact to be made, carries the same penalty, as does the offence of assault occasioning actual bodily harm, when tried in the Magistrates Court. Assault occasion actual bodily harm carries a maximum penalty of 5 years imprisonment or an unlimited fine in the Crown Court. The Courts take violence, whether threatened or actual, towards enforcement officers seriously and in all cases the fact that the behaviour was towards a public servant is an aggravating feature. If an enforcement officer is abused or has violence threatened or offered against him and the police decline to act, I strongly urge that he inform his legal department and that the council, in its role as prosecutor, instigates proceedings against the offender. If the local authority doesn't consider that its staff are worthy of protection why should anyone else?

Children and Fixed Penalties

The last group, I think, deserves a special mention of its own. I want to discuss the position in relation to children. The position in law is clear; a Fixed Penalty can be issued to anyone who is 10 years of age or more. It is also the case that any person who is 10 years of age or more can be prosecuted, but generally there is a desire not to subject children to the full rigours of the court process; there is a very strong preference for dealing with them outside the formal process where that is possible.

Any authority defined as a Children's Service Authority, which includes local authorities, has a duty, imposed on it by the Children Act 2004, to discharge its functions having regard to the need to safeguard and to uphold the welfare of children. That is not to say that enforcement officers should not issue Fixed Penalties to those between the ages of 10 – 17 years, but there is a heightened duty when they do so. For the purposes of serving Fixed Penalty Tickets children aged 16 – 18 years can be treated in the same way as adults but Fixed Penalties, issued on the spot, may not be considered appropriate for children aged 10 – 15 years. Each local authority will have its own view as to how this age group should be treated which will often be informed by input from the Police and from Children's Services' officers, and enforcement officers should be aware of the policy and follow it.

The on-going duty of fairness

Looking at what I have said about who should not be issued, with Fixed Penalty Tickets, a legitimate conclusion might be that Fixed Penalties should only be given to those meek individuals who roll over and offer their name, address and throat to the enforcement officer. It is certainly true that such people are easier to deal with, but local authorities have to be careful that they do not stand accused of picking only the low hanging fruit, pursuing soft targets and finding reasons, real or imagined, not to address the more difficult offenders. Most enforcement policies are clear on this point; all offenders should be tackled and decisions about the appropriateness of proceeding should be an ongoing consideration throughout the interface with the offender.

Issuing the Fixed Penalty and Low Profile Interfacing

When approaching someone, to speak to them or to issue them with a Fixed Penalty Ticket, there are a number of important points to consider;

(1) the nature of the interface with the offender,

(2) gathering such evidence as may be needed to support any legal action that may flow from the interface, and

(3) the personal safety of the enforcement officer.

Taking the points in order, the first is the likely nature of the interface with the offender. Sometimes the enforcement officer will know the offender having dealt with him on a previous occasion or occasions. In such cases, forewarned is forearmed and the enforcement officer will have some knowledge of how he is likely to react. Otherwise the enforcement officer should consider whether the offender is going to be difficult or aggressive, or malleable and put his hands up to the offence. If the offender is with others will he seek to play to the crowd? If so, the enforcement officer must consider how he can separate him from the others so he can deal with the offender in isolation, particularly if the others seek to join in the debate.

The enforcement officer has also got to consider evidence gathering. He will have seen the originating offence and will, hopefully, have been able to gather the evidence that supports his view, but often he will not. He will have to follow up the offence immediately, without the luxury of time, to record the evidence neatly as perfectly constructed contemporaneous notes. If, for example, the offender throws a soft drink can to the floor and walks away, there is no time for the enforcement officer to make notes of what he saw, draw a neat plan of the location and bag and tag the drink can; he will have to go, hot foot, after the offender to challenge him about the incident. Not only must the enforcement officer make a mental record of the evidence of the offence, he must remember that any conversation he has with the offender has evidential value. It is beyond the remit of this book to discuss the PACE 1984 requirements for Interviews Under Caution, but enforcement officers must be aware that if they go beyond asking the offender his name and address, and ask him questions about the offence, the provisions of PACE 1984 Code C, Code of Practice for the Detention, Treatment and Questioning of Persons by Police Officers (as revised) apply and its strict requirements must be followed.

During the encounter the enforcement officer should keep in mind that he may have to change the way in which he deals with the matter. It may be that someone to whom he had intended to give a Fixed Penalty Ticket suddenly becomes aggressive and the enforcement officer may have to withdraw and consider the instigation of legal proceedings. It is important that any evidence he has gathered up to this point should remain admissible and its integrity should therefore be protected.

My third point, although I would not argue with anyone who said it should more properly be the first, is the personal safety of the enforcement officer. This should be uppermost in the mind of the enforcement officer, as it should during any inspection or visit. There is no evidence to suggest that enforcement officers are any more at risk offering Fixed Penalties than when enforcing any other legislation but they should make sure that they monitor the situation carefully; should they feel at any risk they should withdraw. The officer's personal safety is paramount.

Low Profile Interfacing and reducing the likelihood of confrontation

I commented earlier that it would come as no surprise to enforcement officers that most offenders offered the opportunity to accept a Fixed Penalty, even as an alternative to prosecution, may not respond with unmitigated joy. It also will not come as any surprise to most that aggressive enforcement officers will have less success in dealing with alleged offenders than their more amenable colleagues. The attitude of the enforcement officer can be the difference between the offender accepting the Fixed Penalty with a good grace or taking it with a very bad grace or not taking it at all. The decent enforcement officer who does his job in a fair way will be much more successful and will experience many fewer problems than the Self Important Jobs Worth, doing his job with all the subtlety of a sledge hammer. I am not suggesting that enforcement officers should be obsequious and apologise for enforcing the law because they have no need to be. Realistically, they are unlikely to win over the offender by going down the 'This hurts me as much as it hurts you' road, because it clearly doesn't, and if it does, a change of career direction might be in order. That said, there are certainly ways to make the enforcement process easier for both the enforcer and the enforced against.

The key to low profile interfacing is to be polite. Not remorselessly and officiously polite, not blandly polite, and certainly not polite tinged with sarcasm, but just normal, everyday, genuine courtesy. It is actually very hard to be rude to someone who is just polite back to you and politeness tends to take the sting out of what is essentially an undesirable interface. The interface is more likely to take the form of a conversation if the officer is friendly, in the approachable sense of that word, than if he is officious and stand-offish. If the enforcement officer is hostile a conversation can break down into an argument very quickly.

There is another advantage to being polite; it is that the casual observer, watching the interface, would have to report that the enforcement officer was polite and reasonable, even in the face of the offender going off like a firework. That may be useful later if the offender wants to make allegations or lodges a complaint about how he was treated. It is certainly much better than the casual observer reporting that he remembers the enforcement officer and offender stood nose to nose, screaming at each other. Where enforcement officers wear body cameras it is important to remember that not only what they say will be recorded but how they say it; words that on paper appear to be relatively neutral will be recorded in all their deeply ironic or sarcastic glory by the body camera. Being polite will serve you well.

I hope it goes without saying that enforcement officers should avoid being confrontational. However animated the offender is about the pettiness of the law and the small mindedness of those who enforce it, there is no point in getting involved in arguments about the law and its requirements. If offenders want to express their view they can do so, as long as they do so in a civilised manner, but enforcement officers should not get drawn into arguments. Uncontentious acknowledgements by the enforcement officer that he hears what the offender says, without necessarily agreeing with the view expressed, are fine. They show that the enforcement officer is listening and are better than an 'I'm just doing my job' type response. That is a coded version of 'Talk to the hand' and can potentially inflame the offender who may feel that he is just being ignored.

I always advise enforcement officers to remain calm. I accept that it is easier for me to say than for them to do, but it is certainly the case that if an enforcement officer appears to be getting rattled or losing control, an aggressive person will pick up on it and feed off it. Even if the enforcement officer is not calm, as long as he gives the appearance of being in control offenders and witnesses will think that he is and it will help to take the heat out of a potentially escalating situation; as long as it is calm that is measured, rather than just a blank response. There is a difference between calmly refusing to rise to something and pointedly blanking it.

The final comment I want to make is that low profile interfacing does not require the enforcement officer to be passive; he needs to be actively in control of the situation. It is appropriate for him to be firm and to he should ensure that he remains in control of the interface, not allowing the offender to deflect him into argument or debate, and keeping others, who are not involved in the exchange, out of the conversation. Polite but firm is the way to go.

Recording the evidence

I have said, on a number of occasions, that questions of evidence are beyond the remit of this book, but there is one form of evidence that needs consideration. It is the evidence of what the offender says about the offence when the enforcement officer speaks to him. It doesn't take much imagination to see that the content of such a conversation could be extremely important; the enforcement officer will be keen to rely on it if the offender admits to the offence; the 'offender' will be keen to ensure that the court hears about it if he has denied committing the offence, point blank and at the first opportunity. To ensure that the evidence is admissible enforcement officers must comply with the requirements of PACE 1984 Code of Practice C, as it covers the questioning of suspects.

Where an enforcement officer has grounds to suspect that an offence has been committed and wants to ask a suspect questions about it, he must caution him first. There is no necessity for the enforcement officer to administer the caution before he asks general questions such as the suspect's name and address or about the ownership of a vehicle, even though the answers may be very relevant and useful; they are non- controversial and are explicitly

173

excluded by Code C. However once the enforcement officer gets past the non-controversial stuff and wants to talk about the offence itself he must advise the offender that what he says will be recorded and may be used in evidence, and that if he fails to mention something when he is questioned about the offence, that he later mentions at trial, certain inferences may be drawn. The exact words of the caution are printed in enforcement officers' PACE note books and I think that enforcement officers should always try to use the exact words. Whilst the law does not require that the strict wording is used it does demand that the words used are similar in terms and meaning and that is not easy to achieve. It is much easier, and more reliable, to read the caution off a notebook than to try and come up with a new form of words which has the same effect. It is a lot less vulnerable to challenge by a defence lawyer claiming that his client did not understand what was happening, and it is also the case that offenders now recognise the words of the caution. It pops up about ten times a night on television, across the various networks, and even those individuals who have never made a policeman so much as raise an eyebrow recognise the caution and understand, at least in part, what it is about and what happens after the words are spoken.

Merely administering the caution is not enough; the interview that follows must be recorded by the officer so that there is an accurate record of what was said. Recording an interview under caution, while standing on a street corner, is not the easiest thing in the world to do. The officer is required to marshal his thoughts about what he has seen, to ask a series of considered and lucid questions, to consider and weigh the answers he is given and write it all down accurately.

What should the enforcement officer record? He should start with the date and time of the interview, the location at which the interview takes place and the name of the party he is interviewing. It is not necessary for him to write the words of the caution in his note book, words such as 'Caution administered' suffice. He should then record the interview that follows as a series of questions and answers, recording with absolute accuracy what is said. When he has asked all the questions he wishes to ask, he should ask the offender to sign his note book to acknowledge that it is a true record of what was said. If the offender signs as requested, all well and good: if he refuses the enforcement officer should note that the offender was offered the opportunity to sign his note book but declined to do so. If the offender explains why he has refused to sign, the reasons should be recorded but if he offers no reason that should also be noted. If the matter proceeds to prosecution the contents of the interview under caution are part of the evidence. They can be transcribed by the enforcement officer into the body of his witness statement but the better practice is to transcribe them separately and exhibit them to the statement. Having gone to the time and trouble of conducting the interview under caution the enforcement officer is well advised to wring as much value as he can out of it where it supports his case, and to give its contents due consideration where it contains a blank denial; in either case it will be very persuasive evidence.

Back in the office

If the offender pays the Fixed Penalty, whether expeditiously or otherwise, the enforcement officer need take no further action in the matter. That is not to say his interest in it ceases, it does not. It is important that enforcement officers are aware of the names of those individuals who have been offered and have accepted Fixed Penalty Tickets. It was noted earlier in this chapter, that one of the considerations for an enforcement officer when deciding whether to offer an individual a Fixed Penalty is whether the individual has previously been given a Fixed Penalty in respect of a similar matter: it was suggested that if he had, a Fixed Penalty would be inappropriate. To make sure that the same individual is not offered multiple Fixed Penalties, all the officers who enforce the legislation must be able to access the names and addresses of those who have accepted Fixed Penalties in the past. Every time an individual pays a Fixed Penalty the database of recipients should be updated so that the enforcement team is fully informed before disposal decisions are made.

I looked in the last chapter at the varied reasons why someone might not pay a Fixed Penalty but, whatever the reason, the outcome is the same; nothing happens and the ball is back in the local authority court. I would admit that there are those I have advised in the past who have accused me of being litigation mad, but, I have to say, I tear my hair out when I hear of local authorities that fail to follow up offenders who just ignore the Fixed Penalty. I have heard the argument more than once; the Fixed Penalty is only £100, it costs much more than that to follow it up, the authority may not get its money back, resources are limited and blah blah blah. If the system is to be credible, and to act as a proper deterrent to those who would offend, the Fixed Penalty has to be pursued to its proper conclusion. Word will soon spread that only the meek, weak and mugs pay; everyone else will throw their ticket away as nothing will happen and it won't be long before the Fixed Penalty system becomes nothing more than a meaningless shower of paper.

Final Points to Ponder

1. The offer of a Fixed Penalty demands an explicit acceptance. The offender must make a positive decision to accept the Fixed Penalty, knowing the consequences that flow from doing so.
2. Fixed Penalties are not an appropriate disposal mechanism for all offenders. Enforcement officers should be aware of their local authority's enforcement policy and should always exercise their judgement where there is doubt about the ability of the offender to understand the process.
3. Fixed Penalties are not an appropriate disposal mechanism for every set of circumstances. The alternatives should always be considered and the reason for choosing the method of disposal justified.
4. Offering Fixed Penalties does not have to be a hostile encounter. The attitude of the enforcement officer can be all important.
5. Whilst offering Fixed Penalties is no more dangerous than any other part of local government enforcement, the enforcement officer should keep his personal safety at the front of his mind.
6. If the enforcement officer wants to ask questions about an offence he must do so in an Interview Under Caution, taking account of the requirements of PACE 1984 Code of Practice C.
7. Local authorities should follow up unpaid Fixed Penalties in order to maintain the credibility and integrity of the mechanism.

The Authors

Julie Barratt BSc, LLB(Hons) CEnvH qualified as a Public Health Inspector in 1981 and practised environmental health before being called to the Bar in 1993. She has extensive experience of advising and representing local authorities and public bodies. She wrote a legal column for Environmental Health News for over 15 years, is a regular media commentator on legal issues and public health, and is a highly respected legal trainer.

Chris Lewis LLB(Hons) is a solicitor and higher court advocate. He has specialised in crime initially in private practice and then for most of his career working for the Crown Prosecution Service, regularly undertaking trials both in the magistrates and crown court. He is a highly respected legal trainer providing training for local authorities and the police.

By the same authors 'Investigation and Prosecution: practical guidance of local authority enforcement officers' Julie Barratt Legal Training, 2019, ISBN 978-1-9164127-0-5

PATTERN DRAFTING
AND FOUNDATION
AND FLAT PATTERN
DESIGN

- A DRESSMAKER'S
GUIDE -

BY

IDA RILEY DUNCAN

British Library Cataloguing-in-Publication Data
A catalogue record for this book is available from the
British Library

Contents

Dressmaking and Tailoring

Dressmaking and Tailoring broadly refers to those who make, repair or alter clothing for a profession. A dressmaker will traditionally make custom clothing for women, ranging from dresses and blouses to full evening gowns (also historically called a mantua-maker or a modiste). Whereas a tailor will do the same, but usually for men's clothing - especially suits. The terms essentially refer to a specific set of hand and machine sewing skills, as well as pressing techniques that are unique to the construction of traditional clothing. This is separate to 'made to measure', which uses a set of pre-existing patterns. Usually, a bespoke tailored suit or dress will be completely original and unique to the customer, and hence such items have been highly desirable since the trade first appeared in the thirteenth century. The Oxford English Dictionary states that the word 'tailor' first came into usage around the 1290s, and undoubtedly by this point, tailoring guilds, as well as those of cloth merchants and weavers were well established across Europe.

As the tailoring profession has evolved, so too have the methods of tailoring. There are a number of distinctive business models which modern tailors may practice, such

as 'local tailoring' where the tailor is met locally, and the garment is produced locally too, 'distance tailoring', where a garment is ordered from an out-of-town tailor, enabling cheaper labour to be used - which, in practice can now be done on a global scale via e-commerce websites, and a 'travelling tailor', where the man or woman will travel between cities, usually stationing in a luxury hotel to provide the client the same tailoring services they would provide in their local store. These processes are the same for both women's and men's garment making.

Pattern making is a very important part of this profession; the construction of a paper or cardboard template from which the parts of a garment are traced onto fabric before cutting our and assembling. A custom dressmaker (or tailor) frequently employs one of three pattern creation methods; a 'flat-pattern method' which begins with the creation of a sloper or block (a basic pattern for a garment, made to the wearer's measurements), which can then be used to create patterns for many styles of garments, with varying necklines, sleeves, dart placements and so on. Although it is also used for womenswear, the 'drafting method' is more commonly employed in menswear and involves drafting a pattern directly onto pattern paper using a variety of straightedges and curves. Since menswear rarely involves draping, pattern-making is the primary preparation for creating a cut-and-

sew woven garment. The third method, the 'pattern draping method' is used when the patternmaker's skill is not matched with the difficulty of the design. It involves creating a muslin mock-up pattern, by pinning fabric directly on a dress form, then transferring the muslin outline and markings onto a paper pattern or using the muslin as the pattern itself.

Dressmaking and tailoring has become a very well respected profession; dressmakers such as Pierre Balmain, Christian Dior, Cristóbal Balenciaga and Coco Chanel have gone on to achieve international acclaim and fashion notoriety. Balmain, known for sophistication and elegance, once said that 'dressmaking is the architecture of movement.' Whilst tailors, due to the nature of their profession - catering to men's fashions, have not garnered such levels of individual fame, areas such as 'Savile Row' in the United Kingdom are today seen as the heart of the trade.

PATTERN DRAFTING

AS BEFORE STATED, drafting a pattern is generally considered a very complicated process, but, with the following simple system of drafting, it should not be confusing to the average person. At first, it is merely a mechanical process for which explicit directions are given.

Naturally, for the first pattern, it takes more time than using a commercial pattern, but if for no other reason than for fitting, it is a big advantage to have at least a drafted-to-measure foundation pattern from one's own measurements.

Commercial patterns naturally follow the lines of the average figure. But how many of us are average? Commercial patterns are unable to cope with all the irregularities of form, hence they are often too tight in one place, too loose in another, too small here or too large there. From a basic pattern that fits the individual and consequently takes care of her particular needs, one can make simple types of garments such as a plain waist or skirt, children's dresses, alter commercial patterns, make ready-to-wears fit, also use any material one has on hand—in other words, cut the suit according to the cloth—remodel clothes, using part of one garment and part of another, or have certain parts of woven cloth and other parts knitted. These are impossibilities if one doesn't know the basic rules of shaping.

TOOLS NECESSARY FOR PATTERN MAKING

1. Paper on which the pattern is drafted to scale. Manila paper is best, but one may use a cleaner's paper bag, or other wrapping paper, but it should be tough.

2. A soft pencil and an eraser.

3. A T square. If this is not available, use a book or a pad, anything that will help to make a perfect right angle.

4. Several sheets of tracing paper for developing designs.

5. A yard stick.

6. A French curve for armholes, etc. This may be dispensed with if it cannot be obtained.

7. Tape measure.

8. Pins.

9. The chart with measurements listed.

10. Unbleached muslin or any used similar material.

11. Drawing and cutting table. If no other table is available, use the dining or kitchen table.

12. Scissors.

The first pattern to be drafted, to learn the rudiments of pattern making in its simplest form, is a simple waist. It is a plain two-piece waist with normal shoulders, normal armscye, and high round neckline, with only fullness added

to give the necessary amount of ease. This will be a basic pattern, from which may be developed different types of shirtwaists with different structural lines, all types of sleeves and necklines to suit individual needs and the material of which the garment is to be made, waistcoats, jerkins, basque waists, then on to jackets with lapels and skirts of all kinds

So that each step will be readily understood, the same measurements are used throughout. These are not according to any particular size, and belong to an average young adult.

A flat pattern to actual scale is developed first. As was explained when taking measurements, only two dimensions are used; height or length, which are the perpendicular measurements, and the width or breadth, which are the horizontal measurements. Naturally, the roundness or depth is not seen.

That which is seen directly in front is called the front elevation, and that which is seen directly at the back is the back elevation. The average side elevation extends from the curve of the front armscye to the curve of the back armscye. Naturally, the side elevation for a stout figure appears wider and extends beyond the armscye to the bust in front, and beyond the armscye at the back.

7

CHART OF MEASUREMENTS

NOTE.—Measurements taken as prescribed in Chapter 5.

	inches
Waist	26
Waist—underarm seam to underarm seam—back	13
Waist—underarm seam to underarm seam—front	13
Bust—total bust measurement	33
Across the back from underarm to underarm	18
Front bust measurement from underarm to underarm	19
Waist to underarm	8
Shoulder to shoulder	14
Shoulder line or seam	5 1/8
Depth of shoulder	1 1/2
Armscye	18
Width across the back	13—3⊠ down
Width across the chest	13—3⊠ down
Back	
Centre back from neck to waist	16 1/2
Shoulder-line, neck-base intersection to waist	17
Centre front length from neck to waist	14
Shoulder-line, neck-base intersection to waist	17 1/2

NOTE.—No garment is ever made the same as the actual bust measurement. Allowances for ease and movement are necessary. It will be seen from the chart that the bust measurement is 33 inches, while the across the back measurement is 18 inches, and the front bust measurement is 19 inches, making a total of 37 inches.

All garments should fit easily at all times. In a very fitted upper garment, this fullness may be fitted out slightly, but at least 2 to 3 inches more than the actual bust measurement should be left for ease.

BASIC PATTERN FOR WAIST FROM GIVEN MEASUREMENTS

This method is suitable for both women and children.

The drawing is made to the exact scale of the individual measurements.

One piece of the waist is drafted at a time. The back is drafted first because it is simpler than the front; and the drafted back pattern aids when drafting the front, as the front and back are tied together by means of the shoulder to shoulder measurement.

Only half of the pattern is drawn; the other half is traced later. For right angles, use a T square, or a book or pad with true right angles.

The following drafted pattern is constructed from the chart of measurements just given.

CONSTRUCTION OF PATTERN

Back

Follow Diagram 14 for each step.

1. Draw a perpendicular line, AB, for the centre back.

2. With T square or pad placed at right angles to the centre back line, rule another line, CB, to represent the waist.

3. From the waist, CB, using the underarm to waist measurement, which is 8 inches, draw another line, EF, at right angles to the centre back. This is the line to be used for across the back from underarm seam to underarm seam.

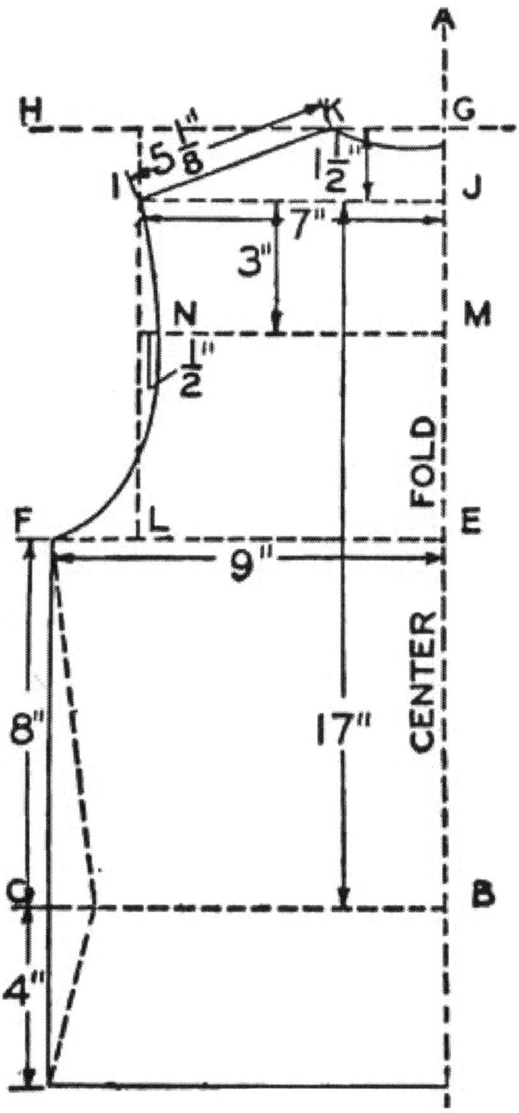

DIAGRAM 14

4. Draw a line, GH at right angles to AB, using the back, shoulder-line, neck-base intersection to waist measurement, which is 17 inches above CB.

5. Draw a line, IJ, at right angles to the centre back, and 1 1/2 inches, the depth of the shoulder, from GH.

6. From E, on the centre back line, measure 9 inches on EF, which is 1/2 the across the back underarm measurement.

7. From J, on the shoulder to shoulder line, measure 7 inches, which is 1/2 the shoulder to shoulder measurement.

8. Place the zero of rule or yard stick at point 1, the tip of the shoulder. At an angle where the measured shoulder length, which is 5 1/8 inches, meets the line marking the shoulder-line, neck-base intersection, place point K. Rule a straight line from the tip of the shoulder, I, to the point K. This is the shoulder seam.

9. From the tip of the shoulder, I, draw a construction line, IL, parallel to the centre back line for a guide for the armscye; also another construction line, MN, 3 inches below I, and parallel to IJ, to mark the narrowest part of the back, and mark N, 6 1/2 inches from M. This is 1/2 the width across the back.

10. *Armscye.* From the underarm at point F, make a very slight curve for 1/2 the width of the armscye, then make a sweeping curve to the narrowest part of the back, N, then out to the tip of the shoulder, I.

11. From K, draw a close-fitting curve, 1/2 an inch deep for the back of the neck.

12. For a plain waist without darts for shaping, add 3 or 4 inches below the waist, according to the amount of material on hand, for sufficient depth below the underarm, or measure in about 1 inch at the waist, as in diagram, and shape; if tighter fitting is desired, make a dart below the shoulder-blades to waist, then to hips. (See Chapter 7 on "Darts.")

13. Using tracing paper, trace the other half, or fold the paper on the centre line, and impression the armscye, shoulder line, etc., on the other side.

NOTE.—Don't cut out the pattern at this stage.

Test

With a tape measure, measure around the 1/2 of the armscye. On an average figure, this is almost 1/2 the required armscye measurement. If much difference prevails, check the shoulder-line, neck-base intersection to waist measurement, also the across the back from underarm to underarm measurement.

FORMULA FOR BACK OF PLAIN WAIST

Follow Diagram 15.

NOTE.—

1. This pattern may be used for foundation pattern for simple garments.

2. Construction lines for only half the back are given; and it is only necessary to shape one side.

3. There are no seam allowances; these to be added later when cutting material.

1. Draw a perpendicular line, AB, for the centre back.

2. With T square or pad placed at right angles to the centre back line, rule another line, CB, to represent the waist.

3. From the waist, CB, using the underarm to waist measurement, draw another line, EF, at right angles to the centre back. This is the line to be used for across the back from underarm seam to underarm seam.

4. Draw a line, GH, at right angles to AB, using the back, shoulder-line, neck-base intersection to waist measurement, above CB.

5. Draw a line, IJ, at right angles to the centre back, and the depth of the shoulder from GH.

6. From E, on the centre back line, on EF, measure 1/2 the across the back underarm measurement.

7. From J, on the shoulder to shoulder line, measure 1/2 the shoulder to shoulder measurement, and mark the tip of the shoulder, I.

8. Place the zero of rule or yard stick at point I, the tip of the shoulder, at an angle where the measured shoulder length meets the line marking the shoulder-line, neck-base intersection, and place point K. Rule a straight line from the tip of the shoulder, I, to the point K. This is the shoulder seam.

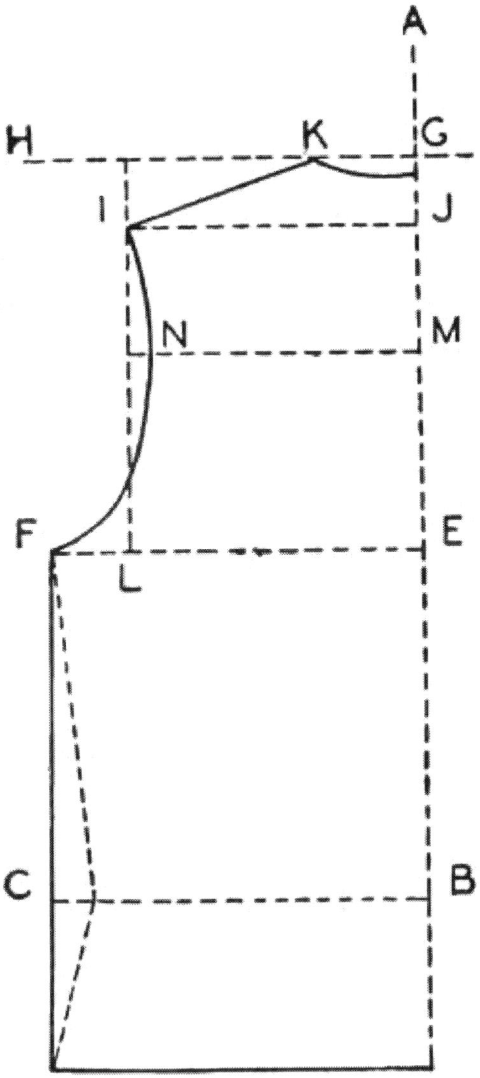

DIAGRAM 15

9. From the tip of the shoulder, I, draw a construction line, IL, parallel to the centre back line for a guide for the armscye; also another construction line, MN, at the narrowest part of the back, and parallel to IJ. Mark 1/2 the width across the back.

10. *Armscye.* From the underarm at point F, make a very slight curve for 1/2 the width of the armscye, then make a sweeping curve to the point marking the narrowest part of the back, N, then out to the tip of the shoulder, I.

11. From K, draw a close-fitting curve, to mark the back of the neck.

12. For plain waist without darts for shaping, add 3 or 4 inches below the waist, according to the amount of material on hand, for sufficient depth below the underarm, or measure in about 1 inch at the waist, as in diagram, and shape; if tighter fitting is desired, make a dart below the shoulder-blades to waist, then to hips. (See Chapter 7 on "Darts.")

13. Using tracing paper, trace the other half of the pattern, or fold the paper on the centre line and impression the armscye, shoulder line, etc., with a tracing wheel or hard pencil.

NOTE.—The edge of the pattern is the stitching line and allowances must be added for seams. 3/8 to 1/2 an inch is a good allowance. This, of course, depends upon the type of seam, but be sure to allow a full seam for all rayons.

Test

With a tape measure, measure around the armscye. On an average figure, this is almost 1/2 the required armscye measurement. If much difference prevails, check the shoulder-line, neck-base intersection to waist measurement, also the across the back from underarm to underarm measurement.

DRAFT OF FRONT OF WAIST FROM CHART OF GIVEN MEASUREMENTS

Salient Measurements

	inches
Waist	26
Bust	33
Across the back from underarm to underarm	18
Front bust measurement from underarm to underarm	19
Waist to underarm	8
Shoulder to shoulder	14
Shoulder line or seam	5 1/8
Depth of shoulder	1 1/2
Armscye	18
Width across the back	13—3⊠ down
Width across the chest	13—3⊠ down
Centre front length from neck to waist	14
Shoulder-line, neck-base intersection to waist	17 1/2

1. Draw a perpendicular line, AB, for the centre front.

2. With T square or pad placed at right angles to the centre front line, rule a line, CB, to represent the waist.

3. Draw a line, GH, at right angles to centre front, AB, using the measurement of the front shoulder-line, neck-base intersection to waist measurement, which is 17 1/2 inches, above CB.

NOTE.—There is 1/2 an inch difference between the back shoulder-line, neck-base intersection to waist measurement and the front shoulder-line, neck-base intersection to waist measurement. This extra 1/2 inch is added to the waist to underarm measurement.

4. From the waist, CB, using the underarm to waist measurement, 8 inches, plus the 1/2 inch as stated above, draw another line, EF, at right angles to the centre front. This is the line to be used for the bust measurement.

5. Draw a line, IJ, at right angles to the centre front, and 1 1/2 inches the depth or slope of the shoulder, from GH.

6. From E, on the centre front line, measure 1/2 the front bust measurement; that is, 1/2 of 19 inches equals 9 1/2 inches, and mark the point X; also from E, mark 1/2 the across the back underarm measurement; that is, 1/2 of 18 inches equals 9 inches, and place the point F.

NOTE.—The front armscye is first constructed from the point F. The extra width for bust is discussed later.

7. From J, on the shoulder to shoulder line, measure 7 inches, which is 1/2 the shoulder to shoulder measurement, and mark I.

8. Place the zero of ruler or yard stick at point I, the tip of the shoulder, at an angle where the measured shoulder length, which is 5 1/8 inches, meets the line marking the shoulder-line, neck-base intersection, and place point K. Rule a straight line from the tip of the shoulder, I, to the point K. This is the shoulder seam.

9. From the tip of the shoulder, I, draw a construction line, IL, parallel to the centre front line for a guide for the armscye; also another construction line, MN, 3 inches below IJ and parallel to it. From M, measure 6 1/2 inches, which is 1/2 the width of the front, and mark N.

10. *Armscye*

NOTE.—For the average figure, the curve for the front armscye is a little deeper than the one at the back, but for a large figure the curve is much deeper in the front.

From the underarm at point F, make a very slight curve for more than 1/2 the width of the armhole, then make a sweeping curve to the narrowest part of the front, N, then out to the tip of the shoulder, I.

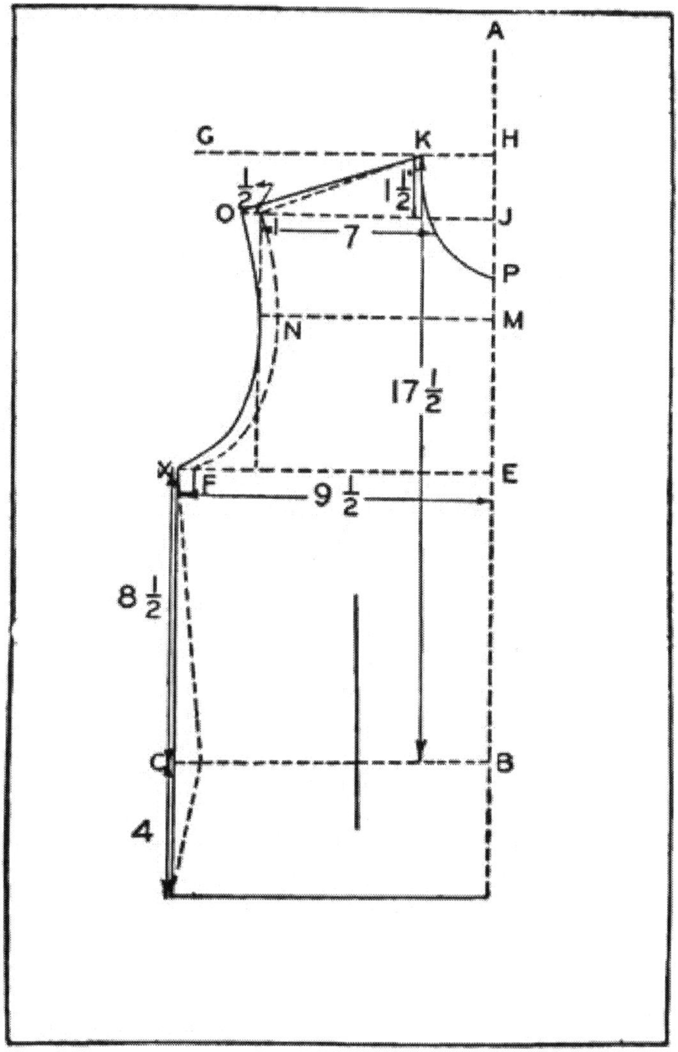

DIAGRAM 16

11. Continue the shoulder to shoulder line for 1/2 inch and mark O. This is the difference between 1/2 the across the back underarm measurement and 1/2 the front bust measurement. Draw a line from this point, O (see Diagram 16), to the shoulder-line, neck-base intersection, K. Rule the new shoulder line from O to K.

12. From the new position of the shoulder tip, O, using tracing paper, or impressioning with a tracing wheel or hard pencil, draw the armscye in new position from O to X.

NOTE.—This extra width at the shoulder may be taken care of by means of a dart, or a yoke may be made, or extra width may be added for shirring, gathering, or tucks, depending upon the texture of the material, the amount of material on hand, and the needs of the individual.

For fine material, when gathering, shirring, etc., generally 1/2 as much more width is added again. This is only a general rule which may become very elastic with need.

Diagram 17 shows how the shoulder seam is drawn when adding extra width.

13. Add 3 or 4 inches below the waist to match the back, or if slight shaping has been made, mark in at the waistline about 1 inch and shape. If front dart is desired for more shaping, make a vertical waist dart from the point of the bust to the waist, then to the hips.

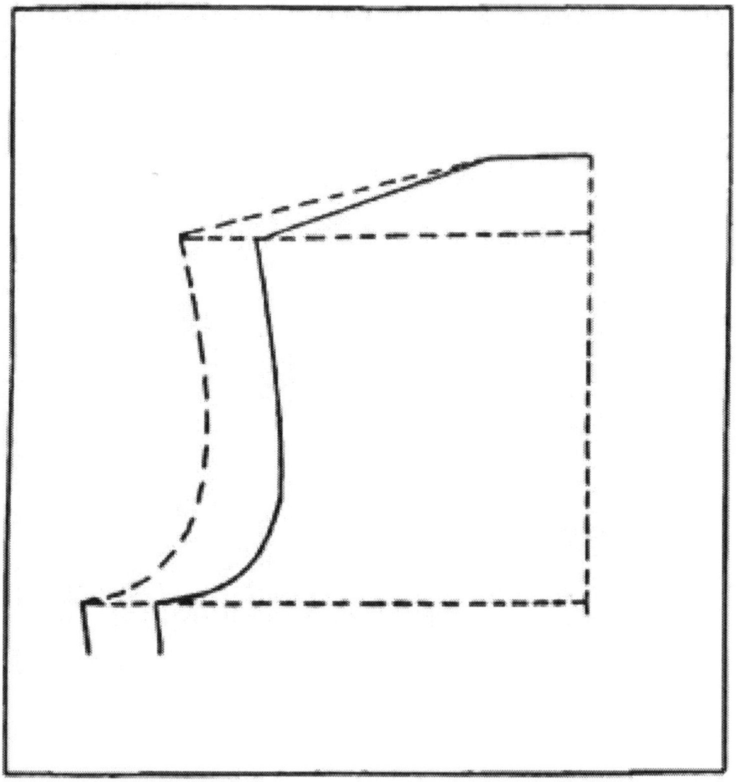

DIAGRAM 17

14. *Close fitting round neck.*—From the shoulder to shoulder line, IJ, draw a construction line parallel to it, and 2 inches below. Mark the point P at the centre front.

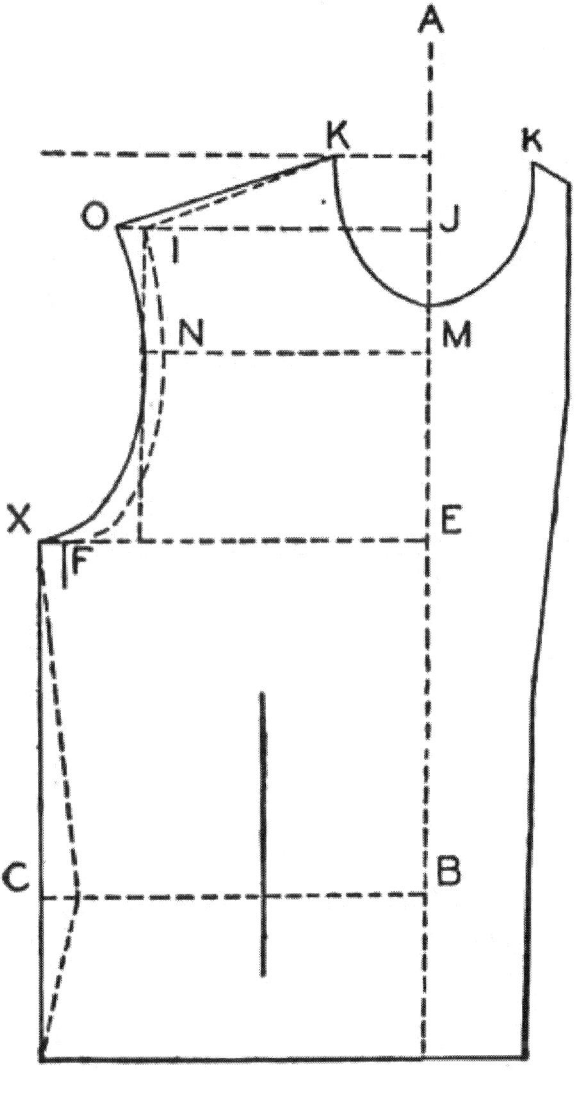

DIAGRAM 18

NOTE.—A high round neckline should be a very full curve, starting and ending almost in a straight line.

Draw the high round neckline.

NOTE.—

1. If the opening is desired, add 1 inch or more to the centre front for the top elevation, then allow a double thickness for the underlapping.

2. Only a narrow extension is needed for snaps.

3. Don't forget to allow for seams.

4. This same neckline will do for a blouse with lapels. The facing may be cut at the same time as the front if there is sufficient width of material; if not, a separate piece may be added, the width to come a little beyond the shoulder seam as in Diagram 18.

FORMULA FOR FRONT OF PLAIN WAIST

1. Draw a perpendicular line, AB, for the centre front.

2. With T square or pad placed at right angles to the centre front line, rule a line, CB, to represent the waist.

3. Draw a line, GH, at right angles to centre front, AB, using the measurement of the front shoulder-line, neck-base intersection to waist measurement, above CB.

NOTE.—The difference between the back shoulder-line, neck-base intersection to waist measurement and the front, shoulder-line, neck-base intersection to waist

measurement is to be added to the underarm to waist measurement.

4. From the waist, CB, using the underarm to waist measurement plus any difference as stated above, draw another line, EF, at right angles to the centre front. This is the line to be used for the front bust measurement.

5. Draw a line, IJ, at right angles to the centre front, and the depth of the shoulder from GH.

Follow Diagram 19.

6. From E, on the centre front line, measure 1/2 the front bust measurement and mark the point X; also from E, mark 1/2 the across the back underarm measurement and place the point F.

NOTE.—The front armscye is first constructed from the point F. The extra width for bust is considered later.

7. From J, on the shoulder to shoulder line, measure 1/2 the shoulder to shoulder measurement and mark I.

8. Place the zero of rule or yard stick at point I, the tip of the shoulder, at an angle where the measured shoulder length meets the line marking the front shoulder-line, neck-base intersection, and place point K. Rule a straight line from the tip of the shoulder, I, to the point K. This is the shoulder seam.

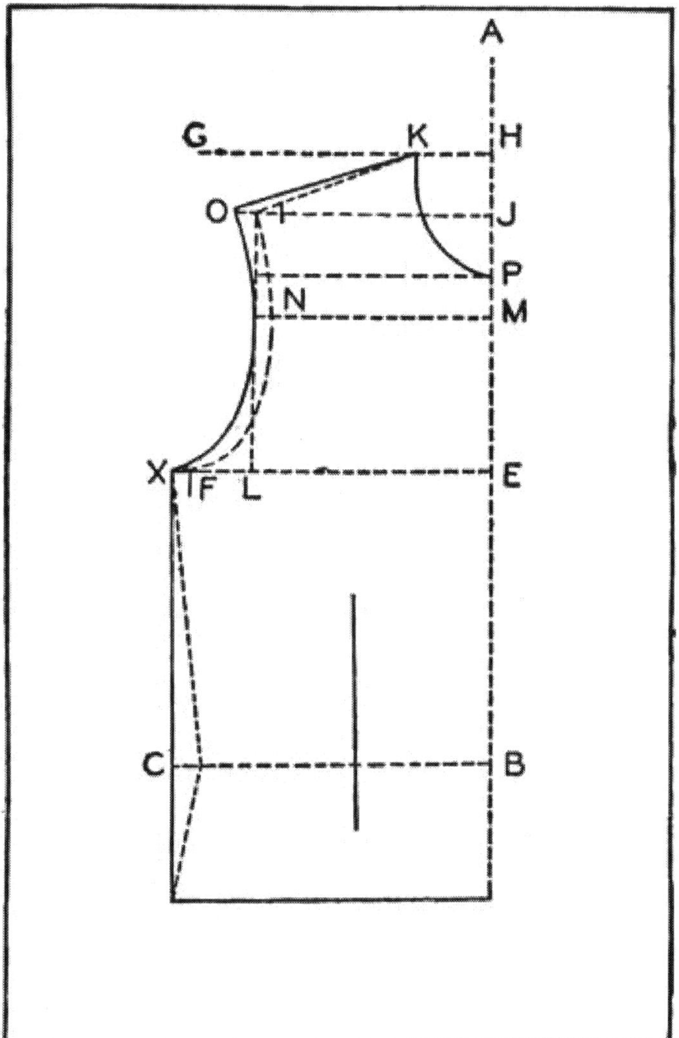

DIAGRAM 19

9. From the tip of the shoulder, I, draw a construction line, IL, parallel to the centre front line for a guide for the armscye; also another construction line, MN, at the narrowest part of the back. From M, measure 1/2 the width of the front, and mark N.

10. *Armscye*

NOTE.—For the average figure, the curve for the front armscye is a little deeper than the one at the back, but for a large figure the curve is much deeper in front.

From the underarm at point F, make a very slight curve for more than 1/2 the width of the armhole, then make a sweeping curve to the narrowest part of the front, N, then out to the tip of the shoulder, I.

11. Continue the shoulder to shoulder line, IJ to O. This is the difference between 1/2 the across the back underarm measurement and 1/2 the front bust measurement. Draw a line from this point, O, to the shoulder-line, neck-base intersection, K. Rule the new shoulder line from O to K.

12. From the new position of the shoulder tip, O, using tracing paper, or impressioning with a tracing wheel or hard pencil, draw the armscye in new position from O to X.

(See Note under 12 in previous draft.)

13. Add 3 or 4 inches below the waist to match the back. If slight shaping is desired, mark in about 1 inch at the waistline and shape. If front dart is desired for more shaping,

make a vertical waist dart from the point of the bust to the waist, then to the hips.

14. *Close fitting round neck*

NOTE.—If in doubt where to place high round neckline, measure with the tape from armscye to armscye in front to the hollow at the throat, then measure the distance from the tip of the shoulder to this point on the armscye.

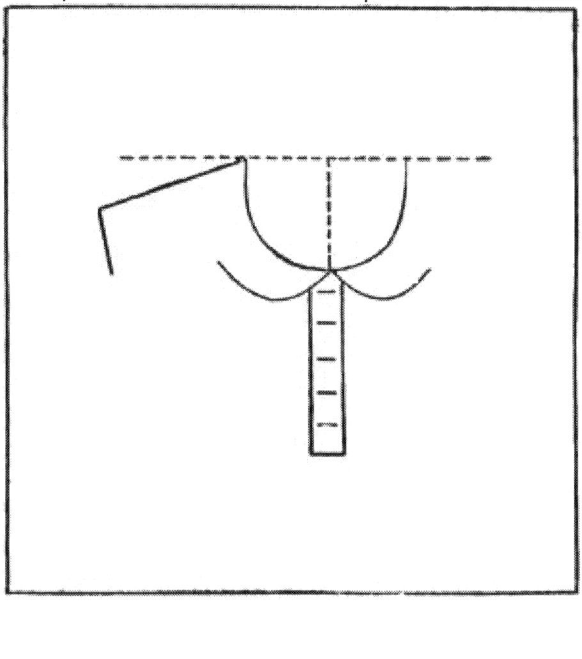

DIAGRAM 20

From the shoulder to shoulder line, IJ, draw a construction line parallel to it, and the necessary number of inches below I. Mark the point P at the centre front.

29

NOTE.—A high round neckline should be a very full curve, starting and ending in almost a straight line.

Draw the high round neckline.

Variations in Completing the Front

1. If opening is desired, add 1 inch or more to the centre front for the top elevation, then allow a double thickness for the underlapping.

2. Only a narrow extension is needed for snaps.

3. Don't forget to allow for all seams.

4. This same neckline will suffice for a blouse with lapels. If there is sufficient width of material, the facing may be cut at the same time as the front; if not, a separate piece may be added to come a little beyond the shoulder seam. (See Diagrams 18 and 20.)

A DRAFTED TO MEASURE FITTED PATTERN FROM GIVEN MEASUREMENTS

(To be used for a foundation pattern if desired)

A fitted draft follows the basic pattern for the front and back of plain waist. Different styles of shirt waists, etc., will be developed later. The reason for this is, that some women may not wish to construct their own patterns or make their own garments, but would like a fitted foundation pattern to use for altering commercial patterns, and so eliminate

many of the problems in fitting, or to aid when making the necessary alterations in ready-to-wears.

A foundation pattern may also be used as a basis for a flat pattern design, as is explained later, and also aids greatly in remodelling and conserving for both women and children, since children's patterns may be constructed in exactly the same way.

Measurements

The same measurements as for the draft of plain waist are used.

DRAFT FOR BACK OF FITTED PATTERN

1–11. Follow the directions for back of plain waist from numbers 1 to 11.

12. Add 3 or 4 inches below the waist, according to the amount of material on hand, for sufficient depth below the underarm, if so desired.

13. The waist measurement from the back underarm seam to underarm seam is 13 inches. 1/2 of 13 inches is 6 1/2 inches.

NOTE.—It is advisable not to make the waist too tight. A slight surplus width is necessary to allow the figure to have freedom for movement. Of course, the amount entirely depends upon individual needs. Always use your

own discretion. A poor figure, large, medium, or small, should never have a too-tight-fitting garment.

In this case, about 2 inches more for the entire waist is allowed; that is, 1/2 an inch added to each side.

6 1/2 inches plus 1/2 an inch equals 7 inches for 1/2 the back of the waist.

14. The difference between 1/2 the across the back underarm measurement, 9 inches, and 1/2 the necessary waist measurement, 7 inches, is 2 inches.

As 2 inches is too much width to take out at the underarm seam, a vertical waist dart, on a line with the shoulder-blade, or gathers may also be used to take out the extra width, the size of each depending upon the figure requirements. (See Diagram 21.)

The shaping for the underarm seam may be considered a dart, like the vertical waist dart, and for an average figure the width will be about equal.

Draw a line for the side seam and mark the position of the vertical dart.

15. From K, draw a close-fitting curve, 1/2 an inch deep for the back of the neck.

16. With tracing paper, tracing wheel, or hard pencil mark or impression the other side.

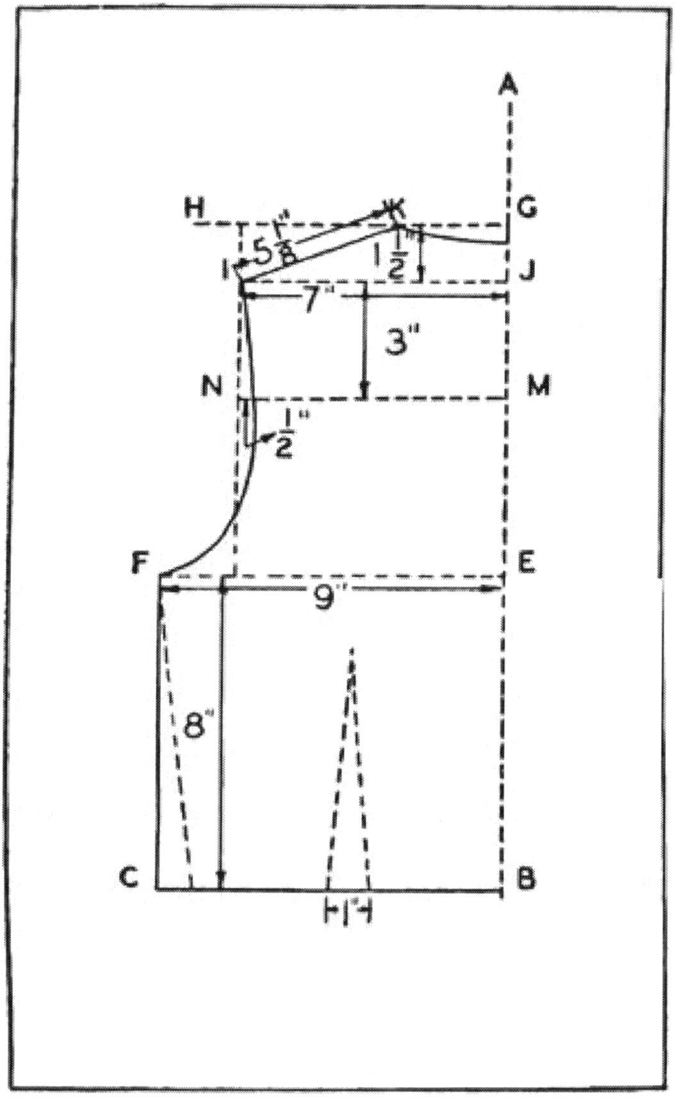

DIAGRAM 21

FORMULA FOR BACK OF FITTED PATTERN

1–11. Follow the formula for back of plain waist from numbers 1 to 11.

12. Add 3 or 4 inches below the waist, according to the amount of material on hand, for sufficient depth below the underarm, if so desired.

13. Subtract 1/2 the back waist measurement from underarm seam to underarm seam, plus the necessary allowance for ease, from 1/2 the across the back measurement. This is the amount which may be fitted out at the waist.

NOTE.—Even on a tight-fitting garment, there must be sufficient ease at the waist to allow for freedom of movement. 2 inches is approximately the amount necessary for an average figure; that is, 1/2 an inch at both sides, back and front.

14. If the amount to be fitted out exceeds 1 inch, it is advisable to use vertical waist dart or gathers, as well as shaping, at the side seam. This, of course, depends upon individual needs. (See Diagram 22.)

15. Draw line from side seam and also mark the position of the dart.

16. From K, draw a close-fitting curve for the back of the neck.

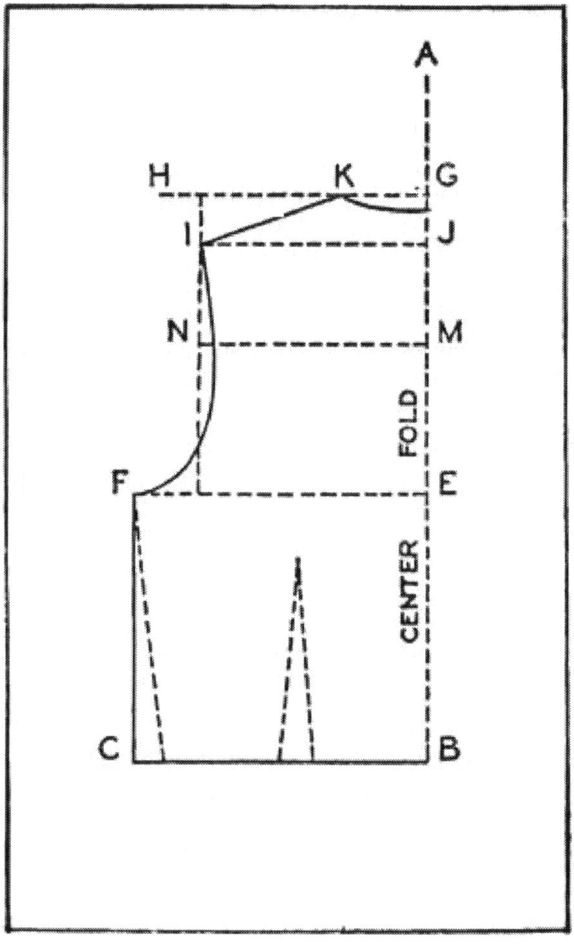

DIAGRAM 22

17. With tracing paper, tracing wheel, or hard pencil mark the other side.

DRAFT OF FRONT OF FITTED WAIST FROM GIVEN MEASUREMENTS

Follow Diagram 23.

1–12. Follow draft of front of plain waist from 1–12.

13. Add 3 or 4 inches below the waist to match the back, if desired.

14. The extra width at the shoulder line from O to K is fitted out by means of a small shoulder dart which tapers to the fullest part of the bust. (See "Shoulder Darts" in Chapter 7.)

The waist measurement from front underarm seam to underarm seam is 13 inches. 1/2 of 13 inches is 6 1/2 inches, plus 1/2 inch for ease equals 7 inches.

15. The difference between 1/2 the front bust measurement, 9 1/2 inches, and 1/2 the necessary waist measurement, 7 inches, is 2 1/2 inches. This to be fitted out at the underarm seam with a vertical waist dart to the bust, or gathers if desired.

As the back underarm seam sloped in 1 inch, it is advisable to slope the front underarm seam 1 inch, which leaves 1 1/2 inches of width to be fitted out by one or two vertical waist darts or gathers. (See "Vertical Waist Darts" in Chapter 7.)

16. Draw a line for side seam and also mark the position of the dart.

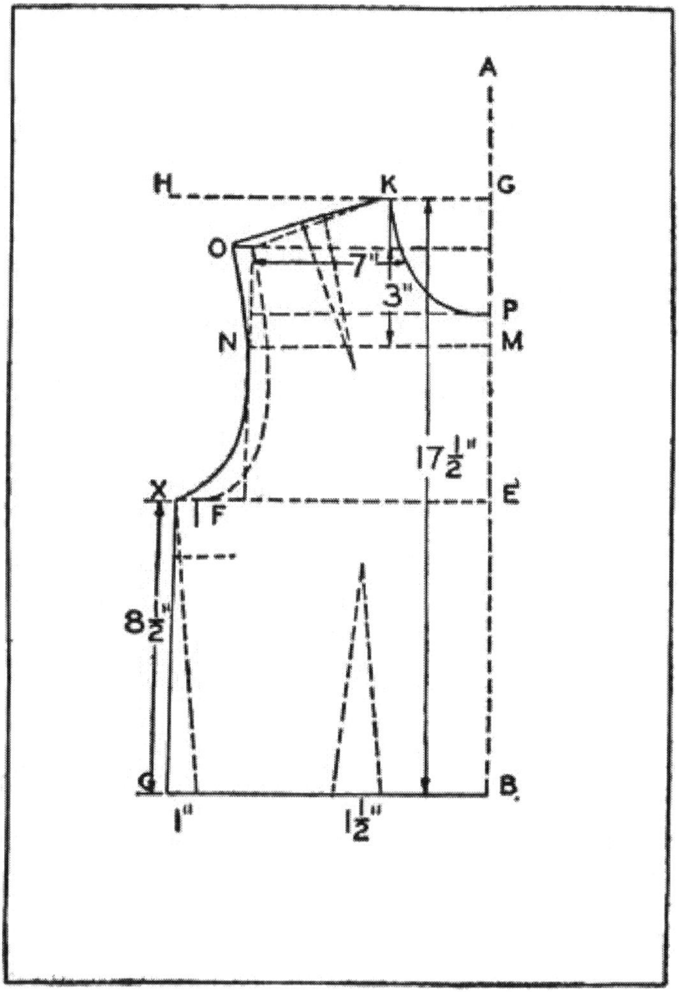

DIAGRAM 23

17. The back underarm to waist measurement is 8 inches. The front length is over 8 1/2 inches. Measure the difference and mark in an underarm dart, so that the underarm seams are the same length. (See "Underarm Dart" in Chapter 7.)

18. *Close Fitting Round Neck.*—From the shoulder to shoulder line, IJ, draw a construction line parallel to it, and 2 inches below. Mark the point P at the centre front.

NOTE.—A high round neckline should be a very full curve, starting and ending in almost a straight line.

Draw the high round neckline.

19. With tracing paper, tracing wheel, or hard pencil mark or impression the other side.

FORMULA FOR FRONT OF FITTED PATTERN

(See Diagram 24.)

1–12. Follow formula for front of plain waist from 1–12.

13. Add 3 or 4 inches below the waist to match the back, if desired.

14. The extra width across the shoulder line is fitted out by means of a shoulder dart, which tapers to the fullest point of the bust. Draw a temporary dart and refit if necessary. (See "Shoulder Darts" in Chapter 7.)

15. To 1/2 the front waist measurement from underarm seam to underarm seam add the necessary allowance for ease, then subtract this measurement from 1/2 the front bust measurement. This is the amount to be fitted out from the waist.

16. Shape the front underarm seam to correspond with the back underarm seam, the remaining width to be fitted out either by vertical waist dart or darts, or gathers. (See "Vertical Waist Darts" in Chapter 7.)

17. Subtract the length of the back underarm seam from the measured length of the front underarm seam, and make an underarm dart the width of the extra length. (See "Underarm Darts" in Chapter 7.)

NOTE.—

(*a*) If the difference is very slight, it may be eased into the underarm seam, or the bottom may be shaped as in Diagram 24.

(*b*) If the amount to be fitted out at the underarm is considerable, the shoulder dart may be dispensed with, and a centre front dart used instead.

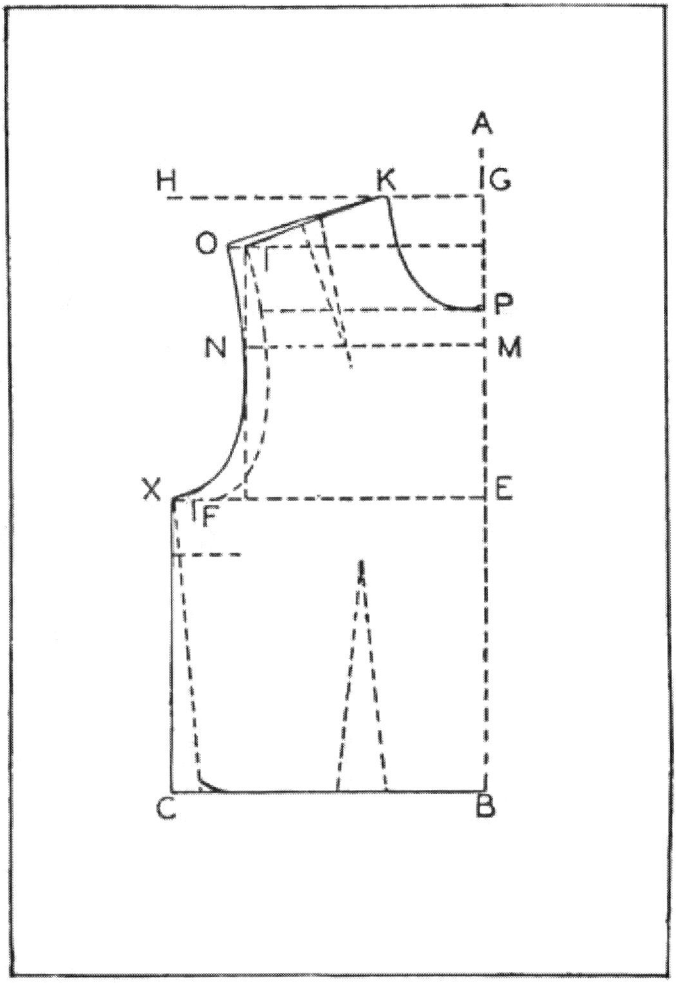

DIAGRAM 24

18. *Close Fitting Round Neck.*—From the shoulder to shoulder line, draw a construction line parallel to it, and the

necessary number of inches below. Mark the point at the centre front.

NOTE.—A high round neckline should be a very full curve, starting and ending in almost a straight line.

Draw the high round neckline.

19. With tracing paper, tracing wheel, or hard pencil mark or impression the other side.

Waistcoats and Jerkins

Waistcoats and Jerkins can readily be drafted from a fitted pattern. The armscye has to be changed—1 inch larger all the way round—therefore the underarm to waist measurement is 1 inch shorter, and the shoulder to shoulder measurement is 1 inch shorter on both sides. The curves for the armholes remain the same.

SLEEVES

All sleeves should have style, be comfortable, and allow for freedom of movement. Naturally, the type of sleeve depends upon the style of the garment, the material of which it is made, the amount of material on hand, and the needs of the individual.

There are many types of sleeves, long, short, tight-fitting, full at the top, wider at the bottom; some have caps that fit comfortably into the armscye with apparently no extra fullness, others have fullness darted into the upper part

of the cap, some have it gathered or shirred, while others have "boxed" tops.

Plain Long Sleeve with Fitted Cap

For the first sleeve pattern we shall consider the simplest sleeve; that is, a plain long sleeve, as wide at the wrist as at the upper arm, and one that fits comfortably into the armhole; a sleeve with a straight sleeve seam gathered into a cuff or wrist band, and a cap with apparently no fullness.

Any sleeve, no matter how tight-fitting, should never be made skin tight. Even for a fairly tight sleeve, cut on the grain of the material, 2 inches should be added to the upperarm measurement for the width, and for a very tight sleeve cut on the bias, it is still necessary to have about 1 1/2 inches of extra width at the upperarm to allow for ease and movement. A generally considered good width for an average person for a plain sleeve set into a cuff is 14 inches, but a little narrower may be used if desired, or if there isn't sufficient material. It is always well to test with the tape measure.

As was explained when taking the underarm to wrist measurement for sleeve, a close fitting underarm measurement is taken. As no armhole should fit tightly under the underarm, this would make the sleeve underarm measurement too long, generally speaking about 1 inch; however, this extra length aids when shaping the wrist, as will be explained later. It will also be noted that no outside

measurement is taken for a sleeve, except the depth of the cap. This simplifies construction and directions are therefore much easier to follow.

In a plain long sleeve the bottom of the sleeve isn't always shaped. A plain long sleeve, without shaping, is drafted first.

Measurements for Sleeve taken from Chart

Total underarm measurement—19 inches

Underarm to elbow—9 inches

Upperarm—10 1/2 inches

Forearm—9 1/2 inches

Bent elbow—10 1/2 inches

Wrist—6 inches

Length of cap—5 inches

DRAFT OF PLAIN LONG SLEEVE

1. Draw a perpendicular line, AB, for the centre line of the sleeve.

2. Draw a line, CB, at right angles to AB, and continue B to D as in Diagram 25. This is the wristline.

3. Draw another line, EF, parallel to CD, the underarm to wrist measurement, 19 inches, from it.

4. As sleeve is to be 14 inches wide, measure 7 inches on both sides of the centre line, AB, from points B and G, on CD and EF.

5. With a rule, join EC and FD.

6. *Cap of Sleeve.*

NOTE.—

1. For any cap that fits into the armscye, add 1/2 an inch in depth to the original depth of cap, to allow for fit over the shoulder.

2. It is very essential that all caps of sleeves, except those cut on the bias, be deep enough so that the grain of the material runs straight around the upperarm, and wide enough so the armscye is not drawn from its true position.

From G on BA measure 5 1/2 inches for depth of cap.

7. Construction lines to facilitate the drawing of the curves for the cap.

(*a*) Join EA and FA.

(*b*) Divide GF at H and GE at I, and draw IJ and HK parallel to the centre line, BA.

8. The lower part of the cap of the sleeve fits into the armscye; therefore, for an average figure, the curve for both the front and back of the cap may be the same as the curve for the back armscye of the waist. This curve may be traced. Then make a good swinging curve for cap as in Diagram 25, the curve extending a little beyond the points, J and K.

NOTE.—

1. It isn't always necessary to add fullness at the back of the cap, especially for small women and children, but it is

always well for a larger figure, then the back should extend 1/4 to 1/2 an inch beyond the front.

2. The cap should not be flat at the top.

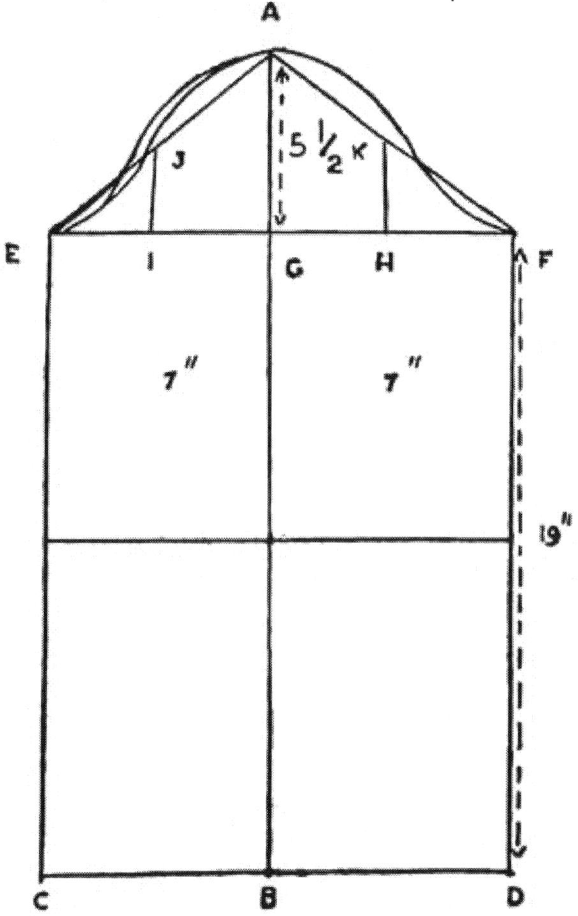

DIAGRAM 25

9. The above is a plain long sleeve, and if a cuff or band is desired, allow 1/2 an inch for puff of sleeve at the wrist, after width of cuff or band has been deducted.

For example, if the underarm sleeve length is 19 inches, and a 2-inch cuff is desired, the actual sleeve measurement would be 17 1/2 inches plus the 2 inches for the cuff.

10. If an opening is desired at the wrist, divide the back half of the sleeve into 1/3s, and place the opening 1/3 from the centre line.

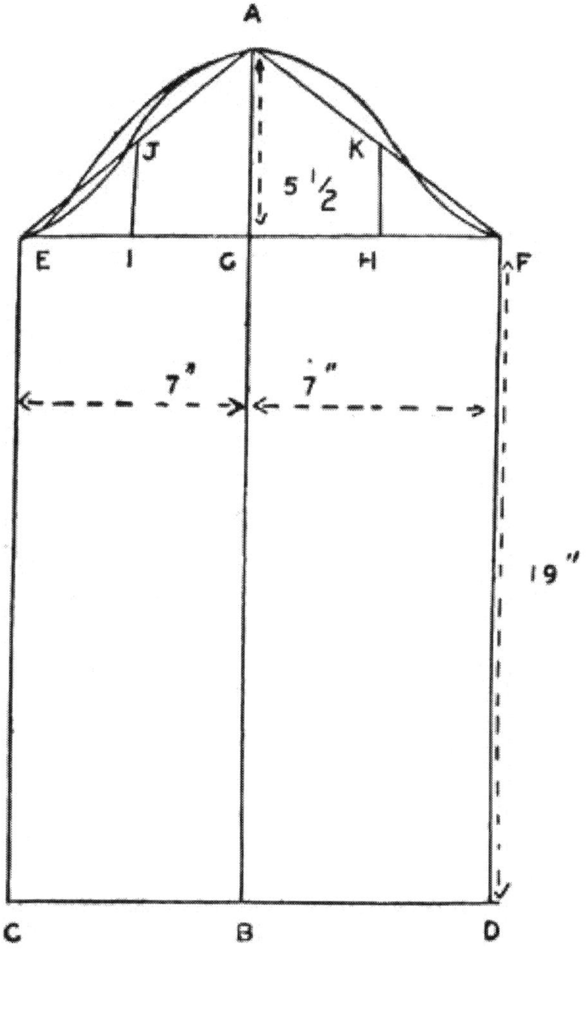

DIAGRAM 26

47

FORMULA FOR PLAIN LONG SLEEVE

Follow Diagram 26.

1. Draw a perpendicular line, AB, for the centre line of sleeve.

2. Draw a line, CD, at right angles to the centre line, for the wrist.

3. Draw another line, EF, at right angles to the centre line, at a distance of the underarm to wrist measurement from the wrist line.

4. On both sides of the centre line, on the wrist and underarm to underarm lines, mark 1/2 the width of the sleeve.

5. Join the underarm seams with rule.

6. *Cap of sleeve.*

NOTE.—

1. The cap of the sleeve is that part of the sleeve above the straight line, drawn from one underarm to another.

2. For any cap that fits into the armscye, add 1/2 inch in depth to the original depth of cap, to allow for fit over the shoulder.

3. It is very essential that all caps of sleeves, except those cut on the bias, be deep enough so that the grain of the material runs straight around the upperarm, and wide

enough so that the armscye is not drawn from its true position.

Continue the centre line above the line marking the underarm to underarm, EF, for the depth of cap plus 1/2 an inch.

7. Construction lines to aid in drawing the curves for the cap.

(*a*) Join EA and FA.

(*b*) Divide GF at H and GE at I, and draw IJ and HK parallel to the centre line, BA.

8. The lower part of the cap of the sleeve fits into the armscye; therefore, for an average figure, the curve for both the front and back of the cap may be the same as the curve for the back armscye of the waist. This curve may be traced. Then make a good swinging curve for the cap as in Diagram 26, the curve extending a little beyond the points, J and K.

NOTE.—

1. It isn't always necessary to add fullness at the back of the cap, especially for small women and children, but it is always well for a larger figure, then the back should extend 1/4 to 1/2 an inch beyond the front.

2. The cap should not be flat at the top.

9. This is a plain long sleeve, and if a cuff or band is desired, allow 1/2 an inch for puff of sleeve at the wrist, after width of cuff or band has been deducted.

10. If an opening is desired at the wrist, divide the back half of the sleeve into 1/3s, and place the opening 1/3 from the centre line.

LONG PLAIN SLEEVE WITH SLIGHT SHAPING AT THE SEAM AND WRIST

Follow Diagram 27.

It is better if the sleeve seam is shaped a little at the upper part of the arm. This is not necessary for a wide plain sleeve, 3 or 4 inches wider than the actual upperarm measurement.

This sleeve is constructed the same as the first plain long sleeve, with the exception of the seam line, which is shaped into the underarm elbow crease and the wristline, thus giving a better fitting sleeve.

1–8. Follow the directions for long plain sleeve, 1–8.

9. Draw a line, LM, 9 inches below EF, the underarm to elbow measurement, and parallel to it.

10. At points L and M on the line, LM, measure 1/2 an inch in toward the centre and mark points, O and N. Join EOC and FND, the new sleeve seams.

NOTE.—More may be fitted out if desired, but at least the bent elbow measurement plus 1 inch must be allowed at the elbow crease.

11. *Wrist.*—Draw a construction line 1 inch above and parallel to CD. (See Diagram 27.) Divide the wristline, CD, into 1/4s at T and S, and draw the new wristline as follows: 1/2 an inch up from D, to 1 inch up at S, to 1/4 inch up at B, on the line at T, and 1/2 an inch up at C.

This gives a back extension at the wrist to allow for the bend of the elbow.

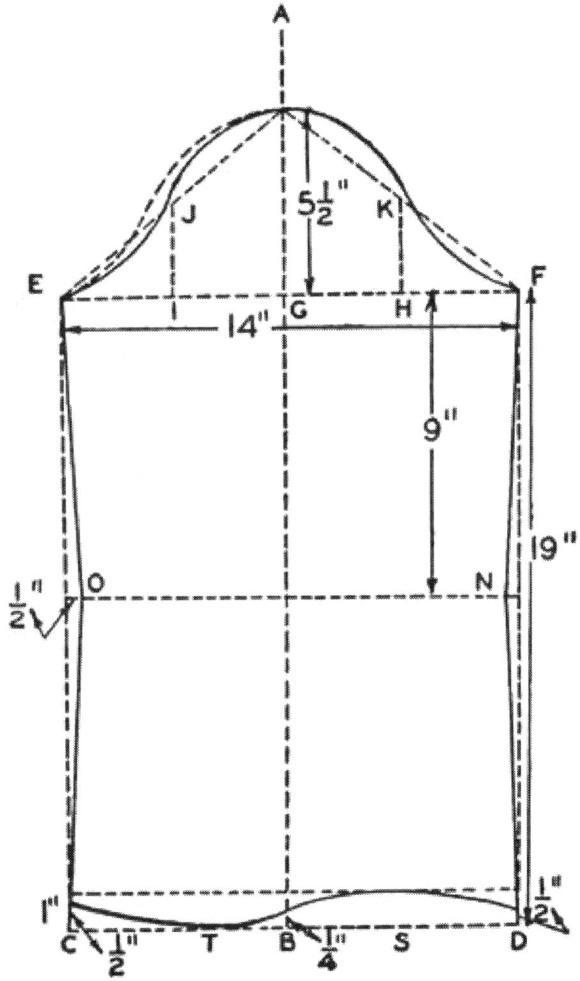

DIAGRAM 27

FORMULA OF LONG PLAIN SLEEVE WITH SHAPING AT THE SEAM AND WRIST

1–8. Follow the formula for long plain sleeves from 1–8.

9. Draw a line parallel to the underarm to underarm line, at a distance of the underarm to elbow measurement from it, and mark it LM.10. At points L and M on the line, LM, measure 1/2 an inch in toward the centre and mark points, O and N. Join EOC and FND, the new sleeve seams.

NOTE.—More may be fitted out if desired, but at least the bent elbow measurement plus 1 inch must be allowed at the elbow crease.

11. *Wrist.*—Draw a construction line 1 inch above and parallel to CD. Divide the wristline, CD, into 1/4s at T and S, and draw the new wristline as follows: 1/2 an inch up from D, to 1 inch up at S, to 1/4 inch up at B, on the line at T, and 1/2 an inch up at C.

This gives a back extension at the wrist to allow for the bend of the elbow.

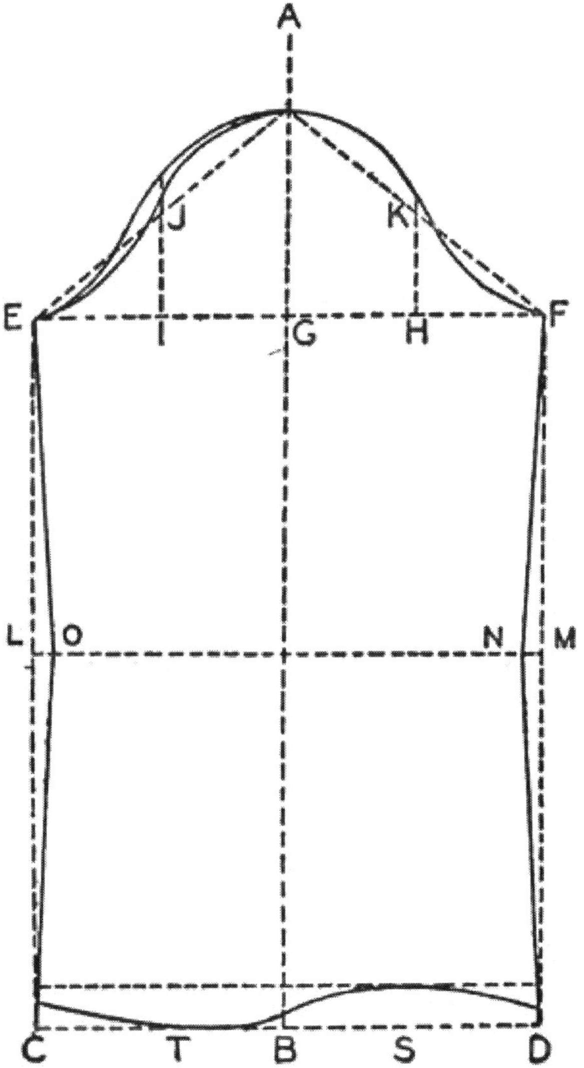

DIAGRAM 27A

DRAFT OF PLAIN LONG SLEEVE OR COAT SLEEVE

(Fitted slightly tighter along the seam and at the wrist.)

Measurements

Underarm to wrist—19 inches

Underarm to elbow—9 inches

Sleeve width at the upperarm—14 inches

Width at the wrist—11 inches

Depth of cap—5 inches plus 1/2 inch

Follow Diagram 28.

1–9. Follow draft for plain sleeve with slight shaping at the seam and wrist.

10. From points L and M, mark N and O, 1 inch in toward the centre.

NOTE.—It is not advisable to shape the sleeve more than 1 inch at the elbow crease for an average sleeve.

11. On the wristline, CD, from the centre point, B, measure 5 1/2 inches, 1/2 the desired wrist measurement, and mark points Q and P.

12. Join EOP and FNQ for the underarm sleeve seams.

13. Curve *at the wrist*.

(*a*) Measure from F on the line, FQ, the total underarm measurement, 19 inches, and place point, R. This will be approximately 1/2 an inch up from Q.

(*b*) Bisect BQ at S and BP at T. Measure up from S 3/4 of an inch; from B, 1/4 of an inch—T remains on the line—and up from P, the same distance as Q to R.

Swing the curve for wrist through these points. This gives a back extension at the wrist.

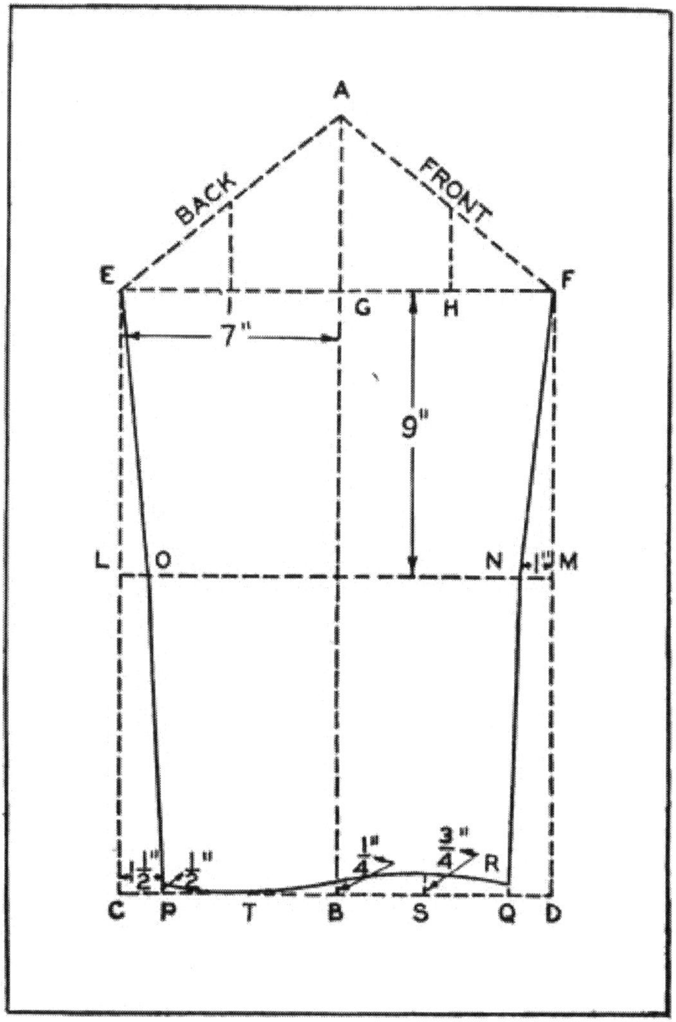

DIAGRAM 28

DIAGRAM 29

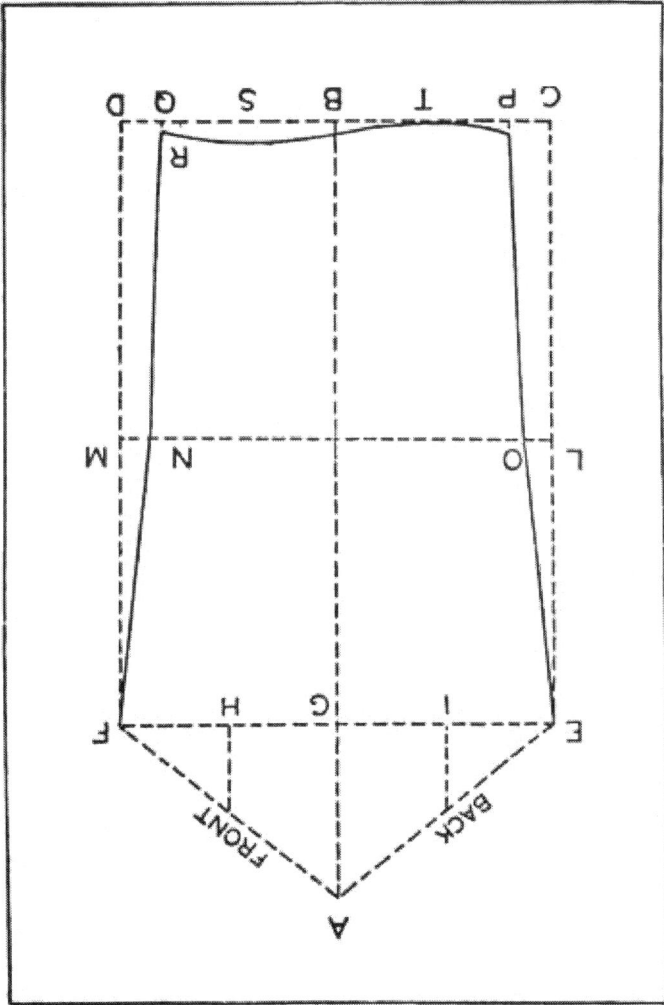

FORMULA FOR PLAIN LONG SLEEVE OR COAT SLEEVE

(Fitted slightly tighter along the seam and at the wrist.)

Follow Diagram 29.

Before starting to draft the sleeve, using the tape measure, decide the width of the sleeve around the upperarm, also the width at the wrist. If remodelling, this depends upon the amount of material one has on hand, as well as texture of material, style, etc.

1–9. Follow formula for plain long sleeve with slight shaping at the seam and wrist.

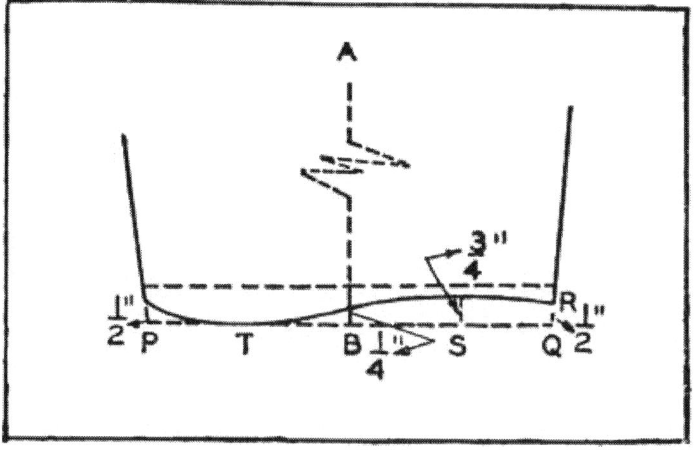

DIAGRAM 30

10. On both sides of the seam at the elbow line, measure 1 inch in towards the centre.

NOTE.—It is not advisable to shape the sleeve more than 1 inch at the elbow crease for an average one-piece sleeve.

11. From the centre of the wristline, measure 1/2 the width of the desired wrist measurement, on both sides.

12. Join the underarm sleeve seams, curving the line out slightly from elbow to wrist.

13. *Curve at the wrist.*

(*a*) From the top of the underarm seams, measure the total underarm sleeve length. Mark the points. They will be approximately 1/2 an inch above the present wristline.

(*b*) Divide the new wristline into 1/4s. Swing the curve for wrist, as shown in Diagram 30. This gives a back extension at the wrist.

DRAFT OF TAILORED SLEEVE WITH DART AT THE WRIST

Measurements
Sleeve width at the upperarm—14 inches
Sleeve width at the wrist—8 inches
1–13. Follow the draft of coat sleeve from 1–13.
14. *To make the wrist dart.*

(*a*) From the centre of the elbow line, ON, measure 1/3 of the distance from the centre line on the back portion of the sleeve. One-third of 6 inches equals 2 inches from the centre line; and mark point V.

Follow Diagram 31.

(*a*) Point T bisects the back half of wristline. Rule a line, VT, for one side of dart.

(*c*) The total desired wrist measurement is 8 inches. P to T is 2 3/4 inches wide; therefore, to make the wrist 8 inches wide, there must be 5 1/4 inches from Q to the other point of dart. Measure 5 1/4 inches from Q and mark W. The dart will be 3 inches wide, the difference between the desired 8 inches for the wrist and the 11 inches as before.

Rule the line, VW, for the second line of dart. The dart lines may curve slightly inward if necessary for full forearm.

FORMULA FOR TAILORED SLEEVE WITH DART AT THE WRIST

Follow Diagram 32.

Before drafting a tailored sleeve with dart at the wrist, measure with the tape to find the necessary width of the sleeve at the upperarm and at the wrist. There must be at least 1 inch difference in the two measurements.

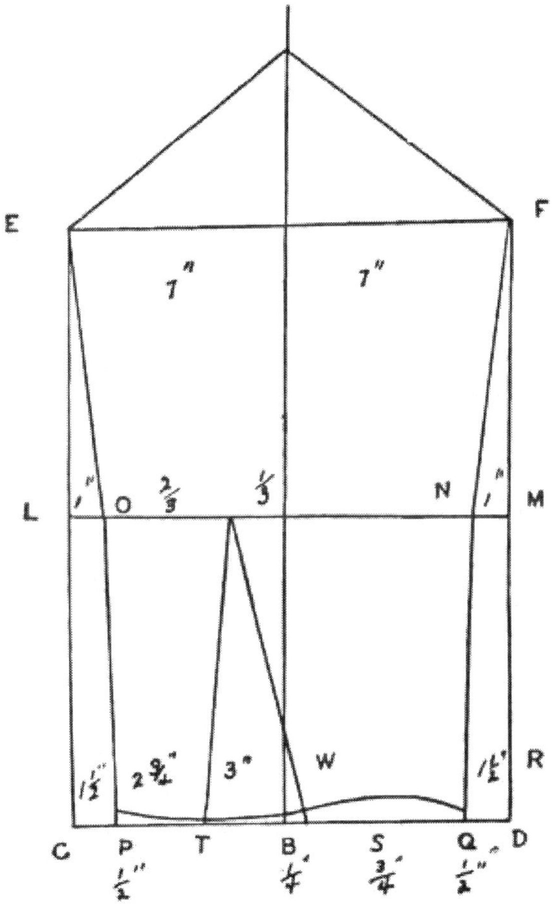

DIAGRAM 31

1–13. Follow formula for coat sleeve, 1–13.

14. *To make the wrist dart.*

(*a*) From the centre of the elbow line, and on the back half of the sleeve, mark in 1/3 of the width from the centre line to the underarm seam.

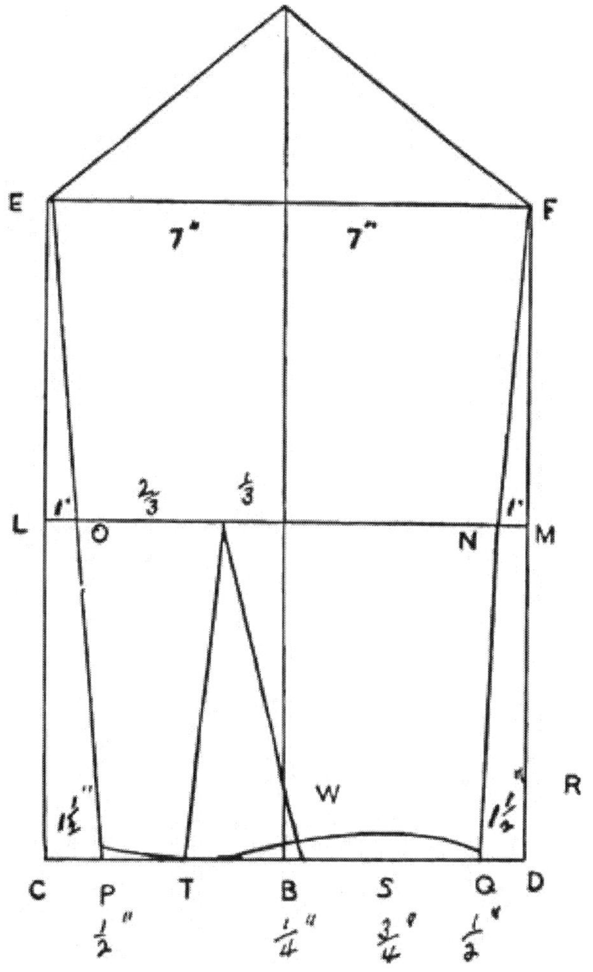

DIAGRAM 32

(*b*) Rule a line from this point, V, to the point T, which bisects the back half of the sleeve at the wrist.

(*c*) Subtract the desired wrist measurement from the width of the sleeve at the wrist. This gives the width of the

dart at the wrist. Mark the other point for the dart at the wrist, W, and rule the other side of the dart.

NOTE.—

1. The lines for the dart may curve slightly in, if it is necessary, giving more room for the forearm.

2. A two-piece sleeve may be drafted by continuing the dart line to the top of the cap.

DRAFT OF FITTED SLEEVE WITH DART AT THE ELBOW

Follow Diagram 33.

1–12. Follow draft of coat sleeve from 1–12.

13. From Q on wristline, QBP, measure 8 inches, the desired width of sleeve, and place point X. Rule a line from O to X, or slightly curve for full forearm. This is the back sleeve seam.

14. Cut out the cap, and front and back seam lines, EOX and FNQ.

15. Measure OX and NQ and make a dart at O, so that OX equals NQ.

16. Fold the two seam lines together and recut the back seam line to match the front seam line.

17. Mark the new centre fold.

18. *Curve at the wrist.*—Reshape the curve with a slight upward curve of about 1/2 an inch in the centre of the front half, and a gradual downward slope to the back.

FORMULA FOR FITTED SLEEVE WITH DART AT THE ELBOW

Follow Diagram 34.

1–12. Follow formula for coat sleeve from 1–12.

13. From the front sleeve seam at the wrist, Q, measure the desired width of the sleeve at the wrist, and mark the point X. Rule a straight line or draw a slightly curved line, if necessary, from O to X. This is the back sleeve seam.

14. Cut out the cap and front and back sleeve seam lines.

15. Measure the two sleeve seam lines from elbow to wrist, and on the back seam at the elbow, make a dart so that the two seams from elbow to wrist are the same length.

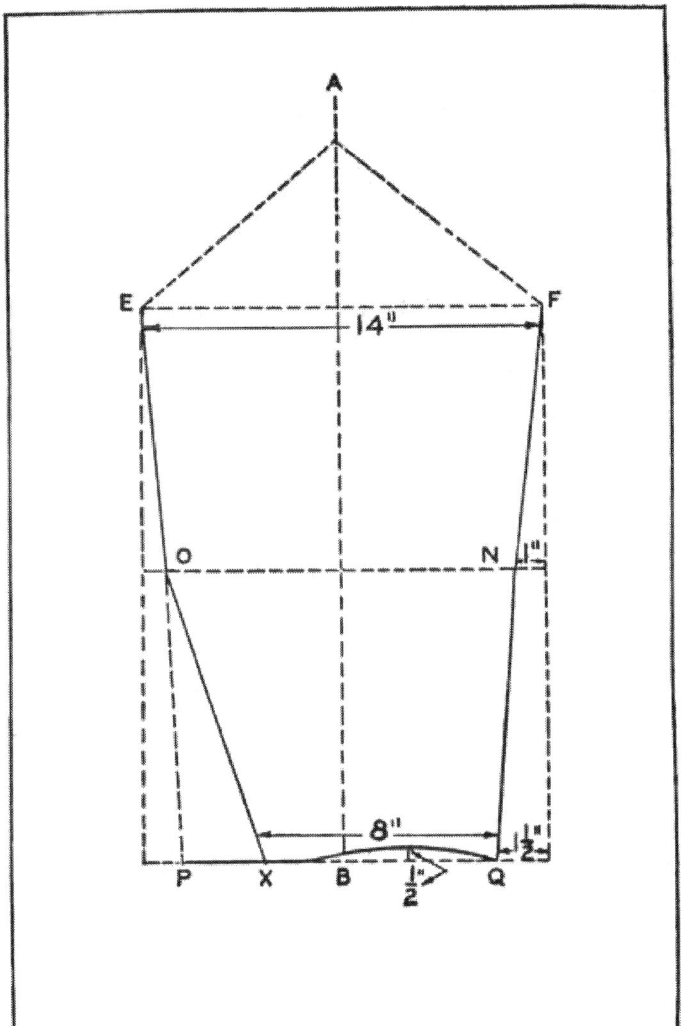

DIAGRAM 33

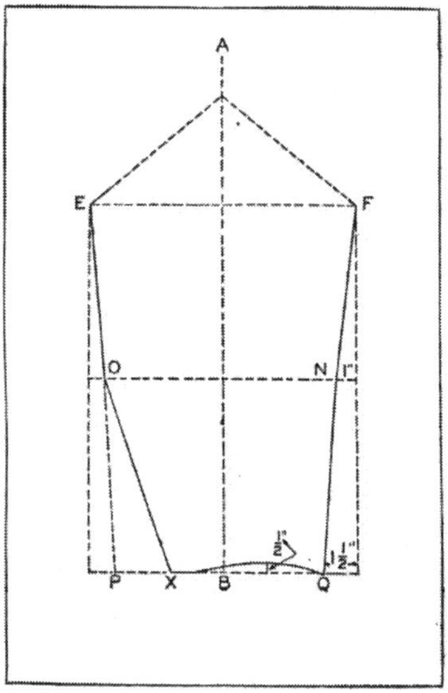

DIAGRAM 34

16. Fold the two seams together and recut the back seam line to match the front seam line.

17. Mark the new centre fold.

18. *Curve at the wrist.*—Reshape the wristline with a slight upward curve of about 1/2 an inch in the centre of the front half, and a gradual downward slope to the back. (See Diagram 34.)

Facts to remember when drafting the tightest-fitting long sleeve.

1. At least 2 inches must be added to the upperarm measurement.

2. 1 inch must be added to the bent elbow measurement.

3. 1 inch to the wrist measurement, and

4. 1/2 an inch to the depth of the cap.

TO DEVELOP A TWO-PIECE SLEEVE FROM A FITTED SLEEVE WITH DART AT THE ELBOW

1. Pin the elbow dart.

2. Pin the sleeve seams, EOX and FNQ together.

3. Flatten the sleeve, and crease along the folds, making the two sides equidistant from the seam lines.

4. Measure in from the folded edges, as in Diagram 35, 1 1/4 to 1 1/2 inches, depending upon the width of the sleeve. Draw lines parallel to the folds or creases.

5. Cut the pattern on these lines for a two-piece sleeve.

NOTE.—If one has a fitted sleeve with dart cut in muslin or similar material, it will be easier to manipulate in order to obtain the pattern of a two-piece fitted sleeve.

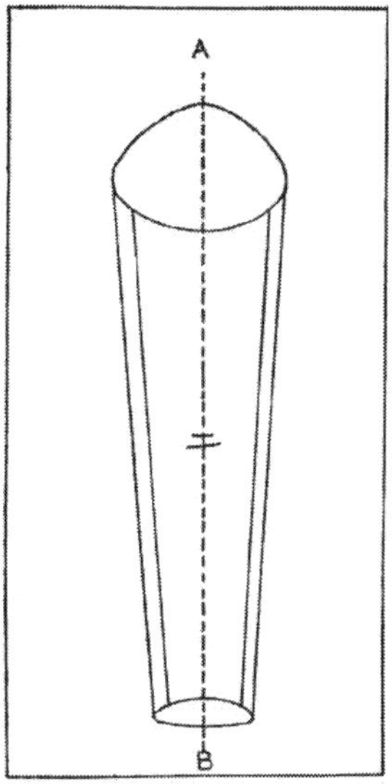

DIAGRAM 35
CAPS OF SLEEVES

It is often erroneously thought that to have a sleeve with a full cap one must have a wide sleeve, the one being analogous to the other. This, of course, is entirely false.

The type of cap of sleeve should depend upon several factors. The first of these is the need of the individual. A cap with gathers or several darts, or boxed top, can do much for narrow shoulders. Just as a cap with too much fullness broadens a figure which is already too wide, or emphasizes faults if it is too narrow.

69

It is the duty of every woman to study her form, and by means of subtle manœuvring in dress, help camouflage some of her deficiencies and make the most of her good points. One of the most important rules in good garment construction is to have a suitable sleeve which hangs straight, and a cap that is deep enough to permit the material to run straight around the arm, and wide enough so that it will not draw.

The type and amount of material is our next guide. Naturally, light, soft, fluffy material may be used with much more fullness than when using her heavier sister; and the extra width may be gathered, shirred, or pleated into the upper portion of the armscye. Darts of different numbers and sizes, as the need arises, are always good for heavier material to give that well-shaped look so essential to some of our smart suits and dresses.

The style of the garment and the occasion on which it is to be worn have also to be considered. This does not mean that a very full sleeve and cap should not be used with a tight-fitting waist. Often this has a very beautiful effect on a beautiful figure; yet one would scarcely for any occasion desire a very full waist with a tight-fitting sleeve and a fitted cap.

Dress is really a matter of common sense. Use a mirror often. Full-length mirror! Your face isn't the only part of your anatomy that needs attention.

Fitted Caps

(See note on fitted caps of sleeves, page 143.)

In the pattern drafting of a fitted cap, it was explained that 1/2 an inch was added to the actual measured depth of the cap, for ease over the tip of the shoulder. (See "Plain Long Sleeve with Fitted Cap," page 141.)

A Full Cap of Sleeve with Light, Soft Material

(To be gathered or shirred at the top.)

For a full cap of light, soft material to be gathered or shirred around the top of the armscye, it is advisable to take the tape measure and judge the amount of extra length necessary to give the desired effect at the shoulder. (See Chapter 5 on "Measurements"—"Cap of Sleeve," page 87.)

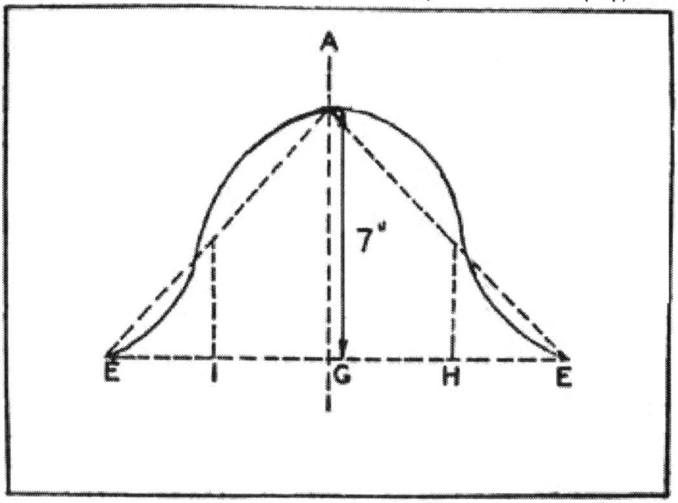

DIAGRAM 36

71

More width may be added by changing the curve of the cap and lengthening the depth. (See Diagram 37.)

It will be seen that when constructing a cap similar to a fitted cap, the width will automatically increase with the length, but if a wider one is desired, construct as in Diagram 37.

A well-fitting cap of any type should fit around the actual curve at the underarm, and the surplus width gathered or shirred around the top of the armscye.

Caps with Pleats

The length of caps of sleeves with pleats may be judged in the same manner as when the fullness is gathered or shirred. The position of the pleats depends upon individual needs, but the fullness should be fitted out at the upper part of the armscye. The depth of a cap with pleats should be the necessary length of the fitted cap, plus the width desired at the shoulder. Watch the grain of the material.

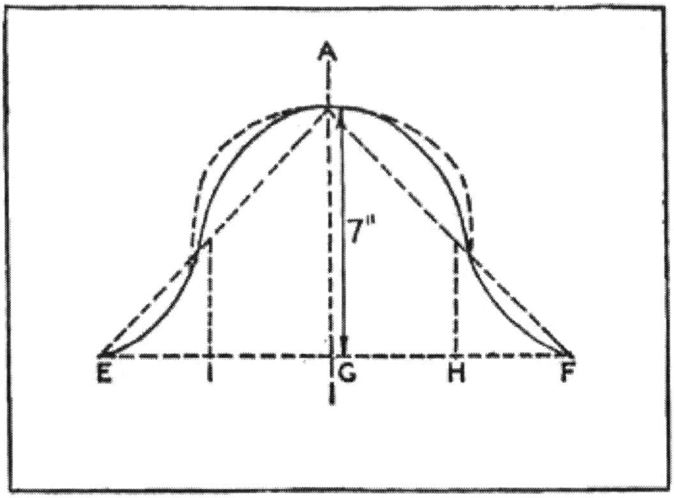

DIAGRAM 37

Caps with Darts

Darts are to give a broadening effect and should not droop below the tip of the shoulder; therefore there should be the measured depth of cap before the shoulder darts begin. In other words, when judging the necessary depth of the cap, add the extra width desired at the shoulder to the depth of a fitted cap. (See Diagram 38.)

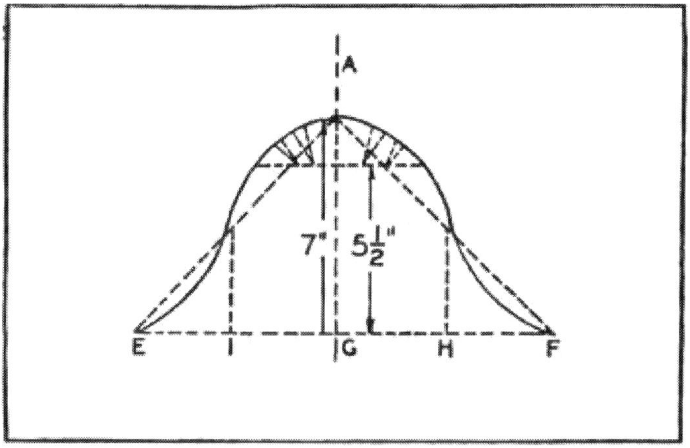

DIAGRAM 38

NOTE.—The number of darts depends upon the needs of the individual, and the amount of fullness to take out. The darts must be even on both sides of the shoulder seam. Several small darts are better than fewer wider ones.

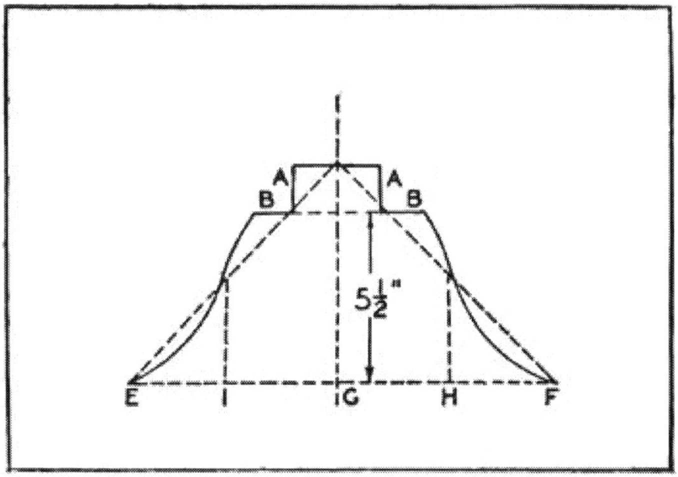

DIAGRAM 39

Caps with a Boxed Top

Caps with a boxed top are constructed the same as the cap with darts, except the fullness at the top is either darted out or cut out to form a square or rectangle at the shoulder to give a boxed effect. It will be seen that the length is again added to the depth of the fitted cap, and the width at the shoulder may vary with need. (See Diagram 39.)

NOTE.—If the box is made by cutting out the top, notice how A and B are equal in length, also don't forget to allow for seams.

OTHER TYPES OF SLEEVES

In the preceding pages only long plain sleeves were drafted. Short, puff, flared, bishop sleeves may all be considered in a similar manner, and with or without shaping at the seam. At first, it is necessary to consider some of the attributes of each.

Short Sleeves

Short sleeves may be many lengths and widths, depending upon individual needs, the kind of material, the amount of material on hand, and the purpose of the garment. They may also be made with or without cuffs or bands.

The length and width of a short sleeve is very important. For a slender person it should not be too tight nor too short. This would emphasize her long thin arm. A stout person usually has a large upperarm. It is better that her sleeve does not fit too closely and is long enough to cover the full part of the upperarm. A 3/4-length sleeve is really better for such a type.

A short, action sleeve is generous in width, about 3 inches more than the upperarm measurement, but not too wide for good styling.

How to Draft Short Sleeves

Measure the necessary or desired width and length for short sleeves and draft as for the upper part of plain long

sleeves. They may or may not be shaped at the underarm seam, and when they are shaped, there shouldn't be too much fullness taken out at the seam. It is well to remember that a short straight sleeve, like a long sleeve, must have at least 2 inches added to the upperarm measurement for width. Cuffs and bands may be used if desired, and the extra fullness gathered into the cuff or band.

The bottom of a straight short sleeve is a straight line, and the cap may be shaped the same as for any long sleeve, the style depending upon the material and the need of the garment and the individual.

A straight sleeve, a little below the elbow in length, can do much to aid in hiding a full upperarm. This should not be flared toward the bottom. It adds width.

Flared Sleeves

Should be chosen with care.

Puff Sleeves

Puff sleeves, as the name implies, are short and wide. Obviously, their choice is limited. Again use the tape measure. For an average puff sleeve, half the width of the upperarm may be added for the width, or twice the upperarm measurement may be used.

If it is desired to have some of the fullness thrown to the lower part of the sleeve, when gathered into a band, the line at the bottom of the sleeve should be curved, the width of the curve depending upon the fullness desired.

Bishop Sleeve

A bishop sleeve is a plain sleeve with a flare toward the bottom and the fullness gathered into a band.

SKIRTS

There are five essentials of a well-fitting skirt. It should allow for freedom of movement; it should have sufficient fullness to allow for comfortable sitting; the style should be suited to the purpose and the material of which it is made; the threads of the material should run correctly; and the hem line should hang evenly.

Every skirt, no matter what style, should have added fullness at the hipline. This amount varies according to the style of the garment, but the slimmer the lines, the greater the amount added to permit ease over the thighline. At least from 2 to 4 inches are added, according to the type of skirt and the need of the individual. If hips and thighs are very large, more may even be necessary. Four inches should be added to the hip measurement when making a straight skirt. The fullness added at the hip in a flared skirt depends upon the amount of flare added from hip to hem. Some flared skirts may fit snugly around the hips, but, even then, there must be 2 inches more than the actual hip measurement. There must be sufficient spread so the skirt does not draw up when sitting. Often a skirt will appear to fit like a glove

when standing, but the fit will be absolutely ruined when sitting down. Any garment must be considered in the light of moving, standing and sitting. If four and six-gored skirts are cut on slim lines, 2 inches should be added to the hipline, although inverted pleats at the back and front of the skirt will help to ease the tight lines.

The waist for any skirt must be small enough to fit the figure. This does not mean that the actual skirt itself should be exactly the waist measurement. Even in a close-fitting skirt, it is necessary to allow a little more to be eased into a belt, etc., just as was necessary for an upper garment; 2 inches is the average amount, but this depends upon individual needs. Often fullness is gathered into a band at a certain place for effect.

A TWO-PIECE STRAIGHT SKIRT DRAFTED FROM MEASUREMENTS TAKEN FROM CHART

Measurements
Waist—26 inches.
Hip—36 inches.
Length, centre front—26 inches.
Length, side—26 1/2 inches.
Length, back—26 1/2 inches.
Waist to hip, centre front—8 inches, therefore

Waist to hip, centre back—8 1/2 inches.

Follow Diagram 40.

1. Draw a perpendicular line, AB, for the centre front.

2. Draw AC at right angles to AB for the waistline.

3. On AB from A measure 26 1/2 inches, the length of the skirt at the side.

4. The hip measurement is 36 inches, plus 4 inches to be added, equals 40 inches for the width around the hips. A quarter of 40 inches equals 10 inches. On AC from A measure 10 inches, and mark C, then draw CD parallel to AB for the side seam.

5. The side, waist to hip measurement is 8 1/2 inches. Draw a line EF parallel to AC and 8 1/2 inches below it, for the hipline.

6. The shaping of the side seam from waist to hip depends upon figure requirements. (See Chapter 7 on "Darts" and read "Vertical Waist Darts.") The actual waist measurement is 26 inches, plus 2 inches for ease, is 28 inches, that is 7 inches for half the front; therefore 3 inches is to be fitted out from the waist to the hips.

7. The figure is generally flatter in the front than at the sides or back. Smaller darts for the front will place the seam on a line with the shoulder seam.

It is advisable to mark temporary side darts, a little over 1 1/2 inches wide, to be changed, if necessary, in the fitting.

Shape the side seam and draw a vertical dart.

8. Measure down from A on AB, the centre front, 1/2 an inch, the difference between the side waist to hip measurement, and the front waist to hip measurement. Mark G and draw the curve for the waist.

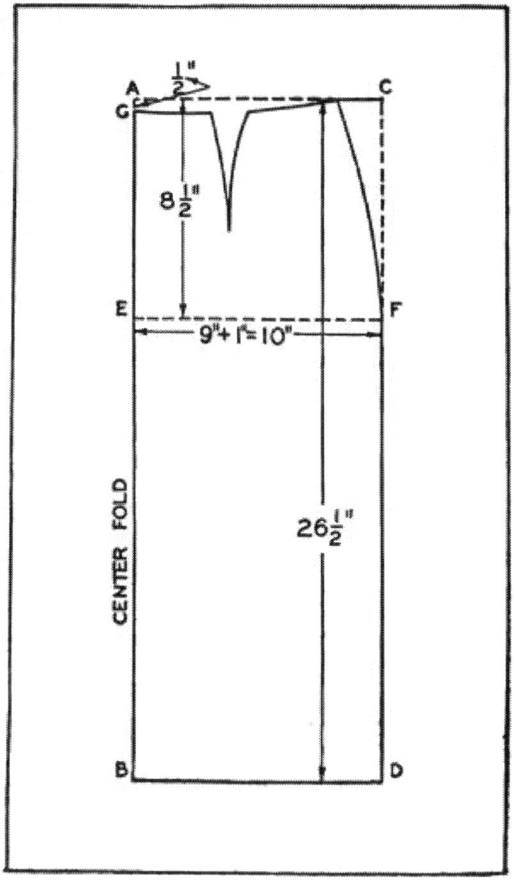

DIAGRAM 40

81

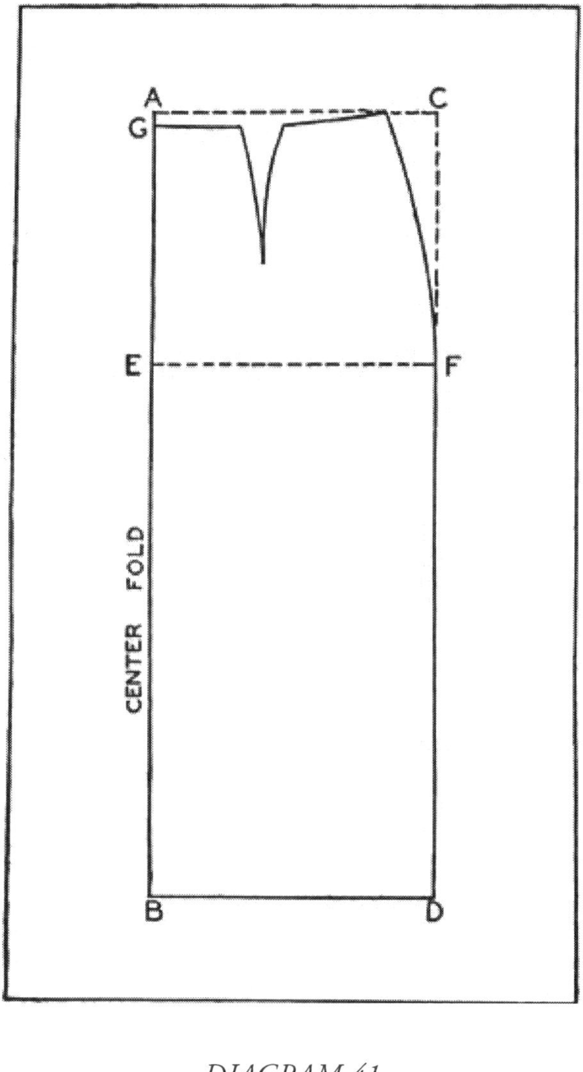

DIAGRAM 41

Pattern Drafting and Foundation and Flat Pattern Design

FORMULA FOR FRONT OF STRAIGHT SKIRT

Follow Diagram 41.

1. Draw a perpendicular line AB for the centre front or fold.

2. Draw a line AC at right angles to AB for the waistline.

3. From the waistline, AC, measure the side length of the skirt, and draw a line parallel to the waist for the bottom of the skirt.

4. To the hip measurement add 4 inches, the necessary extra width for ease. One-quarter of this is the required width for draft.

On the waistline, AC, mark this width from the centre front, and draw a line parallel to the centre front for the side seam.

5. Draw a line EF, parallel to the waistline, AC, the side waist to hip measurement from it.

6. The shaping of the side seam from waist to hip depends upon figure requirements. (See Chapter 7 on "Darts" and read "Vertical Waist Darts.")

Find the amount to be fitted out from waist to hips, allowing ease at the waist.

7. The figure is flatter at the front than at the sides or back. It is advisable to mark temporary side darts, a little over half the amount to be fitted out, at the side seam, this to be changed, if necessary, in the fitting.

Shape the side seam and draw a vertical waist dart.

8. Measure down from A on AB, the centre front, the difference between the side waist to hip measurement, and the front waist to hip measurement. Mark G and draw the curve for the waist.

9. Allow 1/2 an inch seams.

NOTE.—AB marks the centre fold of the material and also the lengthwise grain, and EF the crosswise grain.

TO DRAFT THE BACK OF STRAIGHT SKIRT

The back of a straight skirt is drafted the same as the front with the exception of—

1. The back length of the skirt is used instead of the side length as in number 3.

2. The back waist to hip measurement is used in number 5.

3. The curve at the waist will probably differ.

4. The back vertical darts may be wider than the front vertical darts, but the side seams are the same shape.

(See Diagram 42.)

FORMULA FOR BACK OF PLAIN SKIRT

The back of a *straight skirt* is drafted the same as the front with the exception of—

1. The back length of the skirt is used instead of the side length as in number 3.

2. The back waist to hip measurement is used in number 5.

3. The curve at the waist will probably differ.

4. The back vertical darts may be wider than the front vertical darts.

STRAIGHT SKIRT WITH GORED SIDE SEAMS

Follow Diagram 43.

To obtain a slightly more fitted effect, and extra width at the bottom, the vertical hip dart at the side seam from waist to hip may be continued and flared below the hip. The grain still remains straight around the hips, but the bottom of the skirt will require shaping, and only 2 inches will be necessary for hip allowance.

GORED SKIRTS

Gored skirts may be of many numbers of gores—2, 3, 4, 6, 8, 10—depending upon the desired effect and width of flare at the bottom. A gored skirt may or may not fit closely around the hips. Two inches again should be added to the hip measurement. One may consider that the narrower the skirt and the fewer the gores, the more width is added to the hip measurement.

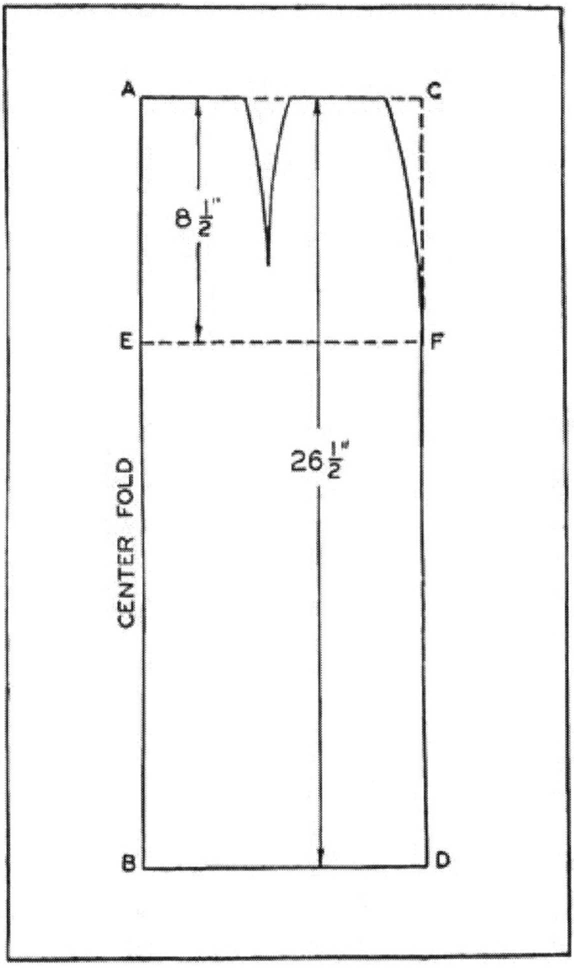

DIAGRAM 42

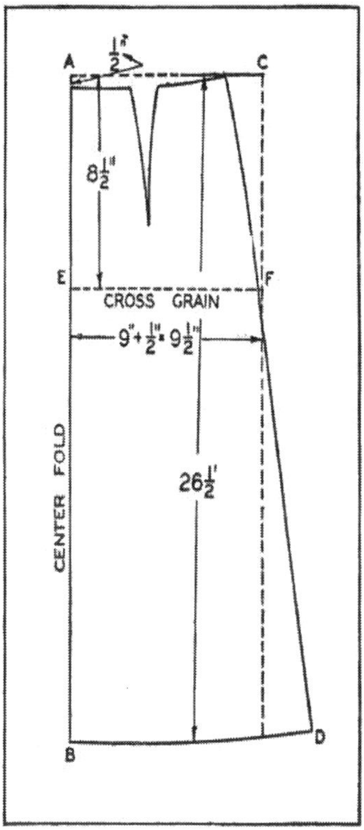

DIAGRAM 43

The seam lines of a gored skirt are really a continuation of the vertical hip darts. These may be ruled lines extending from the hip to the bottom of the skirt, or they may extend from a full curve at the hip to a slanting line toward the bottom, depending upon the fullness desired, and the amount of material on hand.

In gored skirts, the greater part of the grain runs straight around the hips; the greater the slant at the seams,

the greater the drop, hence there is more of the hipline on the crosswise grain in a skirt with many gores.

(Read about "Grains" in Chapter 6.)

TWO-PIECE GORED SKIRT

In a two-piece gored skirt, the grain of the material is straight across the centre front and back and drops at the sides, or it may be straight at the side seams and bias at the front and back. This is sometimes the case with striped or plaid material.

Often extra fullness is added, especially with fine textured material, by widening the gores, and either pleating or gathering the fullness to fit from the hips to the waist, or just in certain places at the waist.

DRAFT OF A TWO-PIECE GORED SKIRT WITH SIDE SEAMS

Measurements

Follow Diagram 44.

Waist—26 inches, to which are added 2 inches for ease—total, 28 inches.

Hip—36 inches, to which 2 inches are added for ease—total, 38 inches.

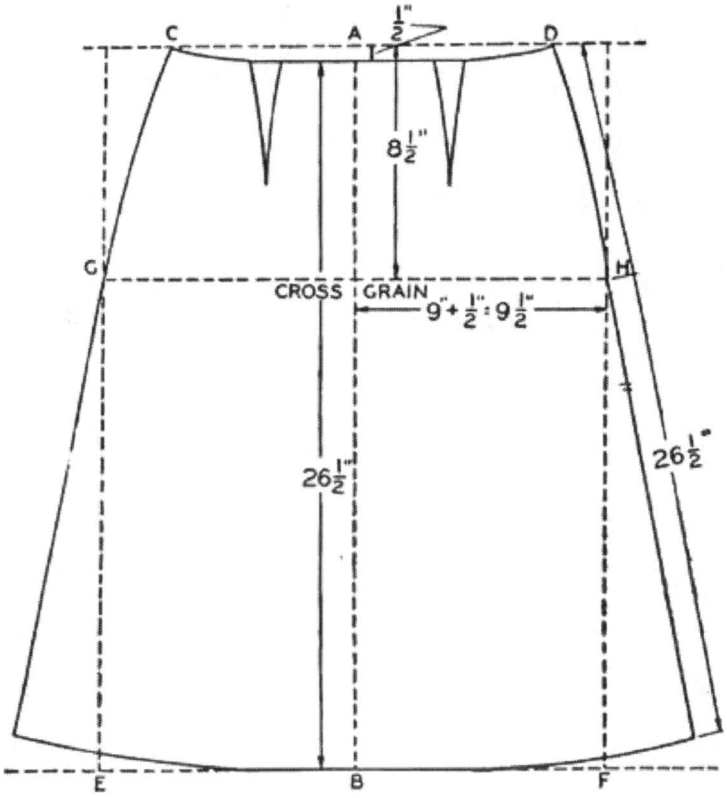

DIAGRAM 44

Length, centre front—26 inches.

Length, side—26 1/2 inches.

Length, back—26 1/2 inches.

Waist to hip, centre front—8 inches.

Waist to hip, side—8 1/2 inches.

Waist to hip, back—8 1/2 inches.

Front Gore

1. Draw a perpendicular line, AB, for the centre line or fold of the front gore.

NOTE.—This marks the lengthwise grain of the material.

2. Draw CD at right angles to AB for the waistline.

3. From A on AB, measure 8 1/2 inches, the side waist to hip measurement, and draw GH parallel to CD.

4. From A on AB measure 26 1/2 inches, the side length of the skirt, and draw EF parallel to CD.

5. The hip measurement is 38 inches, therefore half the hip measurement is 19 inches, 9 1/2 inches on each side of the centre line. Mark G and H.

6. The necessary waist measurement is 28 inches, therefore half the waist measurement is 14 inches, 7 inches on each side of the centre line.

Seven inches from 9 1/2 inches means 2 1/2 inches to be fitted out from waist to hip on each side of the centre line.

7. Try a little over half the amount to be fitted out at the side seam, and the remainder at a front vertical dart, then adjust as necessary in the fitting.

8. From A mark the difference between the side waist to hip measurement and the front waist to hip measurement, then draw the curve for the waist.

9. Continue the curve DH, making a slanting line to suit needs and the amount of material, the side length totalling 26 1/2 inches.

10. From B to I draw a good full curve for the bottom of the skirt.

11. Fold on the centre line, and impression the other side by means of a hard pencil or tracing wheel.

12. Allow 1/2-inch seams.

13. Place AB on the lengthwise fold of the material when cutting.

BACK OF TWO-PIECE GORED SKIRT WITH SIDE SEAMS

The back of a two-piece gored skirt is drafted the same as the front with the exception of—

1. The back length is used instead of the side length.

2. The curve at the waist will differ.

3. The back vertical waist darts may be wider than the front.

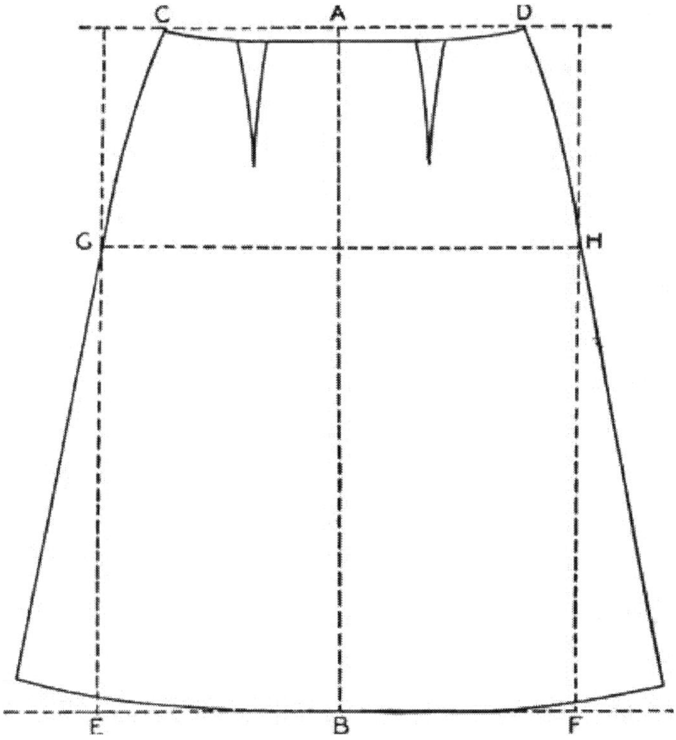

DIAGRAM 45

FORMULA FOR TWO-PIECE GORED SKIRT

(Front Gore.)

1. Draw a perpendicular line, AB, for the centre line or fold of the front gore.

NOTE.—This marks the lengthwise grain of the material.

2. Draw CD at right angles to AB for the waistline.

3. From A on AB measure the side length of the skirt and draw EF parallel to CD.

4. From A on AB measure the side waist to hip measurement, and draw GH parallel to CD.

5. Mark half the required hip measurement on each side of the centre line, at G and H.

6. The difference between the required hip measurement and the required waist measurement gives the amount to be fitted out from waist to hips.

NOTE.—Try a little over half to be fitted out at the side seam and the remainder at a front vertical dart, then adjust as necessary in the fitting.

7. From A on AB mark the difference between the side waist to hip measurement and the front waist to hip measurement, then draw the curve for the waist.

8. Continue the curve DH, making a slanting line to suit needs and the amount of material, and mark I at the side length of the skirt.

9. From B to I draw a good full curve for the bottom of the skirt.

10. Fold on the centre line, and impression the other side by means of a hard pencil or tracing wheel.

11. Allow 1/2-inch seams.

12. Place AB on the lengthwise fold when cutting.

FORMULA FOR BACK OF TWO-PIECE GORED SKIRT

The back of a two-piece gored skirt is the same as the front with the exception of—

1. The back length is used instead of the side length.

2. The curve at the waist will differ.

3. The back vertical waist darts may be wider than the front vertical darts.

THREE-GORED SKIRT

A three-piece gored skirt may be drafted the same as a two-piece gored skirt having side seams, with either the side seams or the centre folds cut on the lengthwise grain of

the material, and generally the front gore cut in two parts depending upon the effect desired.

FOUR-GORED SKIRT

A four-gored skirt is really more satisfactory than a two-or three-gored skirt, and if planned and cut carefully will not use any more material. A not-too-slim, four-gored skirt for an average figure can be made from 7/8 yard of 54-inch material.

A four-gored skirt may be drafted in two ways:

(*a*) Seams at the centre front, centre back and at the sides.

(*b*) The vertical hip darts at the side front and the side back extended into seam lines.

The difference in the two is that the flares, if made slightly full, come in different places; but in both, the grain drops towards the seams.

FOUR-GORED SKIRT WITH SEAMS AT CENTRE FRONT, CENTRE BACK AND SIDES FROM GIVEN MEASUREMENTS

Measurements

Waist—26 inches, to which are added 2 inches for ease—total, 28 inches.

Hip—36 inches, to which 2 inches are added for ease—total, 38 inches.

Length, centre front—26 inches.

Length, side—26 1/2 inches.

Length, back—26 1/2 inches.

Waist to hip, centre front—8 inches.

Waist to hip, side—8 1/2 inches.

Waist to hip, back—8 1/2 inches.

Follow Diagram 46, which represents half the front elevation or one of the front gores.

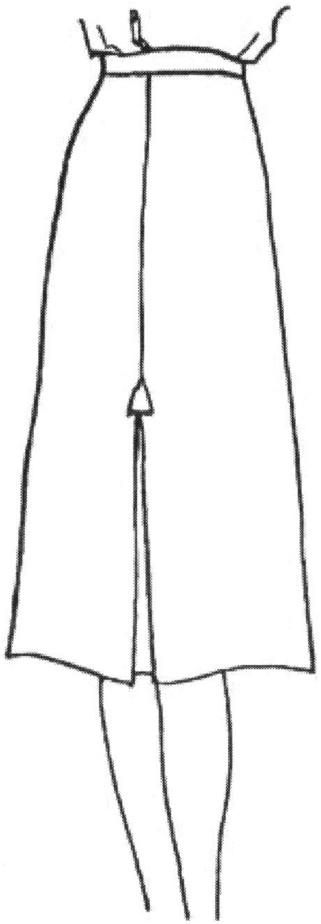

ILLUSTRATION 15

1. Draw a perpendicular line, AB, for the centre line of one of the front gores.

NOTE.—This marks the lengthwise grain of the material.

2. Draw CD at right angles to AB for the waistline.

3. From A on AB measure 26 1/2 inches, the side length of the skirt, and draw EF parallel to CD.

4. From A on AB measure 8 1/2 inches, the side waist to hip measurement, and draw GH parallel to CD.

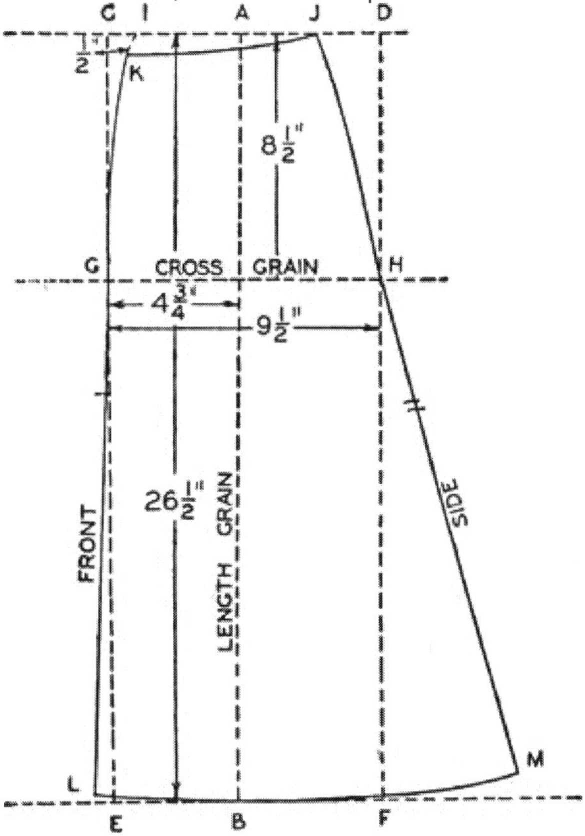

DIAGRAM 46

5. One-quarter of the necessary hip measurement is 9 1/2 inches, 43/4 inches on each side of the centre line. Mark

these points at G and H, and draw CGE and DHF parallel to AB.

6. One-quarter of the necessary waist measurement is 7 inches; 2 1/2 inches are to be fitted out from the waist. The front curve from waist to hip is only slight in comparison to the side curve from waist to hip.

Adjust the seams to meet individual needs and join I to G and J to H. Adjust the lines to suit needs and the amount of material.

7. From I on IL and from J on JM, measure 26 1/2 inches, the side length of skirt. From L to M draw a good swinging curve passing through B for the bottom of the skirt.

8. From I on the line IG, mark the difference between the side waist to hip measurement and the front waist to hip measurement, 1/2 an inch, and mark K. Draw the curve for the waist from K to J.

NOTE.—It is advisable not to cut either the front or side seams from waist to hip too closely, so any necessary adjustments may be made.

9. Allow 1/2 an inch for seams—the line AB marks the lengthwise grain of the material. Mark each gore.

10. Turn the pattern over if both gores are not cut at one time.

FORMULA FOR FOUR-GORED SKIRT

Follow Diagram 47.

Front Gore

1. Draw a perpendicular line, AB, for the centre line of one of the front gores.

NOTE.—This marks the lengthwise grain of the material.

2. Draw CD at right angles to AB for the waistline.

3. From A on AB measure the side length of skirt and draw EF parallel to CD.

4. From A on AB measure the side waist to hip measurement, and draw GH parallel to CD.

5. Mark 1/4 of the necessary hip measurement on each side of the centre line at the hip. Mark these points at G and H, and draw CGE and DHF parallel to AB.

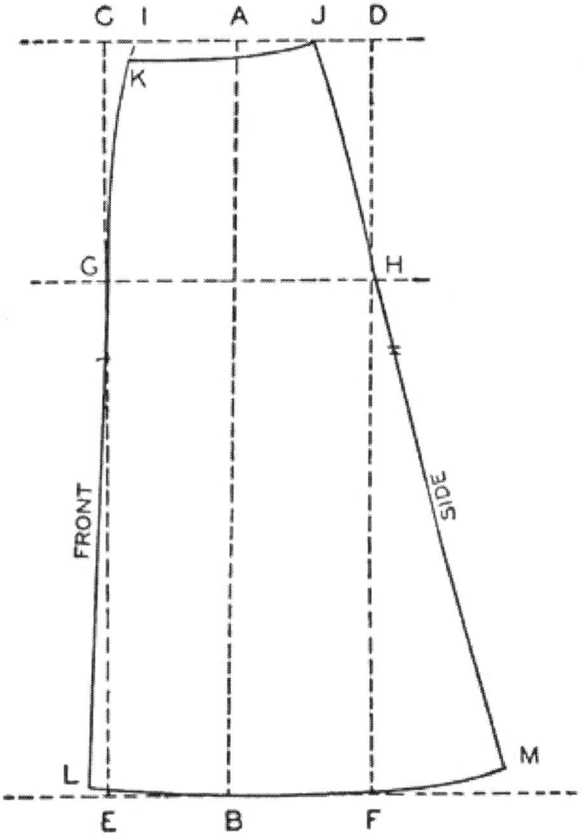

DIAGRAM 47

6. From 1/4 of the necessary waist measurement find how much has to be fitted out at the waist. The front curve from waist to hip is only slight in comparison to the side curve from waist to hip.

Adjust the seams to meet individual needs and join I to G and J to H, and continue the lines to suit needs and the amount of material.

7. From I on IL and from J on JM measure the side length of the skirt. From L to M draw a good swinging curve passing through B for the bottom of the skirt.

8. From I on the line IG, mark the difference between the side waist to hip measurement and the front waist to hip measurement, and mark K. Draw the curve for the waist from K to J.

NOTE.—It is advisable not to cut either the front or side seams from waist to hip too closely, so any necessary adjustments may be made.

9. Allow 1/2 an inch for seams—the line AB marks the lengthwise grain of the material. Mark each gore.

10. Turn the pattern over if both gores are not cut at one time.

Back Gore

The back gores are constructed the same as the front gores with the exception of the length used. The back length of the skirt is used instead of the side length, and the back waist to hip measurement instead of side waist to hip measurement. The side seams will be the same, and possibly the back seam will be more shaped.

NOTE.—

1. If only a skirt is being made from given material, place the front gore pattern on the material as near the selvedge as possible, then cut out the material, then turn the pattern over and place it in the opposite direction from the first gore before cutting; similarly for the two back gores.

2. Test the pattern to see if the flare toward the bottom is too full for the amount of material on hand; if necessary, alter the line from hips down to suit.

3. If the gores must be narrow because of the lack of material, pleats may be added at the centre front and back. (See Chapter 14 for "Pleats.")

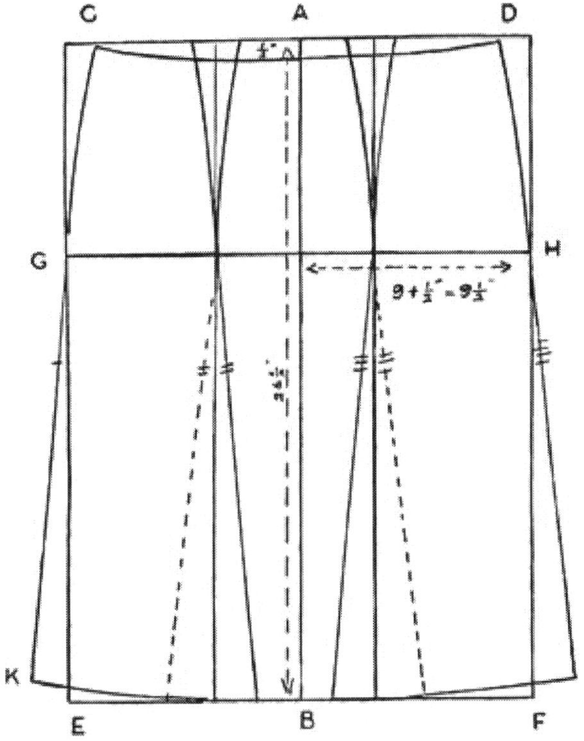

DIAGRAM 48
SIX- AND EIGHT-GORED SKIRTS

Six- and eight-gored skirts keep a goodly portion of the grain running straight around the hips, and because of the slant at the seams, allow the greatest amount of width at the bottom. This amount of fullness may be increased or

105

decreased as one desires by changing the slant of the seams from hips to the bottom of the skirt.

A six-gored skirt has underarm, side front and side back seams, and may readily be developed from a two-gored skirt. (See Diagram 48.)

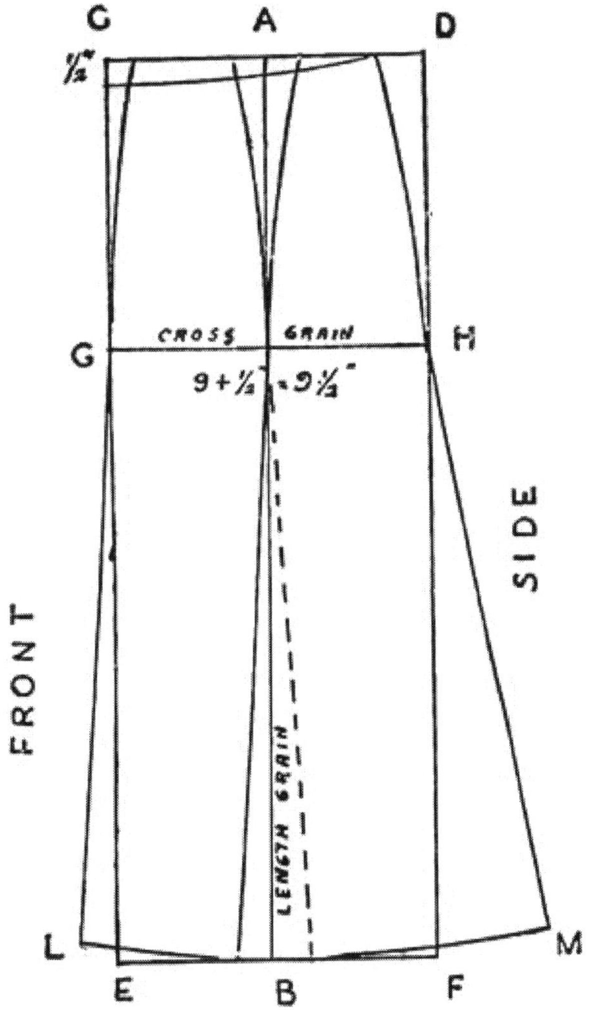

DIAGRAM 49

The three gores depicted are the same size, but they may
be altered at will, and sloped differently toward the bottom,
according to the desired position of the flare.

An eight-gored skirt has centre front and back, side front and back, and underarm seams, and may readily be developed from either a two- or four-gored skirt. Diagram 49 shows how it may be developed from a four-gored skirt. Notice the swing of the skirt at the sides due to the difference in the slant of the side seam.

NOTE.—In either a six- or eight-gored skirt, if the width of each gore and the slant of the seams from the hip to the bottom of the skirt are the same, it is only necessary to complete the draft of one gore from the hip to the bottom, preferably a front gore; and when cutting out; that is, if only a skirt is being made, pin the pattern of the other gores (hip to waist) in turn over the front gore. This eliminates much work and is very satisfactory when cutting out, the same as was explained for the four-gored skirt.

FOUNDATION PATTERN AND FLAT PATTERN DESIGN

DETAILED INSTRUCTIONS AND FORMULAS for drafting a plain waist, many types of sleeves, fitted upper garments and various types of skirts have been given. The question now is, which foundation pattern shall I use and how shall I use it?

Either the plain waist pattern or the more detailed draft for a fitted garment may be used for the foundation

pattern for an upper garment, depending upon the skill and adaptability of the maker, the style of the garment one wishes to create, and the specific need for a foundation pattern.

If one is only desirous of making simple types of garments from one's own pattern or using commercial patterns (either for women or children), it is only necessary to use the plain waist draft with a simple long or short sleeve, and one or the other of the skirt patterns, according to need. It is the armscye, the shoulder line, the width across the back, the width across the chest, the hipline and the length of skirt which are important. However, if one has had experience, and wishes to develop garments of varied structural designs, adding her own individuality and originality, or desires to make more elaborate clothes from commercial patterns, the fitted basic pattern and the sleeve with the elbow dart are better. Or, one may wish to have both on hand, using them for different purposes. It is always advisable to have many types of sleeves; the short tight sleeve, a medium puff sleeve a tailored sleeve or a coat sleeve. From time to time I suggest you add different basic patterns to your store. And it is for you to choose which is more suitable for your own particular needs.

With a foundation pattern, one is able to make simple types of garments, alter commercial patterns, eliminate fitting problems, and take care of any abnormalities in figure, create garments of varied structural designs, re-model

and renovate clothing, using one part of one garment and one of another if necessary, or have part of the garment of woven cloth and the other part knitted.

TRY YOUR FOUNDATION PATTERN IN MUSLIN FIRST

Every draft should have been marked for the lengthwise and crosswise grain of the material. Be sure to check for these before cutting out the muslin or piece of similar material one has on hand.

Material has to be allowed for all seams. On the actual garment the amount depends upon the type of seam necessary for that particular material. (See Chapter 15 for "Seams.") Three-eighths of an inch is average, but 1/2 inch is advisable for some materials. Always allow deep seams for rayon. It is advisable to mark the sewing line of the armscye in pencil. It is most important that the actual sewing is on the line of the pattern. The other seams may be marked in a similar manner or creased over the edge of your foundation pattern with a warm iron. If using the plain waist pattern, gather the front shoulder seam into the back, as explained in the directions; but if the fitted foundation pattern is being used, baste the shoulder dart before joining the shoulder seams. The sleeves are set in seam to seam and one should have no difficulty

in fitting them; in a fitted sleeve, the straight edge comes in front.

If a looser fitting is desired, this depending upon the type of garment one wishes to make, this may be secured by varying the seam allowance. Naturally, this allowance should be the same for all seams.

After the muslin pattern is completed, fit on the form or the person. If any adjusting is necessary, first check the measurements and then draft before altering the muslin pattern. It is possible that the position of the darts may have to be changed to meet individual figure needs.

THE OPPORTUNITIES FOR USING A FOUNDATION PATTERN

1. *Using a Foundation Pattern to alter Commercial Patterns*

NOTE.—When buying commercial patterns and ready-to-wears, always be sure you choose them in the size range nearest to your own figure requirements; women's, and misses', misses' and junior miss—and there are also half sizes for shorter women. This will eliminate many of the serious alterations.

Fitting the Front

The normal shoulder, neck and armscye lines are controlled by the foundation pattern.

Crush the tissue of the commercial pattern where any gathers or shirring has to be made, and pin in the darts, pleats or tucks. If there are any sections, fasten these together before testing. Test each piece of the commercial pattern, making sure that the grain corresponds with the grain of the foundation pattern, and that the underarm curves at the armscye are on a straight line. In a plain waist, there will be no difficulty with the underarm seam, but they must match in a fitted garment; and if the commercial pattern does not lie smooth around the armhole, make an underarm dart or increase the underarm dart until it lies flat. (See "Underarm Dart" in Chapter 7.) Any extra length from underarm to waist must be taken up in the crosswise fold (as explained in Chapter 14) or, if length is needed, split the pattern and add the necessary amount.

Build up or cut out any of the commercial pattern to conform to the foundation pattern.

Fitting the Back

Again be sure that the grain of the commercial pattern corresponds with the grain of the foundation pattern.

Place the centre line or fold of the commercial pattern on the centre line or fold of the foundation pattern with the underarm curves at the armscye on the straight of the grain.

Adjust as for the front of the pattern.

Sleeves

In a simple sleeve, the grain of the material, the depth of cap, the underarm curve, the shape of the cap, and the width of the sleeve are important. Check the commercial pattern with the foundation plain sleeve pattern and alter where necessary. If the commercial pattern hasn't sufficient width, cut and spread to the width of the foundation pattern.

For a fitted sleeve use the fitted sleeve pattern with the elbow dart. Check as above, also the length and curve at the wrist.

To Shorten a Sleeve

Fold a tuck, the necessary amount, in the pattern from underarm to elbow, and from elbow to wrist, as in Diagram 50.

The sleeve should not be shortened all in one place if the measurements do not warrant it.

To Lengthen a Sleeve

Split the sleeve and paste in strips where necessary.

Skirt

I consider a two-gored skirt pattern a desirable one to use for a foundation pattern. It will give one the waist, hip and length measurements. However, if a six or eight, fairly wide, gored skirt is to be tested, the hip measurement may be a little smaller.

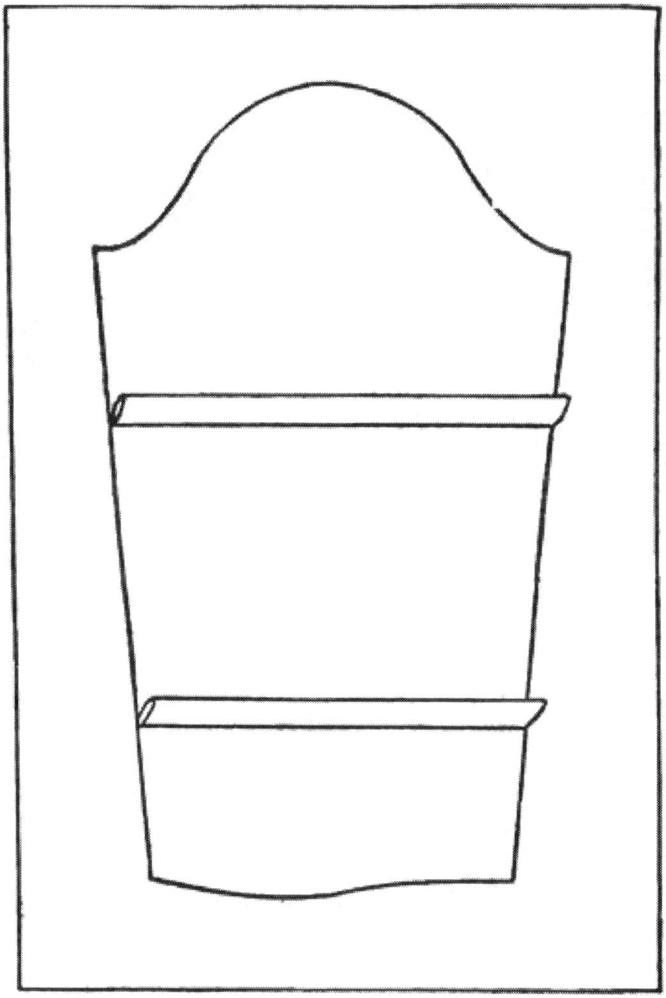

DIAGRAM 50

Pin the gores of the commercial pattern together so that the foundation pattern may be used to the best advantage. Check and adjust where necessary.

2. *Designing from Foundation Pattern or Flat Pattern Design*

From a plain flat pattern practically any design may be developed; simple and complicated patterns for blouses, children's dresses, jackets, skirts, etc. It is genuinely creative work and can give much satisfaction to the creator. Naturally one is not contented with the same type of blouse or dress for all occasions, but with a little thought and manœuvring sometimes, especially if the amount of material is limited, or one has to use two different materials, either new or used, one may design a beautiful garment.

There are, of course, certain design principles which should be adhered to. Design lines are used for breaking up spaces, but these should meet individual requirements; and it is always well to remember that simplicity is the keynote of good taste. It is better, too, if garments are not extreme in styling; then they may be worn for a long period of time without being dated.

There are two types of design lines, structural and applied. Structural lines are those which are incorporated in the actual structure of the garment; seam and hem lines, lines, yokes, pleats, godets, etc.; and each may be curved or straight as necessity dictates. (See development of yokes in blouse patterns, page 199.)

With correct usage structural lines may change the apparent size of the figure, and also emphasize certain good points.

Applied lines are those which lie on top of the actual structure of the garment. They may be flat, such as bands of all types and sizes, appliqué, embroidery, paillettes, bead work, etc.; or they may have depth, such as bows, jabots, cords, tassels, etc.

Much could be said about the principles which govern design, but the first big step is to develop an awareness of becoming lines to meet individual needs, and of the material of which the garment is to be made, remembering that good taste is always in fashion.

"He is best dressed whose dress no one observes."

ANTHONY TROLLOPE

Naturally, we are not satisfied with garment after garment cut on the same lines. This is neither elevating nor satisfying. We can, however, from the previous drafts, develop all manner of garments, according to our ability and the desirability to do so.

One of the first essentials of flat pattern design is to know what one wishes to develop. It isn't necessary to be a costume illustrator in order to design clothes; a mental picture serves equally as well as an illustration. Try to visualize what you wish to create. Of course, flat pattern designing is

equally as effective when copying either a model one has seen or a photograph.

ILLUSTRATION 16

The style should be suited to the type of garment, the person, the material from which it is to be made, and the amount of material or materials one has on hand.

There are certain fundamental lines which practically always remain the same; waist, shoulder, armscye, neck, etc.

ILLUSTRATION 17

In the following pages, the illustrations and diagrams are almost going to speak for themselves. Let us see how a

classic shirt, or a softer blouse for business or dinner, as well as divers dresses of the same line for small daughter may be developed from a simple waist pattern.

The illustration on page 196 with a little extra fullness gathered into the shoulder seams at the front, short sleeves with darted caps, and turned-back collar is one of the simplest to draft from the basic waist pattern.

The added fullness at the front varies with individual needs, and may be either gathered or shirred into the shoulder seam as explained in Chapter 7 under "Shoulder Darts." Diagram 17 illustrates how to draw the shoulder seam to take care of the extra width.

ILLUSTRATION 18

119

The neckline is drawn straighter and higher than the high round neckline to give the straight effect at the top of the lapels, and a straight piece cut on the crosswise grain completes the collar.

All types of sleeves are given under "Sleeves," Chapter 9.

The fussy little bundle which is depicted in Illustration 17 is a counterpart of the woman's blouse. The bottom of the dress is completed with straight pieces of material—the amount depending upon what one has on hand—gathered into the waist.

Illustration 18 is another variation made from the plain waist draft. The yoke has no shoulder seam and the sleeves have a full gathered cap as explained under "Sleeves," Chapter 9. (See Chapter 14 for "Collars.")

Yokes may be any depth, depending upon individual needs; however, they should not be so deep that the armscye of the garment draws across the chest or back. They may also be just in front, or just at the back, or both. They may or may not have a shoulder seam; they may be composed of straight lines; or the bottom of the yoke may be a curved line.

NOTE.—If the yokes are deep, it is advisable to have shoulder seams. This keeps the grain straight.

Diagram 51 shows how to develop a yoke without a shoulder seam.

The required depth of the yoke is first drawn on the draft, then the yoke pattern may be cut out and the shoulder seams placed together as in Diagram 51; or, to save the drafted pattern, the front part of the yoke may be traced on tracing paper, the front shoulder seam matched with the back shoulder seam, then the back portion of the yoke traced.

NOTE.—The shoulder seams are the same width.

The extra fullness allowed in front may be either gathered, shirred, tucked or smocked into the yoke. The tucks or smocking may be completed before cutting the material from the pattern.

The sleeves have a full gathered cap. (See Chapter 14 for "Collars.")

Illustration 19 is a variation for small daughter's dress. It has a narrow straight yoke at the front and back, and fullness smocked into the yoke. (See Chapter 15 for "Smocking.")

The housecoat in Illustration 20 is designed the same as a blouse with a straight yoke in front, short full sleeves with a full gathered cap, and round neckline. A full-length skirt is simply an elongated short skirt, the type of skirt depending upon the kind and amount of material one has on hand.

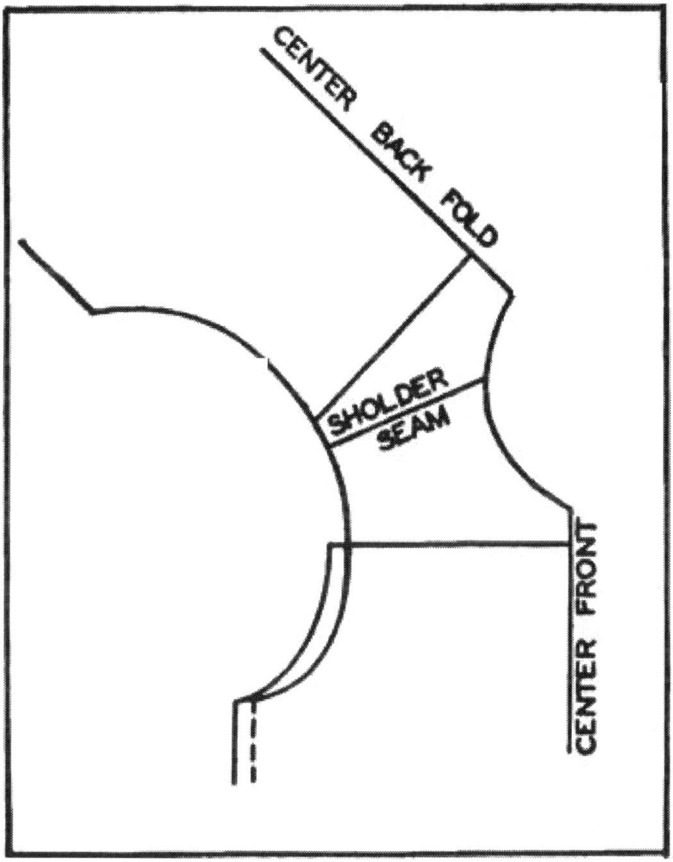

DIAGRAM 51

NOTE.—The seam lines of the skirt are continued to the desired length.

One might have a piece of seersucker, only 3 3/4 yards, tucked away in a drawer. With a knowledge of pattern drafting one can make a housecoat for an average woman from this material. Naturally, the skirt isn't as full as the one

depicted; but it can be made the same as a two-piece straight skirt, using the material cut off at the side seams to widen it toward the bottom, and the remainder of the fullness gathered into the waist.

ILLUSTRATION 19

It has been done, and with seersucker on which was printed huge flowers that were matched in the blouse.

Illustration 21 depicts a softer-looking blouse which could be used for many occasions.

There is a front yoke with a curve at the bottom, and the fullness gathered into the yoke. This line adds width across the chest as well as providing fullness across the bust for a small person.

ILLUSTRATION 20

Diagram 52 shows how the curve for the front is drafted to match the yoke. It will be noted that the longer curve is the same depth as the yoke curve.

ILLUSTRATION 21

Illustration 22 speaks for itself. If one's material is limited, the yoke and sleeves may be made of one colour, the remainder of another. All one needs is a little ingenuity.

If one hasn't sufficient material to make the dress as wide as shown in the illustration, a little narrower won't be any detriment; but always be sure that there is sufficient room to allow for plenty of action. On the other hand, it is equally important not to make children's garments too large, so that they appear to be wearing big sister's. By allowing for growth don't make a small child uncomfortable by making her clothes too large. From very early stages clothes play an important role in life.

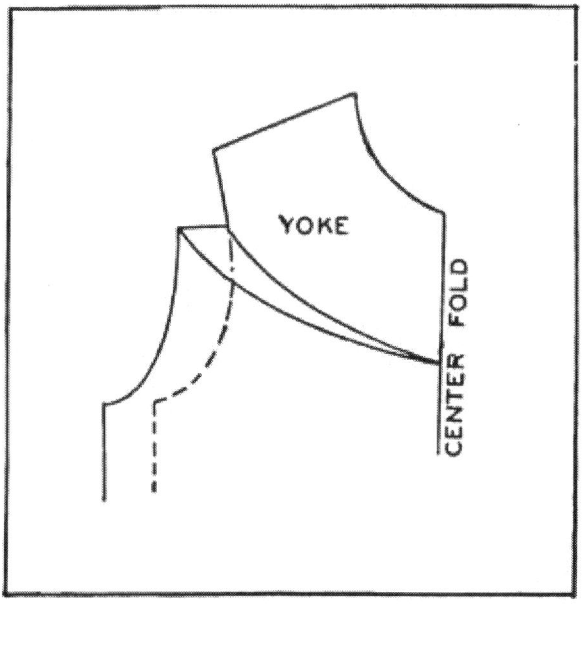

DIAGRAM 52

Simplicity in design and decoration, suitability to the climate, no irritating seams and fastenings, and a colour

which changes with the child's growth and interests are a few of the salient factors which should be considered when making children's clothes.

A dress of the type shown in Illustration 23 should be worn by a person with a good posture and a well-proportioned figure; although, if the waist is not too long, this type of skirt will hide protruding hip bones.

Again, this pattern is readily constructed from the basic fitted pattern.

Notice the small horizontal waist dart at the underarm seam as in Diagrams 53 and 54. The bottom of the waist should be considered in the light of a skirt with the crosswise grain straight around the hips.

If a very tight-fitting upper garment is desired, sew the side seams closer and adjust the darts. Any type of neckline may be used. The sleeves are short and fairly full, with a deep, gathered cap, and a slight curve at the bottom of the sleeve to throw some fullness into the band.

ILLUSTRATION 22

The pieces of material for the skirt are straight with
the lengthwise grain running down. The amount of fullness

depends upon the style desired, and the amount and type of material on hand.

ILLUSTRATION 23

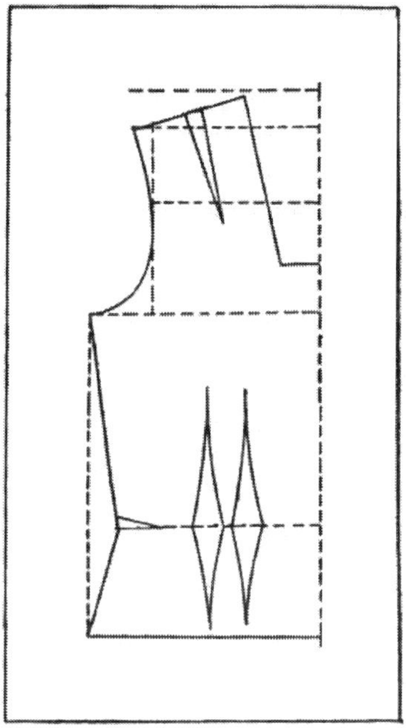

DIAGRAM 53

The dress on page 206 is made of dainty flowered spun rayon with lace insertion at the neck and the bands of the sleeves, through which is interwoven narrow black velvet ribbon.

NOTE.—For a basque waist, continue the front and back shoulder darts over the bust and shoulder-blades until they join the vertical waist darts. (See Diagram 10.)

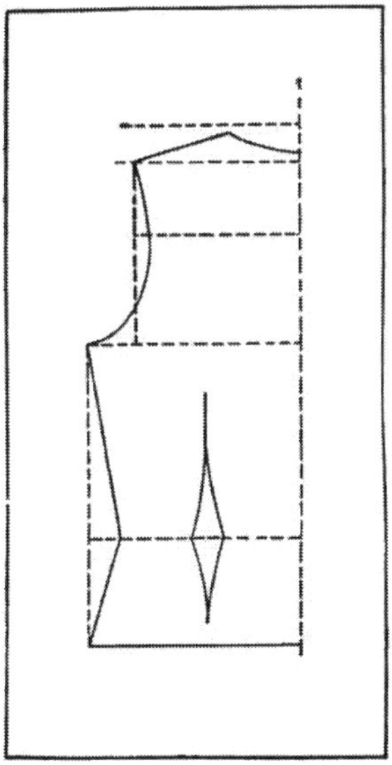

DIAGRAM 54

The design lines of the suit in Illustration 24 are different. They give the shoulders a broadening effect, at the same time lending height to the figure. The curved line at the lapels, collar, epaulets, and centre front are pleasing, and a deviation from the general conception of a tailored suit.

The extra width necessary for the bust is eased into the curve at the top. See Diagram 55. There are also vertical waist darts, and underarm darts to take care of the difference between the underarm measurements, front and back, and also to give the rounded effect for the bust.

ILLUSTRATION 24

DIAGRAM 55

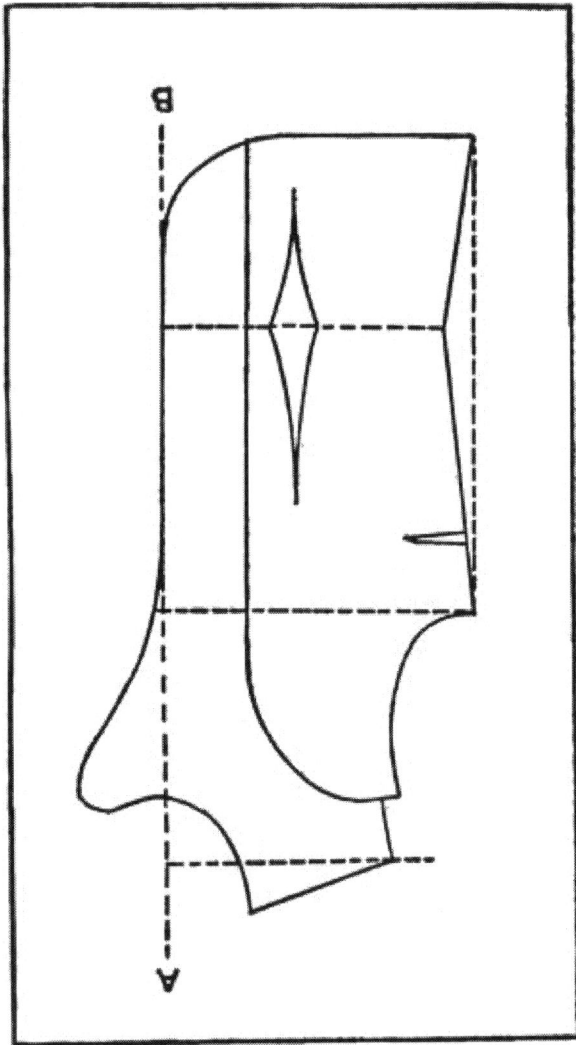

Notice the pocket on the left sleeve. A pocket is a necessity in any jacket, but here it does not detract from the effect of the lines.

The epaulets are 2 inches wide. The shoulder seams are placed together, the same as when drafting a yoke, for the curve at the armholes.

(See Chapter 14 for "Lapels and Necklines.")

3. *Remodelling and Renovating*

Remodelling and renovating are considered at length in the following chapters.

Printed in Great Britain
by Amazon